The making of a northern Baptist college

Peter Shepherd

The making of a northern Baptist college

Peter Shepherd

Northern Baptist College
2004

Cover design: Steve Harvie
Printed by Tyndale Press (Lowestoft) Ltd

© 2004 Peter Shepherd

The right of Peter Shepherd to be identified as the Author of this Work has been asserted by him in accordance with Copyright, Designs and Patents Act 1988

All rights reserved. No part of this publication may be reproduced, stored in a retrieval system, or transmitted in any form, or by any means, electronic or mechanical, photocopying, recording or otherwise, without the prior permission of the author

ISBN   0-9546979-0-1

This book is dedicated to
Anna, Joseph, Thomas, James and Ruth

The making of a northern Baptist college

Contents

List of illustrations	xi
Foreword	xiii
Acknowledgements	xv
Introduction	1
Chapter One. Beginnings: the 1760s	5
Social and economic change	5
Spiritual renewal	6
John Fawcett	8
Dan Taylor	10
The education of ministers	14
Chapter Two. Getting organised: 1770-1804	17
The Bristol Education Society	17
The New Connexion	19
An unprecedented opportunity	21
Dan Taylor's Academy	23
The Lancashire and Yorkshire Association	25
The Northern Education Society	27
The need for an educated ministry	30

Chapter Three. The early work of the Baptist academies. 35

    William Steadman 36
    The Horton Academy 39
    Life in the north of England 44
    A second tutor: Benjamin Godwin 46
    Steadman's resignation 48
    Dan Taylor's Academy 51
    Challenges faced by the academies 54

Chapter Four. From Horton to Rawdon: 1836-1864 59

    Problems at the General Baptist Academy 59
    James Acworth 63
    The search for new premises 65
    The Accrington Academy 66
    Manchester 67
    Rawdon College 70
    Acworth's resignation 74
    Chilwell 75

Chapter Five. The creation of Manchester Baptist College 79

    Baptism and communion 79
    The Baptist Evangelical Society 81
    Chamber Hall 85
    Henry Dowson 89
    Brighton Grove 92

Chapter Six. Raising standards: the 1870s and 1880s 99

    The 1870 Education Act 100
    S.G. Green 102
    Thomas Rooke and an organised student disturbance 107
    Wider links: the *Senatus Academicus* 109
    Thomas Goadby 112
    Back to Nottingham 114
    Thomas Witton Davies 116
    Edward Parker 119

Ministry and mission at the end of the century	124
Chapter Seven. The unsuccessful search for unity: 1891-1904	129
The Baptist Union	129
The first attempt at unity: 1891-1892	130
The second attempt: 1898-1899	137
The third attempt: 1901-1903	141
Reasons for failure	147
Chapter Eight. The Great War and the disappearance of Midland College: 1905-1920	151
Nonconformity before the war	151
Manchester	153
The ministry and the Baptist Union	155
War	158
Henry Townsend	159
Rawdon's centenary celebrations	161
The end of Midland College	165
Educating for ministry	170
Chapter Nine. The inter-war years	175
Changes in society and church	175
Continuity at Manchester	178
Floreat Rawdona!	181
Chapter Ten. The Second World War and its aftermath: 1939-1964	191
The Second World War	191
Kenneth Dykes and changes in the student body at Manchester	193
A.C. Underwood and L.H. Marshall	200
D.S. Russell	204
The creation of Northern Baptist College	207

Chapter Eleven. Northern Baptist College: 1964-1978   221

    Society and church   221
    Getting started   224
    Michael Taylor   228
    The arrival of the Methodists   234
    Developing new courses   237

Chapter Twelve. The Northern Federation for Training in Ministry: 1979-1999   249

    Developing the new pattern of training   249
    Forming a training federation   253
    Brian Haymes: consolidation   255
    New partnerships and a new ecumenical degree   263

Conclusion   271

Afterword   275

Appendix: The college principals   281

Abbreviations   282

Bibliography   283

    1. Manuscript and archival sources   283
    2. Newspapers and periodicals   283
    3. Books, pamphlets, articles, reports and unpublished theses   284

Index   290

List of illustrations

John Fawcett	9
Dan Taylor	12
William Steadman	37
Horton Academy	40
The main entrance to Rawdon College	72
Chamber Hall	87
Henry Dowson	90
Rawdon College library	103
Manchester College	121
Manchester College: staff and students, 1913	155
Midland Baptist College	167
Rawdon College	182
Manchester College: staff and students in the late 1950s	195
Cover of Rawdon College Magazine, 1964	211
D.S. Russell, K.C. Dykes and E.A. Payne at the official opening of the college in 1965, with the Vice Chancellor of Manchester University	215
Old and new premises together at Brighton Grove	225
Michael Taylor	229
David Goodbourn	239
The Brighton Grove community in the 1970s	241
Brian Haymes	255
Richard Kidd	263
Northern Baptist College tutors, 2004	276, 277

Foreword

David S. Russell

Time, they say, marches on. This book traces the history of the Northern Baptist College and its predecessors over the past two hundred years in their work of ministerial training. The task facing the author cannot have been an easy one, involving as it does the sometimes obscure and complicated overlapping accounts of five different institutions in different parts of the midlands and the north of England.

The story the book tells is set against the background of a rapidly changing society and evolving church relations, factors which were bound to affect the work of the ministry and, in particular, the work of ministerial training. The different phases through which such training passed are described in some detail and reflect the felt need to present the eternal Gospel effectively in the changed and changing circumstances of the time.

The opening of the college in 1964, with its new buildings, gave opportunity for the re-assessment of the kind of training appropriate to a new social and religious climate. The way opened up for a much greater ecumenical involvement and commitment on the part of staff and students alike. The words 'relevance' and 'contextualisation' began to be heard more frequently and radical changes began to be effected, linking training more securely with the practical work of the ministry. Residential training largely gave way to alternative programmes, enabling study to be linked with service to a local Baptist church. Emphasis came to be laid on 'lay training' alongside 'ministerial; training', reflecting the Baptist understanding of ministry as something wider than that of the 'ordained ministry'.

The author is to be commended on a difficult task well done. The book will be read not just as a record of past events, but also as a confirmation of present policy and a dedication to future service.

Acknowledgements

Many people have contributed to the writing and production of this book, and I am grateful to them all. I regret not having had the time to hear more from those for whom its contents are not merely history, but part of their lives. I would like to thank in particular the following people: Arthur Bonser, Beryl Dykes, George Farr, David Milner and Eddie Pilling for the chance to pick their brains and their memories; Faith Bowers, David Goodbourn, Brian Haymes, Richard Kidd, John Nicholson, David Russell and Michael Taylor for generously giving their time talking to me, reading the manuscript and making many valuable corrections and suggestions; Sue Mills at the Angus Library and Douglas Wooldridge, archivist of the East Midlands Baptist Association, for their help and co-operation.

The staff at Luther King House and Northern Baptist College have been generous and hospitable in the welcome and help they have given me. I am grateful to the principal, Richard Kidd, and the governors for asking me to take on the project, which I have found enjoyable and rewarding.

My wife, Rita, and my children have patiently put up with my periodic preoccupation with Northern Baptist College, and as with every other aspect of my ministry, I owe them an enormous amount.

A special word of thanks must go to the deacons and members of my church, Broadway Baptist Church in Derby, who have supported me during the preparation and writing of the book. The work has sometimes been time consuming, and although I have tried not to allow it to interfere with my work in the church, it has naturally had an impact. Their encouragement and understanding has made a big difference. In particular I am grateful for them allowing me to take several weeks of sabbatical leave at the writing-up stage.

I am conscious of the short-comings of the end product, but I hope it will bring some satisfaction to these and others who have helped bring it about.

Peter Shepherd

Introduction

This book attempts to describe the development of an institution, or more strictly, several institutions. The story belongs to the people who shaped Northern Baptist College and its predecessors, but their variety and number make adequate portraits of their backgrounds, personalities and motives impossible. The most prominent people are the twenty-nine college principals, but biographical details on even these is sketchy, to say the least. Others, including the students, academic and domestic staffs, officers and family members, also made vitally important contributions, though these were not usually recognised in any official account. Limitations of space and time prevent a proper acknowledgement of the parts they played. In most cases their stories were never told beyond the circle of family and friends, and never will be.

It has also been impractical to investigate thoroughly the theological and educational principles that underlay the formation and evolution of these institutions. Enough hints should be given to stimulate further reading for those who are interested in pursuing these in more detail. Similarly, a full account of the changing position of Baptists in the social and church life of England over the last two centuries, although important in providing the context for the colleges, must be looked for elsewhere.

It must be admitted that the subject matter of this historical survey cannot claim to have any great significance in terms of status or wealth. Small Nonconformist theological colleges in the north and midlands of England do not occupy a central position in church history. Even within their own denomination, they sometimes struggled to make their presence felt.

In spite of these limitations, and perhaps even because of them, the fluctuating fortunes of these institutions constitute a fascinating window through which the history of Nonconformist and Baptist life can be viewed. In striving to respond to the challenges and opportunities of the world in which they were set the colleges, in their own particular way, reflect the broader struggles of the wider Christian community.

Furthermore, the colleges exercised an influence that was more significant than their size and wealth might indicate. Every year they produced a significant number of Baptist ministers whose ideas about ministry and church life had been largely formed within their walls. A few of them went on to play leading roles in denominational or Free Church affairs. More significantly, most of them spent a life-time preaching and leading local churches. The long-term impact of the colleges on church life may often have been indirect and unacknowledged, but was nonetheless substantial.

A number of themes kept cropping up throughout the two centuries covered in this book. One, naturally enough, was the ministry itself, and how its relationship with the rest of the Church was understood. Generally, those who directed college affairs believed that the prosperity of the churches depended very largely on the ordained ministry, and that therefore the training of ministers was vitally important. This view was particularly understandable when the general level of literacy and education was low and congregations needed able teachers and preachers to communicate the message lucidly and persuasively. An emphasis on ministerial education can, however, exaggerate the distinction between the ministry of lay and ordained people, even in a denomination that prides itself on the priesthood of all believers. Generally, lay training did not feature prominently in college life, and it was not until the 1970s that Northern Baptist College began to take it seriously.[1]

The kind of people appropriate for ministerial training, and the nature of the training they should receive, were other constantly present questions. For the most part, an assumption that lay behind the design of college premises and courses was that ministerial candidates should be young, male and single. An informal approach to training, centred on the principal and his household, in which Christian character and a sense of God's calling were all-important, was modified, if not at times transformed completely, by an emphasis on academic ability as the nineteenth century progressed. Although it was sometimes stated that high academic achievement was not necessary for ministry, and that married people and women could be trained, the colleges found it difficult to be flexible, and did little to encourage greater variety in their intake.

Alongside character and piety, preaching ability was almost universally regarded as a prerequisite for an effective and useful ministry. For the most part, a thorough Biblical and theological education was regarded as the main means by which this could be developed and refined. Early in each of the colleges' history, practical experience and training formed an integral part of the course, but this was frequently squeezed out by increasing academic demands. One result was pleas from the churches to include more of it. The tension between the practical and academic demands for ministerial preparation, and the difficulties in combining the two seemed an inescapable part of college life.

Ministerial training was necessarily a co-operative venture, and this raised particular challenges for Baptists, with their commitment to a congregational form of church government. A sense of denominational cohesion was a necessary precursor to establishing effective training institutions. Initially this took the form of Baptist associations and societies, from which the colleges sprang, but by the beginning of the twentieth century, co-operation was extending to a national level as the Baptist Union became increasingly involved in questions of ministerial training. By the end of the century, the provision of training across denominational boundaries had become the norm.

The role of college principals was always crucial. Kenneth Brown may have overstated their role in the steady decline of Nonconformity over the last 150 years or so[2], but it is hard to exaggerate the importance of their personalities as far as the colleges themselves were concerned. The small size and intimate nature of the college communities, centred as they often were on the principal's home and family, made this inevitable. The students frequently took on the role of disciples, receiving instruction and benefiting from the experience of their tutor and mentor, sometimes supported by an assistant. There were some advantages to this system, but it made the colleges unhealthily dependent on their principal. The college authorities were fortunate if resignation or death in office did not result in a major crisis or at least significant disruption.

August 2004 marks the two-hundredth anniversary of the formation of the Northern Education Society in Rochdale, Lancashire. As with the origin of most things, the story starts some time beforehand, in this case at least thirty-five years earlier. That was when two of the leading figures in Baptist history, John Fawcett and Dan Taylor, first met in a remote corner of the Yorkshire Dales to discuss and pray over the task of ministerial training in the north of England. As the story unfolded, it led to London, Bradford, Wisbech, Loughborough, Leicester, Nottingham, Rawdon, Chilwell, Accrington, Bury and Manchester, and involved as many as five distinct collegiate institutions. It contained discontinuities and shifts in emphasis, and it is unlikely that William Steadman, the first principal at Bradford, would find much that was familiar to him at Brighton Grove two centuries after he was first appointed. The continuity rests in the institution itself and in its goal of preparing ministers of the Gospel for the Baptist denomination. Steadman's goal of cultivating in his students that which would make them "acceptable and useful" in the churches to which they believed God had called them to minister is one that few in the colleges could quarrel with, in this or any age[3].

---

1 This is not to say that no lay training took place before this. The evening and weekend "Rawdon lectures" of the 1950s, for example, were designed to provide training for the wider church.
2 Kenneth D. Brown, "College Principals – A Cause of Nonconformist Decay", *Journal of Ecclesiastical History* vol. 38 (1987) pp.236-253.
3 Thomas Steadman, *Memoir of William Steadman* (Thomas Ward, London: 1838) p.318.

Chapter One
Beginnings: the 1760s

The time is the mid-1760s. It is summer. The place is the West Riding of Yorkshire, high in the Pennine hills overlooking the valley of the river Calder, about three miles from the border with Lancashire. To be more precise, it is a small farmhouse in the scattered community of Wainsgate, across the valley from the town of Heptonstall, overlooking Hebden Bridge. It is a bleak but beautiful situation, between the rocks and heather of the windswept moors above and the steep wooded hillside below. Few places in England were more remote. Calderdale boasted no paved roads, and access to Wainsgate had to be either on foot or horse-back. The nearest town of any consequence was Halifax, an hour's hard walking to the east. A couple of hours beyond that was Bradford. A few miles to the west lay the uncompromising spine of the Pennine hills.

Social and economic change

History would subsequently describe the 1760s as a crucial decade for the forthcoming transformation of the social and economic life of England known as the Industrial Revolution. Over the next few decades the residents of Calderdale were to experience this upheaval more dramatically than most. Signs of the changes to come were evident in the world beyond its borders. Colonial expansion was accelerating, bringing unprecedented opportunities for trade and wealth-creation. The Treaty of Paris, bringing to an end the Seven-Year War with France, ceded huge tracts of land to Britain in North America and the West Indies. British rule in India was being consolidated. At home, agriculture was becoming more productive as new methods were introduced. In the midlands and the south, the momentum towards enclosure, that would change agricultural practice and the appearance of the English countryside for ever by the end of the century, was gathering pace. This was the decade in which some of the great figures of the Industrial Revolution, men like Richard Arkwright, James Watt and Josiah Wedgwood, began to implement their far-reaching schemes and inventions. Water and steam power was for the first time being harnessed for the purposes of manufacturing, and the factory invented as a unit of large-scale production.

These momentous events could hardly have been recognised by the people of Wainsgate at the time, even by the few who had the ability and interest to read the news, or indeed the opportunity to think beyond the struggle to scratch a living from the meagre resources of Upper Calderdale. There were some signs of industrial progress, however, even in that isolated part of the kingdom. Work was being done to extend the navigability of the Calder and to construct a turnpike road along the valley bottom. A new bridge at Hebden Bridge was completed in 1771. It was an important step in the long process of opening up the valley for the first time to wheeled transport. Within ten years the route would be complete from Halifax to Rochdale and, for the first time, commercial traffic on a significant scale could flow between Yorkshire and Lancashire through the Calder Valley.

Spiritual renewal

For most local people, however, the most obvious signs of change in the 1760s were not economic or industrial, but spiritual. John Wesley and George Whitefield, who were still conducting preaching tours, attracted huge crowds throughout the West Riding, and made a dramatic and widespread impact. In 1756 Whitefield had preached to an excited crowd of 20,000 in Bradford, at which thousands "vented their emotions by tears and groans".[1] Methodist societies abounded in the area. In 1764 the "great temple of Calderdale Methodism", the octagonal chapel at Heptonstall (still in use today), was erected.

Beginnings: The 1760s

The new evangelical spirit infected the Established Church, especially through the ministries of the Rev. William Grimshaw of Haworth and the Rev. Henry Venn of Huddersfield. Grimshaw and Venn were powerful figures throughout the area and, indeed, throughout the whole of the north of England. Grimshaw, who had died in 1763 after more than twenty years at Haworth, was a well-known open-air preacher throughout the area, and a friend of both the Wesleys and Whitefield. Venn exercised an eleven-year ministry as vicar of Huddersfield until 1771.

Both Grimshaw and Venn were familiar figures to the occupants of the Wainsgate farmhouse. There was still much to be done, however, before the Evangelical Revival could be said to have really changed life in Upper Calderdale. Apart from the influence of Methodism, symbolised by the new chapel at Heptonstall, religious observance was not in a healthy state. One account describes the Anglican church at Heptonstall as "ancient and almost dilapidated", and "among the inhabitants in general, ignorance and vice prevailed in a deplorable degree; there was little appearance of religion".[2]

A remarkable group of people sat together in the main room of the small house, deep in serious conversation. Their Bibles were open on the table before them, together with various other books they had been discussing. Two of them were Baptist pastors, both in their mid-twenties. Their names were John Fawcett and Dan Taylor. Three others were with them, Henry Foster, a young man from the neighbourhood reading Divinity at Oxford in preparation for the Anglican priesthood, John Sutcliff, a youth of fourteen or fifteen helping Taylor as a pupil teacher at his recently opened school a short distance down the road, and Fawcett's wife, Susannah, pregnant with her first child. Fawcett and Taylor had both been recently ordained, Fawcett as pastor of the Wainsgate Particular Baptist Church, and Taylor of the new General Baptist Church at Birchcliffe. The two chapels were about a mile apart. They had both been deeply touched by the Evangelical Revival. They were destined to become leading figures in the Baptist denomination nationally in the years that lay ahead.

John Fawcett

Fawcett was born in Bradford in 1740, and as a young man was apprenticed to a local tradesman. Encouraged by friends who took an interest in him following the death of his father when he was twelve years old, he became an avid reader, and was tutored in Latin by a local Presbyterian, David Pratt. He was sixteen when he first heard Whitefield preach, and as a result made a personal commitment of faith in Jesus Christ.[3] From then on he took advantage of every opportunity to hear Whitefield, Wesley or Grimshaw, associating himself with the Methodists.

Fawcett, however, soon became dissatisfied with Wesleyan churchmanship and theology, and joined a group of Independents meeting in the town. When they decided against forming their own church in Bradford, he was drawn to the newly created Baptist church. It met in Westgate. The pastor, William Crabtree, had been converted under the preaching of Grimshaw and before coming to Bradford had been a member of the church at Wainsgate. Theologically and ecclesiologically, the Independents and most Baptists were closely related. Unlike the Methodists, who, Wesley insisted, were still part of the Church of England, they were committed to a Calvinistic theology and congregational church government. In 1758 Fawcett was baptised by immersion and became a member of the Westgate church. Shortly afterwards he married Susannah Skirrow, a fellow church member. Two years later he made a personal "Covenant with God", writing in his diary:

> I here bind myself, O Lord, to be thine by a sacred and everlasting obligation; I devote myself to be thy servant, to perform the work which thou assignest to me . . . I solemnly devote the powers and faculites of my soul to the service of God.[4]

From 1761 Fawcett's mind turned increasingly towards the work of the ministry, and he began to preach in the Baptist churches of the area. In 1763

Beginnings: The 1760s

John Fawcett (1740-1817), whose visionary commitment to the task of ministerial training lay behind the formation of the Northern Baptist Education Society in 1804

the first minister of the church at Wainsgate, Richard Smith, died, after a thirteen-year ministry. Fawcett was approached by the church with a view to him taking up the position. Smith had been Crabtree's old minister at Wainsgate, and the two men had been friends and colleagues for many years. Fawcett would have known Smith and the situation at Wainsgate well. In May of the following year, after a few months of regular preaching there, he was invited to become pastor. He and his wife took their possessions up the valley and moved into the farmhouse provided for their accommodation. "I have now", he wrote, "made a solemn entrance upon the work of the ministry".[5]

The Wainsgate chapel was dark and damp, seating about 100 people. According to the published history of the church it had been built "in the cheapest manner possible with the result that the place was very uncomfortable particularly in the winter".[6] The people were uneducated – many of them illiterate – and spoke in a dialect almost unintelligible to strangers. Smith had worked hard, often in the face of serious illness, but the church still only had a membership of about thirty. In addition to Smith himself and Crabtree, one other member, James Hartley, had also entered the Baptist ministry; he became the first pastor of the Baptist church in Haworth. The situation was far from easy and demanded all the young Fawcett's ability, tact and energy. He was encouraged by a letter from Whitefield, advising him that "a clear head, and an honest, upright, disinterested, warm heart, with a good elocution, and a moderate degree of learning, will carry you through all, and enable you to do wonders".[7] His gifts as a preacher were soon recognised, and he attracted a growing congregation, many of whom walked considerable distances across the Pennine moors and valleys to hear him.

Dan Taylor

At the time Fawcett moved to Wainsgate, Dan Taylor had been ordained minister of the new Baptist church at Birchcliffe, also in Upper Calderdale, for just a few months. The two chapels were almost within shouting distance of each other. The nearly simultaneous arrival of two gifted young Baptist ministers in the same seemingly unpromising district was a remarkable coincidence. It proved beneficial to both men, and to the Baptist cause in general, that they should have each other's friendship and support during the first twenty years of their ministries in the Hebden Bridge area.

To understand how they came to be neighbours in this way, it is important to understand that the two branches of the Baptist denomination to which they belonged had virtually nothing to do with each other, and are probably best thought of as separate denominations. The Particular, or Calvinistic, Baptists, to whom Fawcett, Smith and Crabtree belonged, were suspicious of their Arminian cousins, the General Baptists. United by baptismal practice, they were divided theologically and organisationally, and had separate histories. It was only during the Evangelical Revival, and through the friendship of men like Fawcett and Taylor, that they began to draw closer together, and ultimately, under the banner of the Baptist Union of Great Britain, to bury their differences.[8]

Dan Taylor was a little older than Fawcett. He was born in 1738 in the parish of Northowram, near Halifax. He showed intellectual potential as a young boy, apparently being able to read the tenth chapter of Nehemiah, complete with "83 hard Hebrew names" before he was five![9] His father was a miner, and when he was still only five, Dan accompanied him down the pit. He continued to work mining coal throughout his childhood and youth, reading as and when he could find opportunity. While Fawcett's life was being changed as a result of the preaching of Whitefield in Bradford, Taylor was having the same experience, walking many miles to hear Wesley, Whitefield or Grimshaw. Like Fawcett, he was drawn to the Methodists, and received his early education from a Methodist teacher, studying Latin, Greek and Hebrew. At the age of twenty he was accepted as a probationary local preacher.

Taylor's career continued to follow the same pattern as Fawcett's when he grew dissatisfied with the organisation of the Methodist societies. He and a few like-minded friends decided to form themselves into an independent church. Taylor was invited to be their leader. They hired a room which was used for services on Sundays and a school for children during the week. It was, by chance, only a mile from the Baptist chapel at Wainsgate. Taylor left mining to devote himself full-time to the work of preaching and teaching.

Dan Taylor (1738-1816), founder of the New Connexion of General Baptist churches and first president of its academy for training ministers

The group were unwilling to join the Independents because it would involve them abandoning the Arminian doctrine they had inherited from Methodism. For a time they were isolated from fellowship with the wider church. During this period Taylor began to investigate the theology of baptism, and became convinced of the unscriptural nature of infant baptism. He persuaded at least one other member of his congregation to accept the principle of believers' baptism by immersion. They were unwilling to baptise each other, and were refused baptism by neighbouring Baptist ministers (Crabtree and Smith probably among them) because of their Arminian theology. One of them, however, told Taylor about the General Baptists, whose baptismal theology and congregational understanding of the Church matched his own. In February 1763 he set out on foot for the nearest General Baptist church he knew about, in Boston in Lincolnshire, with the aim of receiving believer's baptism by immersion at the hands of an ordained General Baptist minister. Boston was about 120 miles away.

In the event, Taylor came across another General Baptist church in Gamston, Nottinghamshire, while *en route* for Boston. After three days in conversation with the church there he was baptised in the river Idle. With the support of the General Baptist Association based in Lincolnshire he reconstituted his fellowship back in Calderdale as a General Baptist church, was ordained minister and, largely with his own hands, built a chapel on land purchased nearby at Birchcliffe. By the end of 1763 he and his new Baptist congregation were established in their new home.

Taylor quickly got to know the General Baptist denomination, attending the annual meetings in London in 1764 and visiting their churches in the Midlands. He soon discovered that while he agreed with much of their theology and churchmanship, there were other aspects that caused him deep concern. Trinitarian orthodoxy was disputed by several General Baptist ministers, and evangelistic preaching was rare. As the 1760s progressed, Taylor increasingly lost hope of being able to continue long in fellowship with the denomination he had joined. There were signs of hope among some of the General Baptist churches and ministers, however, and he had come across many non-Calvinistic Baptists who felt as he did. The notion of launching a new body, or Connexion, in which evangelically-minded General Baptists could work together, formed in Taylor's mind. It was an idea that came to fruition with the creation of the New Connexion in 1770.

Despite their doctrinal differences, Fawcett and Taylor had much in common. They were voracious readers and eager to learn. They had both been profoundly touched by the Evangelical Revival and longed to see lives changed by God through the preaching of the Gospel. It is not surprising that they became close friends.[10]

The education of ministers

So what did they talk about, as they sat together in John and Susannah Fawcett's home? They met as often as three or four days a week, with Foster, when he was at home from Oxford, "to read the classics, to study divinity and to cultivate other branches of knowledge".[11] Their conversations were wide-ranging and serious. No doubt Foster introduced many interesting topics from his studies at Queen's College.[12] Taylor and Fawcett were not only enthusiastic about learning themselves, but eager to encourage others to do so too. In 1769 they formed a Book Society in Heptonstall. Conscious of the widespread illiteracy around them, they were grateful to those who had helped them discover the riches of the Bible, the classics and other literature. They were keen to help others, like their young friend John Sutcliff, in the same way.

They had both become Baptists as a result of personal convictions, and were naturally concerned about the future of the Baptist churches in their area, and the Baptist cause nationally too. They wanted to enable Baptists, and particularly Baptist ministers, to enjoy the benefits of a proper education, in order to make the most of the opportunities presented to them by the new openness to spiritual matters made evident by the Methodist revival. The English Universities had been closed to Baptists, as to all Nonconformists, for over 100 years, and other opportunities to pursue learning at anything more than a very basic level were haphazard.

The Dissenting Academies provided a high standard of education for many people, including many Nonconformist ministers, throughout much of the eighteenth century. These included the Northampton Academy, an institution that flourished under Philip Doddridge's leadership in the 1730s and 1740s, and the Tewkesbury Academy, where several leading Anglicans were educated. By the 1760s, most of them were past their peak, and those that maintained high educational standards were often associated with doctrinal unorthodoxy. Joseph Priestley's Warrington Academy, for example, was avowedly Unitarian.

The Independents, recognising the need for ministerial education in the north in particular, had formed a Northern Education Society in 1756. It supported an academy in Heckmondwike (in the West Riding) for forty years. Dr John Ward bequeathed some money for the education of Protestant Dissenting ministers at Aberdeen University when he died in 1758. The Countess of Huntingdon's famous college at Trevecca was opened in 1768.

Among Baptists, the only institution for training ministers was the one associated with the Broadmead Church in Bristol. Hugh Evans, who was appointed pastor of Broadmead in 1758, was attempting to broaden its work and appeal, encouraged in 1765 by news of the establishment of Rhode Island Baptist College in the American colonies. A few other attempts to address the need for an educated ministry had been made. From 1720 the Particular Baptist Fund had devoted some of its resources to supporting the training of ministers, mainly at Bristol.[13] Another society based in the capital, the London Baptist Society for Assisting Young Men in Grammar and Academic Learning, had been founded in 1752, but failed to win support and within about twenty-five years had "lapsed into a state of inaction and neglect".[14] For Fawcett and Taylor, the sad fact was that ministerial education was not regarded as a priority by most Baptists. In some quarters it was positively frowned upon. There were virtually no opportunities for young Baptist men (let alone women!) to receive a systematic education in the north of England.

The conviction that ministerial education was vital to the future effectiveness of the Baptists, of whatever theological hue, in their God-given task of proclaiming the Gospel and building the Church of Christ, became indelibly etched in the minds of these two men during this period. It was to become a key priority in their future ministries. Fortunately, they both had the ability and determination and would have the opportunity to do something about it.

1 J. Fawcett, *An Account of the life, ministry and writings of the late John Fawcett, DD* (Baldwin, Cradock and Joy: London, 1818) pp.18-19.
2 *Ibid.*, p 120. There had been a Baptist presence in the Heptonstall area for some years, consisting of the small churches at Stone Slack and Rodhill End. These were the results of the itinerant preaching of David Crosley and his cousin William Mitchell in an earlier generation.
3 Fawcett kept a portrait of Whitefield at his bed-side until the end of his life.
4 J. Fawcett, *An Account*, pp.45-6.
5 *Ibid.*, p.111.
6 *A Short History of the Baptist Church at Wainsgate* (Yorkshire Baptist Association: no date) p.6.
7 Fawcett, *An Account*, pp.35-6.
8 The Baptist Union was formed by the Particular Baptists in 1813. At its re-constitution in 1832, the door was opened for General Baptists to join, and they played an increasing role in the Union as the nineteenth century progressed. In 1891, the General Baptist Association, representing the bulk of General Baptists, decided to disband itself and amalgamate with the Baptist Union. For most Baptists, the older doctrinal differences had by then ceased to be meaningful.
9 W. Underwood, *Life of Dan Taylor* (Simpkin, Marshall and Co.: London, 1870), p.2.
10 Adam Taylor, *Memoirs of Rev Dan Taylor* (London, 1820), p.31.
11 *Ibid.*, p 23. See also J. Fawcett, *An Account*, pp.131-9.
12 Foster was ordained as a deacon in London in 1767 and went on to become a popular preacher and lecturer, re-establishing regular contact with Taylor on the latter's move to the capital in 1785.
13 The Fund was established in London in 1717.
14 George P. Gould, *The Baptist College at Regent's Park (founded in Stepney, 1810): A Centenary Record* (Kingsgate Press: London, 1910).

Chapter Two
Getting Organised: 1770-1804

The Bristol Education Society

In 1770, two events took place which were to have important consequences for the future of ministerial education among Baptists in England. One was the formation of the Bristol Education Society by Hugh Evans, minister of the Broadmead church, and the other was the creation of the New Connexion among the General Baptists. Under Evans' ministry, which commenced after the death of Bernard Foskett in 1758, Broadmead and its college for ministerial training had felt the touch of the Evangelical Revival. Evans, "an eloquent and forthright Welsh preacher"[1], was keen to expand the college and train more "able, evangelical, lively, zealous ministers of the Gospel"[2]. In 1770 he wrote to Baptist churches throughout England and Wales inviting them to support the Society he and a few other Bristol ministers had decided to establish in order to achieve this ambition.

From the start, the Bristol Education Society was concerned with more than simply training young men for the ministry. It wanted to involve the churches in seeking out suitable candidates, and to encourage them in evangelistic activity, working closely with the Western Association. It soon became a key factor in enabling Baptists throughout the country to benefit from the new spiritual openness, and many of the most influential ministers in the denomination at this decisive stage of its history were trained either under Evans or his son Caleb, who succeeded him as Principal. Among them was John Sutcliff, the young man who had shared in the conversations at Wainsgate between John Fawcett and Dan Taylor and received much of his early education at their hands. By 1770 he was a member of the Wainsgate church and, showing signs of promise and a call to the ministry, walked to Bristol for training two years later. Subsequently, as minister of the Baptist church in Olney[3], he was to play a leading role in the formation of the Baptist Missionary

Society in 1792 and to be one of its most prominent supporters. He also established an academy of his own where young men were educated, some in preparation for the ministry.

The Bristol Education Society was not the first such society among the English Baptists[4], but it was the first seriously to put the education of ministers on the denomination's agenda. It was an inspiration to Fawcett at Wainsgate. Within two years of its founding he had begun receiving men who showed promise for ministry into his own home for training[5]. A year later, in 1773, he and his friend John Sandys made the first attempt to establish a Baptist college in the north of the country. With the encouragement of Hugh Evans, and no doubt motivated in part by the example of John Sutcliff's long walk to Bristol for training in the previous year, the two men wrote to their ministerial colleagues in the north urging the formation of an Education Society in that part of the country. "The grand design we have in view," they wrote, in words that are almost a direct quotation from Evans, "is to furnish the churches of Christ with lively, zealous, judicious, disinterested ministers of the Word"[6]. The proposal came to nothing, partly because the Baptists in the north did not yet possess either the strength or organisation to embark on such a co-operative venture, and partly because of suspicion in some quarters about the effect education might have on men God might call to the ministry.

Fawcett himself was undeterred by this disappointment. His Wainsgate home had been enlarged to accommodate students, but soon proved inadequate for the task of education, both of ministerial candidates and other students, to which he was increasingly committed. In 1776 he left the farmhouse, which had been the family home for twelve years, to take up residence at Brearley Hall, a mile or two down the valley. Although "in a most ruined, dilapidated state"[7], it had in its day been quite a grand house, and provided ample accommodation for Fawcett, his wife Susannah and their children, as well as the students living with them. He received financial help from the short-lived London Baptist Education Society for at least one of his students[8]. Brearley Hall had the advantage of adjoining the new Halifax to Lancashire road which, although not yet completed, made it more readily accessible than the remote Wainsgate hillside[9]. In the orchard Fawcett erected a small cell, in which he kept a skull, under which was the inscription:

> In this unpolished, lonesome cell,
> From noise and interruption free,
> My thoughts on solemn subjects dwell,
> Death, judgement and eternity.[10]

Here he thought and prayed about the task of educating Baptist ministers, and the benefits it could bring to ministers and churches alike. Although he continued to play his personal part in the fulfilment of this dream, it was to be nearly thirty years before it was secured on a more permanent basis.

The New Connexion

As pastor of the General Baptist church and school at Birchcliffe, a short walk from both Wainsgate and Brearley Hall, Dan Taylor's standing among the General Baptists steadily grew. He was a regular participant at their annual national meetings. Increasingly dissatisfied with the doctrinal unorthodoxy and lack of evangelistic zeal of many of his fellow-ministers, in 1769 he proposed the formation of a New Connexion of General Baptists. His aim was to create a body which could effectively support the churches and ministers who felt as he did. In 1770 the New Connexion became a reality and held its first general meeting in London. It was destined to be an important influence in the future development of the Baptist denomination as a whole, both Particular and General wings. Taylor was from the start the prime mover and shaper of this new institution.

By 1770, the Birchcliffe church had grown to about seventy members[11]. It organised itself along the lines of a Methodist society, with small group "experience meetings". It was joined in the New Connexion by nine other General Baptist churches, some from the Lincolnshire Association and others from London, and by a small but lively group of non-affiliated Baptist churches centred on Barton-in-the-Beans in Leicestershire. The Barton group had its origins in the Methodist revival, like Taylor's own church. In their case it was the influence of the Countess of Huntingdon and the preachers she supported, rather than Whitefield, that had been the most important influence. The group had adopted Baptist baptismal practice in 1755.

Taylor drew up a statement of faith in Six Articles for the New Connexion. This was mainly intended to prevent the new organisation being weakened by the doctrinal laxity that distressed him so much about other General Baptists. It included statements on the Person and Work of Christ and Salvation by Faith[12]. Taylor's ties with the older General Baptists were not entirely broken, and he continued to be a prominent participant in their annual Assembly for many years. His energies, however, were increasingly devoted to the development and growth of the new body.

The New Connexion grew quite rapidly in size and effectiveness, attracting other existing General Baptist churches into membership, establishing new ones, and putting in place organisational structures that would guarantee its long-term survival. Taylor himself travelled widely, provoking complaints from the Birchcliffe congregation about his frequent absences from the pulpit. His preaching tours were partly aimed at raising funds for the expansion of the work into new areas. A letter written by Taylor in 1777 suggests that Fawcett too may have been critical of the apparent neglect of his Yorkshire congregation. Taylor wrote to his old friend of damaging and upsetting reports of the way he was treating his people and clearly suspected that Fawcett was responsible[13].

The provision of training for New Connexion ministers was an important issue for Dan Taylor from the start. Adam Taylor, in an early history of the movement, wrote:

> The propriety of endeavouring to assist young men, who were called to the work of the ministry, in obtaining useful learning, seems early to have occupied the minds of the most judicious and zealous supporters of the New Connexion.[14]

In 1779 Taylor submitted to the annual meetings of the Connexion a plan for assisting the study of young men preparing for ministry, already being involved personally in running a weekly class for men who "wished to learn how to preach" in his own church[15]. Nothing substantial, however, seems to have occurred as a result of this.

In 1782 a new General Baptist church was opened in Halifax. It was not the usual practice for New Connexion ministers to move from one church to another, but the Halifax church was strategically situated in a growing centre of population, and its members were keen to secure Taylor's services. The question was submitted to the General Association (the annual meeting of the Connexion), and their advice to Birchcliffe to "let brother Taylor go" settled the matter[16]. Unfortunately for Halifax, this precedent led to them losing Taylor two years later.

The General Baptist cause in London was weak, and reckoned by some to be "hastening towards extinction"[17]. The only prosperous New Connexion church, in Whitechapel, was led by the elderly John Brittain. He successfully argued that Taylor's gifts could be more effectively used as his assistant, and ultimately his successor, in the capital, and Taylor was persuaded after a long debate in the Connexion to move to London. Although the bulk of the New Connexion churches were in the Midlands, Taylor's ministry, as its leading figure, was national in scope, and a London base was considered important for this. After eight days' journey with his wife and nine children in a borrowed wagon he commenced his ministry there in 1785.

An unprecedented opportunity

Spiritual renewal was most evident at this time within Methodism, but it was also becoming widespread within the Baptist and Independent denominations. Among the Particular Baptists, the last two decades of the eighteenth century brought substantial growth and renewal. Much of this was centred on the Northamptonshire Association. Urged on by Andrew Fuller, John Sutcliff and others, this association was largely responsible for the creation of the Baptist Missionary Society in 1792. Throughout the country, new churches were being formed, new associations were coming into existence, making co-operative ventures easier, and evangelistic initiatives undertaken.

One of the features of church life during this period was the breakdown of many traditional denominational loyalties. The birth of Methodism itself was an example of this. Within Nonconformity, interplay and movement between the various groupings were commonplace. Some of the most important initiatives were inter-denominational, such as Sunday Schools and the London Missionary Society. Even between Nonconformity and the Established Church, the spirit of co-operation was strong among those who were evangelically minded. In Bedfordshire, the Union of Christians organised village preaching and established new churches on a genuinely ecumenical basis. However, it was among the Nonconformists, especially the Independents, but also the Baptists, that the impact was chiefly felt.

Part of the reason for this new openness and vigour were the momentous events taking place on the national and world stage, creating a widespread sense of excitement and threatening traditional certainties. At home, it was becoming clear that the Industrial Revolution would leave few areas of social or economic life untouched. Overseas, the independence of the American colonies had been formally recognised at the Treaty of Versailles. Many Nonconformists in England had strong religious affinities with the colonists and had supported their cause during the War of Independence. Six years later the outbreak of the French Revolution sent shock waves throughout the country. In its early stages, before its bloody course led to revulsion and fear, it received considerable sympathy within the Nonconformist churches in England. Influential Baptist ministers such as Robert Robinson and his successor in Cambridge, Robert Hall, spoke out forcefully in favour of the freedoms the Revolution sought to establish[18].

These events were viewed with grave concern by many of those who were most closely associated with the traditional institutions in English society, but for many others they seemed to open the door to unprecedented opportunity. New possibilities, previously unimaginable, were opening up for those who had the courage and imagination to grasp them. The campaign for ministerial education among Baptists may seem insignificant compared to these global developments, but it is against this background that it should be viewed. For those who were involved, though they might not have understood the significance of all that was going on around them, it was a matter of vital importance. Without ministers who had been effectively educated and trained, there was a real danger that Baptists would not be able to take advantage of the opportunities before them.

Dan Taylor's Academy

The New Connexion was finally provoked into action over the education of ministers by the decision of the old General Baptists to form an Education Society for the training of young men for the ministry in 1794. Two years earlier, one of their number, Stephen Freeman (who according to W.T. Whitley was the first Baptist minister to be styled "Reverend"), "having been applied to as a proper person to instruct young men who have abilities for the ministry", had agreed to provide such instruction, and the churches had been requested to "exert themselves in their contributions towards this important undertaking"[19]. By 1799, just three students had been admitted for training, under the guidance of either Freeman or John Evans, but hopes were expressed that the scheme would gradually remedy the shortage of General Baptist ministers[20].

In 1796 the question of an equivalent society within the New Connexion was raised at its annual Association meeting in Boston, Lincolnshire. It was agreed to support a scheme of instruction and churches were invited to send subscriptions. Twelve months later the Association formally resolved that it was "highly necessary to do something to instruct young men in biblical knowledge, in order to fit them for the work of the ministry"[21]. Taylor, who was approaching sixty, was at first reluctant to take on the responsibility of being tutor but, when he realised that there was a danger of the whole scheme collapsing if he refused, accepted the invitation. A committee was set up, £175 was raised and a letter appealing for support was sent to the churches. At the beginning of 1798 an Academy was opened under his superintendency in the Mile End Road. Taylor ran it as an independent institution within the New Connexion until 1812, during which time nineteen students received instruction. The first to be enrolled was his own nephew, James Taylor.

An interesting account of the instruction provided by the first students at "Dan Taylor's Academy", as it was known, was given in the story of the Goadby family by Bertha and Lilian Goadby[22]. Joseph Goadby was baptised at the Barton church in 1793 and joined Taylor and two other students in Mile End in 1798 for six month's training. Studies commenced at 6 o'clock in the morning with lectures on a broad range of subjects given by Taylor, including Hebrew, Greek, English, History, Geography and Moral Philosophy. In order to fulfil his duties, Taylor reportedly drew up a 450-page manuscript of 135 lectures, together with others on miscellaneous subjects[23].

The committee required the students to spend two hours walking in the afternoon. Goadby visited various places of interest in the capital, including the House of Commons, where he heard Pitt speak, the British Museum, a Jewish funeral and a public hanging. He heard prominent London preachers, such as the Particular Baptist, John Rippon, in Southwark. While studying, Goadby procured a licence to be a Dissenting preacher and preached at Taylor's own church when Taylor was absent, which was a frequent occurrence, and elsewhere. After six months, he returned to Barton. Under the direction of its minister he took up pastoral charge of a small congregation in the area, and was ultimately responsible for establishing several new causes in the Leicestershire area, in particular the church at Ashby de la Zouch.

Taylor's achievement, as a largely self-educated ex-miner from Halifax, setting about the task of providing a broad education for students, and introducing them to the cultural life of the capital, alongside his many other activities, is impressive. He had many personal qualities from which those he taught could benefit, and was totally committed to the cause of ministerial education. His standing within the New Connexion was unrivalled, and he presided at almost all of the annual Associations he attended, frequently promoting the cause of the academy. As well as a vigorous preacher, he was a prolific writer of pamphlets and was not afraid of controversy. He had a reputation for stubbornness, but his sympathies were broad, and he maintained friendships with Baptists of most shades of opinion as well as members of other denominations. During his ministry in London he had opened a book-shop in Bishopsgate Street and compiled a hymnbook.

William Underwood has drawn attention to Taylor's "immense industry". He worked hard and continuously from the age of five until his death at seventy-eight. According to Underwood, amongst all his varied activities, as a teacher, farmer, shop-keeper and author, among others, "his preaching faculty was pre-eminent". He was, however, "a grave-looking and plain-speaking man ... employing a style which was utterly devoid of verbal ornament"[24]. There must be some doubt, then, as to whether his lectures gripped the imagination of his students. It is easier to think of him tramping the moors of the north to a preaching station, or engaging in a lively debate with an opponent, than behind the lectern of a classroom.

When Taylor started work as the New Connexion's tutor he was fifty-nine. Despite his "intrepidity of mind" and "physical hardihood"[25], it was really the work for someone younger. He had fairly recently suffered the loss of his first wife and from the mid-1790s suffered from intermittent poor health. At the time of his appointment he was struggling to make a success of the new *General Baptist Magazine*, of which he had been appointed editor in 1797[26]. In 1804, tired and in indifferent health, and needing to hand on at least some of his responsibilities to others, he was still active in most areas of the life and work of the Connexion, including the teaching and running of the academy.

The Lancashire and Yorkshire Association

In the meantime, the Particular Baptists of the north were also making progress in the provision of education for young ministers. A decisive step was taken with the revitalisation of the Lancashire and Yorkshire Baptist Association in 1787. This provided an effective organisational basis for promoting the cause of ministerial education and gaining the breadth of support necessary to make it successful in the long term.

By 1787 Fawcett was no longer minister of the Wainsgate church, having moved the short distance down the steep hillside to new premises in Hebden Bridge, the Ebenezer Chapel, in 1777. The new building was a huge improvement on the damp, cramped premises at Wainsgate built by Richard Smith in 1750. It seated between 500 and 600 people and was prominently situated at the heart of the growing town. Many of his congregation joined Fawcett in the move. It was a sign of substantial progress, both for Fawcett personally and for the Baptist cause in the area. His influence, both through his preaching and his writing, was being increasingly felt throughout the churches of Lancashire and Yorkshire. Several churches, including those at Rochdale, Bingley and Lockwood, owed their origin to his ministry, and the Wainsgate and Hebden Bridge chapels were familiar venues for association meetings. Fawcett was keen to deepen relationships with other ministers in the area and developed a particular friendship with the minister of the Byrom Street Church in Liverpool, Samuel Medley. Among his various publications, one of the most influential was his first hymn book, which appeared in 1782.

Between them, Fawcett and Medley were primarily responsible for revitalising association life within Lancashire and Yorkshire. It was at a low ebb, and at the annual meetings in Preston in 1786 they called on the church representatives from the two counties to make a new commitment to effective co-operation. They realised that a greater degree of unity was necessary if existing churches and ministers were to fulfil their potential, new churches were to be founded and new ministers trained.

Fawcett's establishment at Brearley Hall provided a general education, and was not exclusively geared towards the ministry, as is evident from an advertisement appearing in 1794:

> At Brearley Hall, in Midgley, near Halifax, a very pleasant and healthy situation, youths are genteely boarded and trained up, with diligence and fidelity and care, in the several branches of literature necessary for civil and active life, by J. Fawcett and assistants.[27]

A number of ministers were trained by Fawcett, either at Brearley Hall or at his later residence, Ewood Hall; these included William Ward, the editor and printer of a paper in Derby, who went on to become one of William Carey's companions in Serampore in India. Some, like the essayist John Foster, moved on for further training to the college in Bristol. Important though Fawcett's efforts at Brearley Hall were, they could not secure the future of ministerial education without being established on a surer basis. Gifted people like Fawcett, or his fellow

Baptist minister in Rochdale, Thomas Littlewood, who also ran a successful school, could pass on their experience and learning in private academies, but this was evidently inadequate as a long-term solution to the need for trained ministers[28]. A proper education required resources of time and money which could only be released by the churches working together.

Following Medley and Fawcett's efforts at the Preston meeting, the Lancashire and Yorkshire Association of Baptist Churches was reconstituted at Colne the following year. Seventeen churches from the two counties became inaugural members of the new body. From then on, reports and a circular letter were issued each year and the debates at the annual meetings took on a new importance[29]. The association became an important stimulus for change and development[30].

Fawcett's ministry at Ebenezer Chapel in Hebden Bridge and at Brearley Hall until 1796, when he moved to the nearby Ewood Hall, was varied and active. He wrote pamphlets, including one, an *Essay on Anger* that came to the attention of the King. For a few years he operated his own printing press. Although, unlike Dan Taylor, he refused invitations to leave Calderdale for ministries in larger centres, his reputation was soon established as a national denominational figure. In 1792, following the death of Caleb Evans, he was invited to become the Principal of Bristol College, but, regarding fifty-two as too old for the task, declined[31]. After the formation of the Baptist Missionary Society in the same year, he became an enthusiastic supporter, becoming Secretary of the local auxiliary at Halifax. His own indirect influence in its formation was not inconsiderable through the early education and encouragement of John Sutcliff, to whom the Society's formation owes as much as to anyone.

The Northern Education Society

It was not until 1804 that definite moves were made to establish a co-operative venture in the training of ministers in the north. Fawcett's age may have been a factor, as he faced the prospect of his own educational efforts at Ewood Hall coming to an end. Another factor was the example of Baptists and Independents in other places. The Independents were making significant progress in ministerial education in Yorkshire. An academy in Rotherham had been opened in 1795, taking the place of the one at Heckmondwike which had closed in the previous year. In 1800 another scheme was launched for training ministers at Idle, a few miles north of Bradford.

The example of the Baptists in London was also significant. During the summer of 1804 a new Education Society was formed, largely through the work of Abraham Booth, minister of the Prescott Street Church. Booth was, like Fawcett, an enthusiastic supporter of the Baptist Missionary Society and committed to the importance of an educated ministry[32].

According to Benjamin Evans, the decision to form a Northern Education Society started with a conversation between Fawcett, Littlewood and James Bury, a calico printer from Pendle Hill, Lancashire, early in 1804[33]. The importance of Bury's involvement was that he had financial resources to devote to the cause, offering £500 to help get the society off the ground. The annual meetings of the association were due to be held at Fawcett's church in May of that year, and the three men, together with the appointed preacher for the occasion, Thomas Langdon, minister of the Leeds church, used the opportunity to advocate the benefits of a society being created. At a specially convened meeting, it was unanimously agreed:

> That it is our opinion that there is a great want of able ministers of the Particular Baptist Denomination in this part of the Kingdom.
> That the Academy at Bristol and other institutions of the same kind have been singularly useful in assisting and bringing forward candidates for the work of the Ministry.
> That we form ourselves into a Society, under the denomination of the Northern Education Society, for the purpose of encouraging pious young men, recommended by the churches to which they belong, persons of promising abilities for the Ministry[34].

A membership subscription of one guinea was decided. Littlewood was appointed secretary and Bury treasurer. A letter from Fawcett was sent to the churches of the association and subscribers and friends were invited to a further meeting three months later, at which subscriptions would be paid and a committee formed. At this gathering, held in Rochdale in August 1804, Robert Hall of Cambridge preached and the society was formally constituted. The committee consisted of seventeen men, evenly divided between Yorkshire and Lancashire, and was entrusted with the task of finding a qualified tutor. The location of the proposed institution would depend on who was appointed tutor. It was assumed that he would combine his duties with the pastorate of a local church, which was the pattern in other similar institutions. In the event, both the appointment of a tutor and the finding of a location proved difficult to resolve. Persuading men with appropriate gifts, most of whom ministered in the south of the country, to come north, was not easy, and the competing claims of Yorkshire and Lancashire made the decision about location a sensitive one.

Determining the exact starting date for what we know today as Northern Baptist College is not easy. Claims could be made for the start of Fawcett's work of training young men at Brearley Hall in 1776, or even 1773, although the education he provided was of a more general nature than geared specifically for the Baptist ministry. Some might argue that the establishment of the New Connexion's academy under Taylor in 1797 is the correct date. The link between that establishment and the present college is a real one, as we shall see, but for most of its first hundred years it belonged to a distinct strand of Baptist life and should probably be thought of as having been grafted on to its younger relative rather than providing the original stock. The best claim to a "birthday" can be made for 1 August 1804, the day of the first General Meeting of the Northern Education Society in Rochdale. The story from that day to this is a continuous one, in spite of the changes the intervening years have brought.

An interesting sidelight on the discussions in Hebden Bridge and Rochdale in 1804 is shed by the opening in that year of the Calder canal linking the West Riding to Manchester. It went through both towns, and was the second major link between the two counties along the valley. It was to prove the most successful of the trans-Pennine canals. It enabled goods such as coal, iron and cloth to be transported in far greater quantities and more cheaply than had been possible by road, and was both a sign and a stimulus of industrialisation[35].

The need for an educated ministry

Before leaving the story of the beginnings of ministerial education among Baptists in the north of England, one observation needs to be emphasised and one question asked. The observation relates to the importance of organisation and co-operation among the churches. In the case of both the New Connexion of General Baptists and the Particular Baptists of Yorkshire and Lancashire, the ability of the churches to act in a united way was a necessary precursor to the provision of training for ministers. This may seem an obvious point to make: in the sense that few, if any, individual congregations could be expected to have the necessary resources to take up the task. It is important to recognise, however, that the need for ministerial education was one of the driving forces behind the move towards effective associating and greater denominational cohesion amongst Baptists at this time.

The familiar Baptist tension between a congregational understanding of the Church and the need to act together has often been most keenly felt in questions relating to the ministry. The significance of this tension can be seen with the development of institutions for ministerial training between 1770 and 1810. The way that Baptists expressed their desire to co-operate, whether in mission or in training for ministry (the two were not, of course, unrelated) was usually through societies. These had the effect of institutionalising denominational unity. Their committees inevitably attracted funds and powers and were to exercise considerable influence over future developments in denominational life. However, this is to look ahead. The significant factor at the beginning of the nineteenth century is the link between the provision of ministerial education and the new spirit of denominational co-operation[36].

The question relates to the motivation of men like Taylor and Fawcett. Why did they take the question of ministerial education so seriously? The most natural answer is that they were concerned about the welfare of the churches and the effectiveness of their mission, and saw a well-educated and properly trained ministry as indispensable for this. There was no doubt that the shortage of men who had the ability to speak in public, whether evangelistically or within the context of a Christian congregation, was a serious handicap to church life and growth. Some of the churches, like Rodhill End, where John Sutcliff's parents were members, and, indeed, Wainsgate itself before Fawcett became its minister, were at times not able to hold regular weekly services because of the unavailability of preachers to fill the pulpit. The general level of education was low and many church members were illiterate, so even those with promising ability needed considerable help in order to sustain a regular ministry. There were, then, very practical reasons for concern about ministerial education.

These pragmatic considerations must be considered against the background of the importance historically placed by Baptists on the office of minister within the local congregation. Although lay people could, according to the Baptist view of the Church, officiate at any service, and ultimate authority lay in the Church Meeting, the place of the minister, whose primary task was as a preacher of the Gospel, had always been highly regarded. The call to a local pastorate was taken very seriously as one of the most important decisions a church could take. This was surely part of the reason why Taylor and Fawcett regarded the study of Latin, Greek and Hebrew as important in their own education, and as necessary for other prospective ministers in giving them access to the original Scriptural texts and the writings of the Church Fathers.

This does not, however, entirely explain their inclusion of the classics, nor Taylor's insistence on introducing his students to the cultural life of the capital. It seems that he, and Fawcett, had a love of learning and culture for its own sake, and recognised the value of education not just for its usefulness in ministry but also for its own sake. They loved literature and were involved in printing and book-selling. This was partly the consequence of the excitement of discovery they underwent in their reading and conversations in the Wainsgate farmhouse in the 1760s. They longed to share this experience with others, confident that it would enhance not only the ministry, but also the lives, of those who came to them for training.

---

1   Moon, *Education for Ministry*, p.10.
2   *Ibid.*, p.11.

3   Fawcett preached at Sutcliff's ordination at Olney in 1775.
4   The London Baptist Education Society was founded in 1752.
5   Perhaps it was partly Fawcett's commitment to the task of ministerial training in the north that led him, after considerable heart-searching, to turn down the invitation to lead a prestigious London church following the death of its minister John Gill in 1772.
6   Fawcett, *An Account* p.176.
7   *Ibid.*, pp.220-1.
8   The Minute Book of the society records that in 1776 a grant of £25 was given to enable Michael Parker to study with Fawcett (Minute Book of the London Baptist Education Society, 1 March 1776).
9   Old Brearley Hall still stands next to the A646 between Halifax and Hebden Bridge.
10 Fawcett, *An Account* p.226.
11 Adam Taylor, *History of the English General Baptists, part II: The New Connexion of General Baptists* (1818), p.79.
12 The relationship between the New Connexion and the older General Baptists is somewhat ambiguous between 1770 and the complete break that came in 1803. An attempt in 1784 to heal the breach between them failed because the New Connexion could not unite with those who denied "the proper atonement of Christ for the sins of men" and justification by faith (Whitley, *Minutes*, p.183).
13 Taylor's letter was dated 21 February 1777 (John Rylands Collection, Manchester: ref. ENG.MS.371/f.118). It is unclear whether or not he was justified in his suspicions.
14 Adam Taylor, *History* p.329.
15 W. E. Blomfield, *Yorkshire Baptist Churches*, p.106.
16 Adam Taylor, *Memoirs of the Rev Dan Taylor* (London: 1820). From quite early in the eighteenth century an important centre for the manufacture and trading of textiles, Halifax experienced the dramatic changes connected with the early industrial revolution as much as any northern town. It was at the eastern end of the new turnpike linking the West Riding and Lancashire (completed in 1781) and this, together with technological developments in manufacturing, was rapidly transforming the town during this period. The famous Piecehall was opened in 1779. The new General Baptist Church was established largely as a result of Taylor's own efforts.
17 Adam Taylor, *Memoirs*, p.125.
18 Raymond Brown, *The English Baptists of the Eighteenth Century* (1986), p.134.
19 W.T. Whitley (ed.), *Minutes of the General Assembly of the General Baptists 1731-1811* (Baptist Historical Society: London, 1910), p.209.
20 *Ibid.*, p.233.
21 Adam Taylor, *History*, p.330.
22 Goadby, *Not saints but men*, Kingsgate, 1908?
23 Adam Taylor, *Memoirs*, pp.314-5.
24 Underwood, *Life of Dan Taylor*, pp.98-9.

Getting organised: 1770-1804

25 *Ibid.*, p.46.
26 The *General Baptist Magazine* only lasted for three years, ceasing in 1800. In 1802 a new periodical, the *General Baptist Repository*, was begun under the editorship of Adam Taylor.
27 The advertisement appears in *BQ* vol.6 (1932-3) p.231, without any indication of where it originally appeared.
28 Littlewood's Townhead school in Rochdale educated young women as well as men. It survived his death in 1817, eventually closing in 1860.
29 The Association may have needed a new impetus in 1787, but its meetings were not entirely moribund before that. The annual meetings at Halifax in 1764, for example, included discussions on a range of issues brought forward by the churches; and appreciation was expressed by church representatives for the opportunity provided by the Association for consultation and fellowship (see Raymond Brown, *English Baptists*, pp.86-89).
30 In the south-west, the Western Association played an important role in the development of Bristol College. The vitality of the Northamptonshire Association was, in the 1780s, transforming attitudes towards mission and was a necessary precursor to the formation of the Baptist Missionary Society.
31 Fawcett, *Life*, pp.271-2.
32 The London Baptist Education Society did not immediately start its own training institution. This occurred in 1810 with the establishment of a college at Stepney. Booth's name and address was circulated as a contact for Londoners who wanted their support for the work of ministerial education among Baptists in the north.
33 B. Evans, *Historical Sketch* (1854) p.28.
34 Minutes of Northern Education Society, 24 May 1804. It was a significant sign of the non-denominational spirit of the times that the Society did not designate itself as a Baptist institution.
35 There was a clear correlation between Nonconformist growth and the development of the new industries. The places of residence of virtually all the members of the first committee of the Northern Education Society followed a line of growing industrial towns from Hull in the east to Liverpool in the west, going through Leeds, Bradford, Rochdale and Manchester along the way.
36 It is worth noting that neither Fawcett nor Taylor had a Baptist upbringing. The spirit of independency that was strong among some of the Baptist dissenters of the seventeenth and early eighteenth centuries was not part of their own personal background. Their early Christian experience was within Methodism, which had a much more connexional ecclesiology than the Baptists and Independents of Old Dissent.

Chapter Three
The Early Work of the Baptist Academies

It was not easy for the Northern Education Society to find a tutor for its proposed academy. After the encouraging meeting in Rochdale in August 1804 Thomas Littlewood, the society's secretary, wrote to Baptist ministers in the Lancashire and Yorkshire Association asking for suggestions. It was clear that they would have to look south for a suitable candidate. In October they decided to approach James Hinton, the minister of New Road Baptist Church, Oxford, and a friend of John Sutcliff at Olney. If he refused, they agreed to contact Joseph Kinghorn of the St Mary's Baptist Church in Norwich[1]. This was ambitious, as Hinton and Kinghorn were two of the foremost figures in the denomination at that time. In the event, they both declined the invitation. The committee met with the same answer from at least three others, including William Steadman of Plymouth Dock (Devonport)[2]. The unattractive prospect of coming to such a remote northerly part of the Kingdom no doubt played its part in their decisions. The invitation to Steadman seems to have been a last resort. Littlewood told him that the society would have no prospects left if he answered in the negative. Nevertheless, he declined.

Possibly more in desperation than for any more positive motive, the northern brethren refused to take no for an answer from Steadman. He received several appeals at least to visit them to discuss the matter further. They told him that there were two or three churches needing a pastor in the area, and that the plan was for a joint appointment as tutor and pastor, the location of the church determining that of the academy[3]. Sensing their genuine need, and the opportunities such a situation afforded, Steadman felt unable to let the matter rest. He informed his church at Plymouth Dock about the approaches he had received. They agreed that, if the society was unable to secure a tutor in another three months, they would "then take the matter into serious contention"[4]. Encouraged by this, Littlewood told Steadman that the society had not the least prospect of getting anyone else.

William Steadman

In June 1805 Steadman arrived in Leeds to meet the committee and visit the area. He preached at Rawdon and Bradford, the meeting house at the latter, which held 700, being crowded on each of the three Sunday services. Initially, the prospects of a base in Manchester seemed good, as the church there was without a pastor, but these virtually disappeared when William Gadsby was appointed in 1805. Gadsby was of a strictly Calvinist persuasion and vigorously opposed the new moves towards Baptist co-operation for evangelistic and training purposes. The Back Lane Chapel, where Gadsby ministered for nearly thirty years, was the only Baptist church in Manchester, and his influence in the area was considerable. If Steadman had arrived a few months earlier, the story, not only of the academy, but of Baptist life in the north as a whole, might have been very different. Some of the Lancashire brethren still urged Steadman to consider coming to Manchester, but the challenge of forming a new church as well as getting the academy established was unrealistic. With the recent retirement of William Crabtree, the founder and first pastor of the Bradford church, the Yorkshire town now seemed the most favourable location. The church members were keen to secure Steadman's services.

Steadman was impressed with the eagerness of the people he met, and with the extensive opportunities for missionary work in the area. He was told he would have freedom to lead the academy in the way he wanted. In July the society wrote to his church at Plymouth Dock asking for their agreement to his resignation as pastor, and within a month the matter was settled. Just over a year after the society had been created, it was decided to house Steadman, and establish the new academy, in rented premises at Little Horton, a mile or two south of Bradford.[5]

Steadman was born in 1764 near Leominster in Radnorshire. His father was a farm labourer. An aunt paid for his early education at a

The early work of the Baptist academies 37

William Steadman (1764-1837), the first president of the Horton Academy

school run by Baptist minister Joshua Thomas, and later hired him as her servant, during which time he learned the trade of beehive making. The Countess of Huntingdon's Trevecca College was a few miles away, and he sometimes heard its students preach at the house where his uncle was employed as a coachman. In 1784 he was baptised and became a member of Thomas's church in Leominster. He was by this time employed as an assistant teacher by a local clergyman, and was encouraged to pursue his education further. Having been given the opportunity to preach in his own church, and encouraged to pursue a possible calling to ministry, he entered Bristol Baptist College at the age of twenty-four for training. The president of the college at that time was the evangelically minded Caleb Evans. Caleb was the son of Hugh Evans, who had done much to make Bristol a leading institution in the revival of denominational life towards the end of the eighteenth century. Two years after entering Bristol, Steadman was invited to become the pastor of the church at Broughton in Hampshire. One of his Baptist neighbours there was John Saffery, the pastor of the church in Salisbury. The two men became lifelong friends, and their correspondence is one of the best available contemporary sources of information about Steadman's work in Bradford.

Influenced by the evangelical spirit of the times, which lay very much at the heart of his training at Bristol College, Steadman established a preaching station at Stockbridge while in Hampshire. He welcomed the creation of the Baptist Missionary Society in 1792 and became a keen supporter. In fact he was urged by Samuel Pearce, Baptist minister in Birmingham and one of the leading figures in the founding of the society, as well as a fellow-student of Steadman's at Bristol, to become a missionary himself. Being deterred, partly by sensitivity to the feelings of his young wife Sarah, he was nevertheless eager to take part in the society's evangelistic endeavours. Under its auspices he undertook several preaching tours of Cornwall from 1796 with Saffery. They found the Cornish tinners "as civilised and intelligent a race of men as can be found amongst the labouring classes"[6]. John Rippon's *Baptist Register* gave an account of the tour, in which Steadman encouraged more itinerant preaching on the part of Baptist ministers. In 1798, after another Cornish tour, Steadman moved to Plymouth Dock. As minister of the Liberty Street church there he could continue his interest in mission work in the county more easily.

Steadman was described by his son Thomas as "wholly destitute of imagination . . . endowed with a large share of discrimination, and with a great facility of acquiring and retaining ideas of every kind". He had a strong sense of "the obligations of duty" and a "passion for the useful". His sermons were "devoid of rhetorical embellishment, their chief ornament was a natural and easy simplicity". He was an easy public speaker, and it was said of him that he could "shake a sermon from the sleeve of his coat"[7]. John Ryland, who succeeded Caleb Evans as president of Bristol College in 1793, described Steadman as a "great lump of goodness"[8].

Steadman's personality, training and experience suited him well for the challenge he had accepted in Bradford. It would nonetheless demand all his resources of character. Upon his shoulders lay the primary responsibility for the success or failure of the vision of John Fawcett and his colleagues. They were fortunate to have a man who not only possessed intellectual capacity and evangelistic zeal, but also the ability to communicate effectively with the working people of the growing industrial towns of the north.

The Horton Academy

Steadman found the premises rented for the president's home and academy at Little Horton "very pleasant and healthful". There was a good garden and a meadow large enough to support two cows[9]. It had previously been used as the home, factory and warehouse of a cloth and worsted goods manufacturer. Other evaluations of its suitability were not as generous as Steadman's. Benjamin Godwin, who came to assist him in 1822, described the students' accommodation as "of a very inferior kind", and Steadman's house as "a little low building"[10]. Later descriptions of the premises as basic, dark and damp, and possessing "not a single recommendation"[11], probably reflected the different standards of a succeeding generation, and did not take sufficient account of the type of accommodation available in the Bradford area in 1805.

Some modifications to the premises had to be made, and it was not until the beginning of 1806 that the first students could be welcomed. The old workshops and warehouses became a lecture hall, studies and bedrooms. According to Benjamin Evans, later a student at Horton, the studies were "singularly uncomfortable". They were each five or six feet square, with access off a single passage, and separated by wooden partitions. There was no heating and no floor covering. As student numbers rose, the bedrooms were able to accommodate between six and eight students each. The dining room was on the basement floor: "A long table ran from end to end, with benches on each side; and one or two chairs, and a small table in the centre, completed the furniture. We had

The Horton Academy, established near Bradford in 1805

no pictures, no papering; indeed nothing could surpass its baldness. Here all our meals were taken". It was in the dining room that students gathered and Steadman's guests enjoyed conversation while smoking their pipes[12].

At the beginning of 1806 the first student, James Viney, arrived at Horton, and by March he was joined by a second, Isaac Mann. Local ministers were encouraged to take advantage of Steadman's assistance as tutor, and if they paid for their board, could be accommodated on the premises for short periods. In the summer of 1806, two Scottish students were admitted. The numbers gradually rose, so that by the society's annual meetings in 1808 Steadman could report on the progress of eight students, three from Scotland and five from England[13]. None was accepted without the recommendation of his home church.

Upon Steadman's shoulders rested the major responsibility for administration and fund-raising as well as lecturing. His wife Sarah conducted the domestic affairs of the establishment. He drew up the curriculum over the first few years, no doubt using his experience at Bristol as a guide. He was also, throughout his time as president, pastor of the Bradford church. In the summer of 1809 the academy's rules and curriculum were drawn up and included in the society's minute book. Steadman's approach to the task of training was essentially pragmatic. He wrote to an American enquirer,

> I endeavoured to form as correct an idea as possible of the state of those churches with which the young men were likely to be connected after their studies closed, with a view to cultivate that in them which would be likely to make them acceptable and useful.[14]

Steadman's primary emphasis was on helping the students become proficient at preaching. A first priority was competence in English, and English grammar was taught in the first year, a necessity for many in view of the general poor standard of education. The "learned languages" were taught if there was "any rational prospect of success", Latin in the first year and Greek, both New Testament and classical, from the start of the second year[15]. Some time in the third year Hebrew could be attempted. Other subjects covered included logic, rhetoric, composition, geography, natural philosophy and chemistry, as well as theology and the Christian church.

What standard of teaching Steadman was able to provide, and how he managed to sustain such a syllabus, is difficult to know with any degree of certainty. His son Thomas wrote that he rarely required the students to present proof of their attention. Students were examined on their progress around the time of the society's annual meeting in July, but Godwin's later experience suggests that this was not a very effective exercise. Steadman, it seems, was remembered more for the tenderness of his prayers and his parental solicitude for the students' welfare than the effectiveness of his lecturing. He began each day by leading devotions, and each lecture with prayer, and frequently wrote to them with advice after they had left the academy. Each week an essay and a sermon were given by a student. Benjamin Evans describes this experience from the student's perspective in vivid terms:

> The doctor . . . in one hand was the large slate . . . ever and anon the pencil was used, and every stroke touched the nerves of the poor reader. . . . No countenance could more fully indicate the inward workings of the mind than the doctor's at this time. . . . Very soon the slate was filled, and with unusual energy placed upon the desk . . . we saw the clouds gathering around his massive head, and every moment we expected the thunder to roll. Endurance was at last exhausted. Suddenly the reader was stopped. 'Have you nothing about Christ in it?' said the doctor.[16]

Academic studies were frequently interrupted by preaching engagements. Steadman was always eager to accept requests for students to preach from churches in the area. Sometimes this involved time-consuming journeys on Saturdays and Mondays, often on foot, and not infrequently absences for several weeks at a time[17]. Perhaps in recognition of the problems these interruptions could cause, in 1809 the committee stipulated that students should not be allowed to go out as supply preachers during their first year[18].

Steadman's letters to Saffery showed his personal concerns and priorities. One of the main factors that had attracted him to the north was the "almost boundless" opportunities for village preaching[19]. These existed throughout West Yorkshire and South Lancashire, particularly in the Leeds area, where there was a population of about 20,000 within easy walking distance of the city. The correspondence is full of references to Baptist life in the area. His opinion of the quality of churches and pastors was low. On the ministers, he wrote that most of them were "illiterate, their talents small, their manners dull and uninteresting, their systems of divinity contracted, their maxims of church discipline rigid, their exertions scarcely any at all"[20]. Of his own church members in Bradford, he said that some of them were inclined to a way of proceeding in church "more resembling the ferocity of savages than the meekness of Christians"[21]. The Yorkshire people, he thought, compared unfavourably with the Cornish tinners:

> ...except for a few instances, whoever settles among the Baptists in this side of the Kingdom must make up his mind to great poverty, and to great vulgarity of manners. Delicacy, or what we in the south would be

only deemed civility, has scarcely any place here except in some of the larger towns; a Cornish tin miner would pass for a gentleman."[22]

Steadman soon took on a leadership role among the northern Baptists. He wrote the Association's annual letter to the churches on five occasions, more often than anyone else. He founded and led an itinerant society for the encouragement of evangelistic preaching throughout Yorkshire and Lancashire. The close link between this society and the academy is clear from the Education Society's Minute Book, which refers to several joint meetings between the two societies[23]. The students were often to be found engaged in door-to-door visiting and personal evangelism.

Steadman was frequently called upon to preach at the ordination services of his students. One example was in October 1818, when he gave a Pastoral Charge to George Sample at his ordination at Westgate, Newcastle-upon-Tyne. The three great qualifications of a Gospel minister, he said, were "courage, love and wisdom". He believed that preaching was "by far" the most important part of a minister's work, and that its primary object was "the conversion of sinners to God". He believed that it was worth risking everything, even life itself, in order to attempt the conversion and salvation of souls. He warned the new minister against criticising other denominations, exhorting him to see the enlargement of the borders of Zion, rather than the increase of his own denomination, as his goal[24]. He also warned him against an excess of study. It was necessary, to avoid shallowness and repetition, but a minister should not, he thought "smell too much of the lamp" [25].

Because of the wide knowledge of the northern churches he soon gained, Steadman was approached increasingly by churches and ministers for help with ministerial settlement, not only when his students or ex-students were involved, but also more generally. His strategic overview of Baptist life and concern for the welfare of the churches in general is obvious. References to the churches in the larger centres, such as Manchester and Liverpool, are frequent in his letters to Saffery. He was particularly troubled about the situation in Lancashire, and in Manchester especially. "The state of the Baptists in Lancashire is lamentable", he wrote in 1807. "There is scarcely a church in any town except Rochdale and Liverpool"[26]. In 1809, "Manchester seems more discouraging than ever"[27]. By 1816 things had not improved: "Manchester is in a melancholy plight . . . the congregation nearly annihilated"[28]. In 1820 the situation in Lancashire was still "mortifying"[29]. Generally in the association, church membership was growing throughout this period, but the progress of the Kingdom of God was not nearly as evident as Steadman would have liked.

Until about 1820 the academy seemed to be a source of satisfaction for Steadman and to pose few major difficulties for him, except that he would have liked more students. There were thirteen attending for at least part of 1814-15, and fifteen in 1816-17. It appears relatively infrequently in his correspondence, and he seems to have regarded it as just a part of his ministry rather than the major element of it. We can imagine it being like an extended family, with meals being shared by students, visitors and the president's family, frequent discussion on the state of the churches, an informal and frequently interrupted programme of learning and regular expeditions by individuals and groups to preach near and far.

Life in the north of England

Bradford itself was a rapidly expanding district in the early nineteenth century, although rather overshadowed by Leeds, its larger neighbour to the east. With a population of 8,000 to 9,000 in 1805, it was surrounded by growing industrial villages, which it gradually engulfed. Weavers and woolcombers abounded in every direction, Steadman told Saffery, as did iron men and colliers, both frequent attenders at his preaching services. For many, working life was exhausting and difficult, with long hours and dangerous conditions. Women and children faced constant peril alongside men in the narrow shafts and low passages of the West Yorkshire mines. Population growth in the northern cities was particularly rapid in the 1820s, and it was in the latter stages of Steadman's ministry that the true nature and scale of the industrial revolution going on became apparent.

By the time Benjamin Godwin arrived at the academy in 1822, the population of Bradford had risen to around 26,000. He found the town

The early work of the Baptist academies 45

to be full of carts, wagons and drays laden with coal, stone, lime, timber, ironwork and wool. If you escaped the din of those "rattling and lumbering vehicles you probably only exchanged it for the more regular clacking of the shuttle and the incessant whirling of spindles". By night the town was lit by smoking oil lamps. The villages in the neighbourhood were "swarming with population, smelling of mill oil, rattling with spindles and shuttles, black with mud and clouded with smoke". The country around was "broken with coal pits and iron mines", rendering the fleeces of sheep "dingy almost to blackness"[30]. This contrasted with the loveliness and beauty of the Yorkshire scenery, and the generous hospitality of the people — if the visitor could understand what they were saying!

Steadman showed some awareness of the social problems around him, describing the riots of 1812[31] and the construction of new mills in the area[32]. There is no evidence, however, that he involved himself directly in the political and social turmoil going on. One of the advantages of Little Horton was its detachment from Bradford's dust and smoke, although this was increasingly threatened as the years went by. The social and industrial changes going on provided an ever-present backdrop to the academy's life and work. The constant influx of weavers and combers from other parts of the country gave the area a cosmopolitan character that was reflected in the academy. Students came from Wales, Scotland and the West Country. The congregations, sometimes of many hundreds, to which Steadman and his students preached, were made up of men, women and children who faced a new kind of poverty and exploitation. This deepened with the process of industrialisation. The five-month 1825 woolcombers' and weavers' strike, which E.P. Thompson described as "the bitterest strike of Bradford's history"[33], involved 20,000 strikers and resulted in total defeat for the workers. As a result they were condemned to unhealthy home-working. Professions that had carried considerable status earlier in the century no longer carried respect and became poorly rewarded. Many people found consolation and a restored sense of personal worth listening to the revivalist preachers of the Baptists and the Methodists. Others rejected religion in any form as providing a solution. Some were ready to welcome the dangerous proposals of political radicals like the

Chartists, many of whose leaders came from the weavers of West Yorkshire.

A second tutor: Benjamin Godwin

The Education Society's minute book summarises the major developments that took place during Steadman's presidency. Trustees for the society were appointed in 1810, mostly connected in some way or other with the cloth trade. In the following year Steadman's annual salary was increased from £70 to £100. The academy was given a substantial boost when John Sutcliff of Olney bequeathed his library to the society in 1814. In 1816 Thomas Key, a wealthy patron, donated £1,000 to enable the buildings at Little Horton to be purchased, and this was done in the following year. One of the consequences of this was that, on Key's insistence, the word Baptist was inserted into the title of the society, so that from 1817 it became the Northern Baptist Education Society[34]. By 1817, twenty-three students had been through the academy, in addition to the sixteen then in training.

The academy had to contend with opposition from some quarters to the whole idea of providing education and training for ministers, and the society's annual reports often sought to answer this criticism. Baptists' lack of growth in Lancashire, especially in comparison with the Independents, was blamed on their objections to an educated ministry. It was pointed out that nationally, the Independents had ten "respectable seminaries" compared to the Baptists' three. The academy was not trying to make ministers, but to provide opportunities for "prayer, meditation and the diligent perusal of the sacred scriptures" for those whose "views are directed to the Christian ministry"[35]. In 1821 the committee disclaimed "all ideas of imposing ministers upon the churches, or of interfering in the future settlement of those they have educated, any further than by way of friendly advice"[36]. Two years later another lengthy defence of the academy, and other similar institutions, was given[37].

By this time, it had become clear that Steadman could not continue to cope with all the demands of teaching on top of his other responsibilities, and he was given permission by the committee to "employ any assistance in the classical department he can obtain"[38]. Initially this involved recruiting one of the academy's very first students, Isaac Mann, who was by then the minister of the Shipley church. Within two years a more qualified tutor was found in the person of Jonathan Ryland, the son of the principal at Bristol. His appointment did not prove a success, however, and lasted only three years. His successor, Benjamin Godwin, arrived from the pastorate of Great Missenden in 1822, and worked alongside Steadman as classical tutor until 1834.

Godwin's contribution to the academy was a significant one. He is also to be credited with a description of its life and work in his letters to his son. The immediate impact of his appointment, however, was financial. The resources of the society were stretched to the limit by the appointment of a second tutor, and more than once in the 1820s it had to limit the number of new students because of the exhausted state of its finances. Generally the number at the academy had grown to over twenty, but when, in 1829, the annual meeting heard that the society owed Steadman nearly £900 for students' board over several years, it decided that the academy could not accommodate more than sixteen unless income improved. The financial health of the academy was not helped by Steadman's eagerness to admit as many students as possible. The committee felt it was necessary to limit numbers, both for financial reasons and also for the sake of the quality of education the students received[39].

Godwin was twenty-one years younger than Steadman. In the year that he arrived in Little Horton, Steadman celebrated his fifty-eighth birthday. The combined burden of leadership in academy, church and association was too much for him, and responsibility for teaching and student life fell increasingly onto Godwin's shoulders. If his own account is to be believed, he developed the language work remarkably, covering not only a wide range of Greek and Latin authors, but also Hebrew and Syriac. He also taught Biblical criticism, mathematics, including algebra, geometry, philosophy and natural philosophy, illustrated by experiments. He introduced a preparatory class for those who needed more elementary help, and a comprehensive programme of annual examinations. Godwin brought in new ideas, and helped to raise academic standards.

In 1824 a second Baptist church in Bradford, "Sion", was opened. Its formation was largely the work of Godwin, and he was invited to be its first pastor, combining this with his work as tutor. The society's ownership of the Little Horton property enabled it to put some substantial improvements into effect, rebuilding both the principal's house and the students' studies. In 1825 the society's treasurer, Samuel Broadley, died, leaving the academy £5,000 in his will. An additional £5,000 was also designated by him for distribution by the society to needy ministers and their families. Unfortunately, several years of legal argument about the terms of the bequest prevented Steadman from seeing much benefit, but ultimately the legacy gave the academy a degree of financial security that enabled it to face the future with greater confidence.

Steadman's resignation

In his later years as president, Steadman faced increasing health problems, which cut down on his preaching. The academy also faced financial anxieties. Tensions arose within the student body, a consequence, perhaps, of Steadman's inability to provide the kind of energetic leadership required for a house full of young men cooped up for long periods in study. In 1828, at Godwin's initiative, the students were each called before the committee to be interviewed regarding "the unhappy differences between them". Three were immediately expelled and five others put on probation, with Godwin and Steadman being given the power to dismiss any "whose impropriety of spirit and conduct may threaten to disturb the peace of the house"[40].

A complicating factor for the academy was the large number of Welsh students. In 1832, having admitted students from Aberystwyth, Talybont and Carmarthen, the committee decided they could not admit any more. They later limited the total number in the academy at any one time to two. A major part of the problem was that many needed special help with English, but the fact that Steadman expelled one for getting into debt and another for "want of veracity and upright principle"[41] suggests there may have been other difficulties too.

The early work of the Baptist academies 49

In 1834 the situation at Little Horton became critical. Steadman's health was precarious. Expenditure was running substantially above income and domestic arrangements in the academy were inadequate. Godwin resigned as tutor, to take up full-time responsibility for the Sion church. His decision was hastened by a dispute with the students. The committee felt unable to appoint a permanent replacement in view of the uncertainty about Steadman's future, and called a special meeting of subscribers and friends in 1835 to consider the situation. Steadman, now over seventy, admitted he could not carry on, and offered his resignation. As his inability to lead the academy effectively was probably the main cause of its problems, this was immediately accepted. A fund-raising committee was set up and a decision taken to make the domestic management of the academy the responsibility of a matron rather than the president and his wife. The minister of the Leeds church, and a member of the committee, James Acworth, was invited to become president, and a month later he accepted the invitation. He had been trained at the college at Bristol and then taken an MA at Glasgow University[42]. During his twelve-years ministry at Leeds he had built a new chapel on South Parade and seen a dramatic growth in membership.

The transfer of leadership from Steadman to Acworth represented a major step for the academy. Steadman's contribution had been enormous. He had established the academy as a widely respected institution in Baptist life, making it a vital component of the revival of Nonconformity in the north, and won a position of influence and leadership for its president. In total, 157 students had been trained at Horton under him, of whom over 100 were, at the time of his retirement, still in ministry. At least one was serving with the Baptist Missionary Society overseas. He had preached at most of their ordination services and, by providing trained ministers, had done much to enable Baptists to respond positively to the unique opportunities presented to them during the first three decades of the nineteenth century. His generous character and common sense had ensured him a personal welcome throughout the country. The work of the academy had so far depended on Steadman's personality and gifts, but the appointment of Acworth was a sign that the society had matured into an institution not dependent on one man and was ready to face the changes the future would bring.

For Baptists, as for many others, circumstances were very different in 1835 from those in 1805. In terms of ministerial training, a London academy had been opened in Stepney. A regular journal, the *Baptist Magazine*, was providing denominational news for Baptists throughout the country. The Missionary Society had gained a full-time secretary and a London headquarters. New associations and societies had been created, and in 1832 the Baptist Union, originally formed in 1813, had been reconstituted into an effective national body for all Baptists. Numerically, both in terms of churches and church members, Baptists were growing quickly, as were the Independents and the Methodists. Actual numbers are notoriously difficult to assess for this period, but it seems likely that the number of Baptist churches at least doubled between 1800 and 1830[43]. There was a growing sense of denominational identity as denominational institutions proliferated. The easy-going ecumenical spirit of the turn of the century had disappeared.

Nonconformists were beginning to gain in confidence in the wider social and political sphere, encouraged by the general national spirit of reform. Lord Sidmouth had failed in his attempt to curb the activities of Nonconformist itinerant preachers in 1811. This Parliamentary defeat was partly the consequence of Nonconformist opposition, which included several leading Baptists. This was followed in 1812 by the repeal of the Conventicle and Five Mile Acts, and sixteen years later, after a lengthy campaign, by the repeal of the Test and Corporation Acts. Pressure for Parliamentary reform increased after 1830, and was rewarded by the Reform Act of 1832. This increased Parliamentary representation for the middle classes and the growing cities of the north.

Events such as these, news of which was disseminated through the expanding religious and secular press, encouraged Nonconformists to feel that they were no longer entirely excluded from the power structures of society. The removal of hindrances to political participation encouraged thoughts of unprecedented influence. Other developments promised other kinds of social change. Not least was the arrival of rail transport. The first regular steam train for passengers in the world started operation between Manchester and Liverpool in 1830. This was perhaps the most obvious sign that industrialisation was going to transform life for the whole population.

Changed times meant that it was an appropriate time for a change of leadership at Horton. Quite apart from questions of Steadman's health and age, he belonged to a generation ill-equipped to tackle the challenges and opportunities of mid-nineteenth century England.

Dan Taylor's Academy

Like Steadman, Taylor exercised a parental authority over the students in his charge. The work of his academy was hindered by his own ill health, particularly after his seventieth birthday at the end of 1808, and by the remoteness of London from most of the New Connexion churches. Of the seventy or so churches, over fifty were in the Midlands or Lincolnshire. Taylor was, furthermore, widowed three times between 1808 and 1816. The number of students he had responsibility for at any one time was small, generally between two and four, and the course of study short but intense. The students were expected to read through the Old Testament three times and the New Testament six times, during their first year. The principal object of the training was "to give suitable young men a competent knowledge of the English tongue, of the Bible, and of the true work of the Christian ministry"[44]. Other subjects, including history, geography, moral philosophy, Greek and Hebrew were taught as and when appropriate. In total, Taylor trained nineteen students during the sixteen years of his Presidency.

Management of the academy was in the hands of a private committee elected by its supporters. In 1812, dissatisfaction with this arrangement was expressed openly at the annual Association. It had been growing for some time. The committee resigned, and at the request of the subscribers, the Association assumed direct control. A new committee was appointed at the 1813 meetings. The church representatives felt obliged, in view of Taylor's "very advanced age, the natural decays of his constitution and intellect, and his domestic circumstances", to start looking for his successor. Joseph Jarrom, pastor of the Wisbech church and an exstudent, was asked to take over as tutor, and he accepted the position. This meant that the academy's work had to leave London for the Cambridgeshire town.

As a location Wisbech was not exactly central, but it was closer to most of the churches than London. Under Jarrom, the number of students at first slowly increased. In 1817 the Association heard that five students had been admitted. Concern was frequently expressed about the churches' lack of interest in the academy, especially in failing to encourage suitable young men to apply for training. In 1819 J. Bissill appealed in the Association's annual circular letter on behalf of the academy for "young men of a more cultivated mind . . . of better circumstances, and better education"[45]. In 1824 the churches were told that "the encouragement of young men to the ministry is much neglected"[46].

As at Horton, some students trained at Wisbech became missionaries. They served, not with the Baptist Missionary Society, which lay within the Particular Baptist tradition, but with the General Baptist Missionary Society, established by J.G. Pike of Derby in 1816. James Peggs, one of Jarrom's first students, sailed to Orissa in 1821 to establish the Mission's work there.

An insight into the training provided by Jarrom at Wisbech is given in an exercise book of one of his students, Thomas Hopley, who entered the academy in 1818. Although the book is described as a "sermon class notebook", it is much more than this, recording lectures on such subjects as "general rules for sermons", "a definition of the terms in theology", "a comparison between the Arminian and Calvinistic schemes", and "a comparison of the advantages and disadvantages of learned and unlearned ministers", as well as a fairly comprehensive course of systematic theology. Hopley was taught that the Christian ministry required first of all grace, then "a degree of material capacity or genius" and "an acquired knowledge in every branch of learning". Specifically, these branches of knowledge should include divinity, the languages in which the scriptures were written, composition, general knowledge and "knowledge of men". He was urged to add to these requisites diligence, and to "keep a constant guard against levity, and a bandying about of religious things".

Hopley's notebook was carefully written, as if it is a fair copy of notes taken during lectures. It reads as if it is a verbatim account, and includes such phrases as "in this lecture we shall. . .". It reflects a style

The early work of the Baptist academies

of teaching that seemed to allow little room for independent thought. It was obviously kept as a treasured possession by the author, who was minister at Hemel Hempstead between 1823 and 1845. The lectures cover a period of three years, which may well have been the extent of the full course[47].

The move away from London was popular, but the academy in Wisbech still struggled to win support from many General Baptists. Student numbers fell, until by 1824 Jarrom had responsibility for just one. Questions were asked about whether it could not be moved to a more central location, and whether academic studies and active ministry could not be combined in the training given[48]. Major change was not realistic as long as Jarrom was tutor, so the critics brought matters to a head by forming a separate society, by means of which, they believed, more effective training could be given. The General Baptist Education Society was formed in 1825 "to afford such instruction to brethren apparently gifted with ministerial talents as shall tend to qualify them to become more useful preachers of the everlasting Gospel"[49]. The society was given responsibility for supervising the training of men who were not able to devote themselves to whole-time training, as well as full-time students. At the start it was understood that students would spend three months of each year working with the Home Missionary Society, but after a few years this practice was discontinued because it was felt to interfere with their studies. Thomas Stevenson, pastor of the church in Loughborough, was appointed president and tutor of the new institution. One of his first students was his son John who, following further studies at Glasgow University, became classical tutor between 1830 and 1832.

Between 1825 and 1838 the General Baptists of the New Connexion maintained two ministerial training establishments, one, under the direction of the Association, in Wisbech under Jarrom and the other, under the direction of the new society, in Loughborough under Stevenson. In 1835 the Association formally recognised the Loughborough institution, and accepted that churches could choose which of the two they wanted to support. Given the number of churches in the Connexion, this situation was unsustainable, and when Jarrom was forced to resign in 1837 on health grounds, steps were taken to combine the two academies. Stevenson agreed to assume overall responsibility in

Loughborough, and his committee agreed to "cheerfully resign the direction of our institution to the committee appointed by the Association" in 1838[50].

One major difference between the General Baptist Academy and Horton was that the former became the responsibility of the denomination as a whole, while the latter had a greater degree of independence from its parent body, the Lancashire and Yorkshire Association. In part, this was because of the deeper sense of unity among the General Baptists, itself a product of their roots within Methodism. It was possibly also the result of the larger size and greater financial resources of the Yorkshire institution. Apart from this, however, the basic pattern of training seems to have been similar. Both developed the aim of having two tutors, although it was to be some time before the General Baptists could afford to appoint one. Tutors combined their teaching responsibilities with those of ministry in a local church[51]. The range of the curriculum was broadly similar, with an emphasis on the practical skills needed for ministry, especially that of preaching.

Challenges faced by the academies

Both academies faced similar problems in the provision of ministerial training. One was coping with the competing demands on students. On the one hand they needed sufficient time for their studies, but on the other the need for preachers in the churches was sometimes desperate, and opportunities for fruitful evangelistic activity were many and varied. It was, however, not just a matter of conflicting demands; it was also a question of how the training should best be delivered. Steadman worked on the basis that preaching engagements, preaching tours and short-term placements in churches were not so much interruptions to the training process as part of it. Taylor seems to have had the same approach. As academic standards were raised, the need for a more rigorous and systematic approach to study made this harder to sustain.

Another common problem was the almost complete dependence of the academies on their presidents. As advancing age restricted the capacity of both Steadman and Taylor, their academies suffered. An attendant problem was achieving a smooth succession to a new president.

This was partly an inevitable consequence of inadequate pension provision and the absence of any clear retirement age. It would probably have been better if Steadman, Taylor and Jarrom had all retired before they did, rather than continuing until poor health made the step essential. The problem of succession was exacerbated by the fact that the president was responsible not only for teaching and financial management, but also, with his wife, for domestic affairs and the spiritual and pastoral care of the students. The academy was, in effect, an extension of his home and family. It was impossible to conceive of an unmarried man fulfilling the duties of the presidency. Because his personality was an integral part of the students' training, a change of president meant, in effect, a change of academy, even if the location remained the same. In the case of the General Baptists, of course, it meant a change of location, from London to Wisbech, and then to Loughborough.

A third problem was the ever-present need to raise money. For the General Baptists this was alleviated somewhat when the denomination as a whole accepted responsibility for the academy. It was not an easy task to convince the churches of the need to provide funds in order to secure a trained ministry, and the task of raising money was constant and time-consuming.

The educational challenge facing the academies and their tutors was enormous. Given the basic level of educational provision generally in the country, the demands on them were almost impossibly broad. Needs ranged from the basic skills of reading and writing to classical Greek and Hebrew, from geography and history to sermon preparation and delivery. Two factors made the situation worse. One was that, for the most part, students were accepted regardless of their prior educational achievements. The second was the small size of the establishments, which meant that one tutor, or at the most two, had to shoulder responsibility for almost all the teaching. One cannot help but be impressed with the seriousness with which Steadman and Taylor went about drawing up a curriculum and writing lectures, but the practical usefulness of their teaching under such circumstances must have been severely limited.

The success of the academies, or colleges, as they became increasingly known, in the forthcoming Victorian period would depend on their ability to confront and overcome these difficulties.

---

1   NES Minute Book, 3 October 1804. It seems that Fawcett made his own approach to Hinton before this. A letter from Hinton to him declining the Presidency, and dated 21 September 1804, is in the John Rylands collection (ref ENG.MS.378/f.953).
2   B. Evans: *Historical Sketch*, given at the Jubilee Memorial services of Horton College in 1854 (pp.31-2 of the book produced to commemorate the occasion, published by J. Heaton and Son, Leeds).
3   See William Steadman's letter to John Saffery, dated 26 March 1805 (Angus Library).
4   *Ibid.*
5   NES Minute Book, 3 August 1805. There is some ambiguity about when the precise location of the academy was decided upon, as there are two minute books covering the early meetings of the society's committee. One states that the decision to establish it at Little Horton was taken on 3 August; the other merely says that the committee and tutor were asked to "look out for a proper situation" in Bradford at the annual meeting on 7 August.
6   Thomas Steadman, *Memoir of the Rev. William Steadman* (Thomas Ward and Co.: London, 1838), p.147.
7   *Ibid.*, pp.458-60.
8   Cited in Michael A.G. Haykin, *One Heart and One Soul: John Sutcliff of Olney, his friends and his times* (Evangelical Press: Durham, 1994), p.214.
9   Steadman to Saffery, 21 October 1805.
10 Benjamin Godwin to his son (letter number 35: 1855).
11 *Historical Sketch* in Jubilee Memorial, 1854, p.34.
12 *Ibid.*, pp.46-8.
13 NES Minute Book, 6 July 1808.
14 Thomas Steadman, *Memoir of the Rev. William Steadman*, p.318.
15 John O. Barrett, *Rawdon College 1804-1954: A Short History* (Carey Kingsgate Press: London, 1954) p.11.
16 Evans, pp.59-60. Steadman received an honorary doctorate from Brown University in America in 1815.
17 Godwin, letter 36, p.370.
18 NES Minute Book 4 July 1809.
19 Steadman to Saffery, 3 March 1806.
20 From his diary, cited by J.O. Barrett, *Rawdon College* (1954).
21 Steadman to Saffery, 22 June 1807.
22 Steadman to Saffery, 24 October 1809.

The early work of the Baptist academies 57

23 e.g. NES Minute Book, 25 August 1813 and 31 August 1814.
24 It was significant that the ordination service took place in an Independent chapel, and that Independent ministers took part.
25 College sermons, no.3 (21 October 1818) in the Rylands Library, ref. NBC S72.
26 Steadman to Saffery, 22 June 1807.
27 *Ibid.*, 21 August 1809.
28 *Ibid.*, 20 January 1816.
29 *Ibid.*, 3 March ?1820.
30 Godwin's letter to his son, written in 1855 (letter number 36).
31 Steadman to Saffery, 19 May 1812.
32 Steadman to Saffery, 5 January 1815.
33 E.P. Thompson, *The Making of the Working Class* (Penguin Books, Harmondsworth: 1968) p.312.
34 One of the features of the early period of revival within Old Dissent was the absence of any rigid denominational demarcation between Baptists and Independents. As the nineteenth century wore on, the sense of denominational identity grew, especially as denominational institutions proliferated.
35 Horton College 1820 Annual Report, pp.6-13.
36 Horton College 1821 Annual Report, pp.5-6.
37 Horton College 1823 Annual Report, pp.4-19.
38 NES Minute Book 25 December 1816. The fact that the committee was willing to meet on Christmas Day sheds an interesting light on how attitudes towards this festival have changed.
39 Godwin, letter number 35. Godwin's account of his invitation to the academy makes fascinating reading. Steadman made it quite clear to him that he was not at all keen for any second tutor to be appointed for financial reasons, but Godwin was persuaded not to withdraw by members of the committee, who were determined that it was necessary.
40 NBES Minute Book, 15 and 20 April 1828.
41 NBES Minute Book, 16 May 1832.
42 Education at the Scottish Universities was the only way Nonconformists could gain university degrees in Britain before 1836, when London University received its charter, as Oxford and Cambridge were open only to members of the Church of England.
43 E.A. Payne gives figures of 445 for the number of churches in 1798, and about 1,000 for 1832 (in *The Baptist Union, a Short History*, p.267). Briggs gives figures of 369 and 924 for the same years (excluding New Connexion Baptists) (John Briggs, *The English Baptists of the Nineteenth Century*, p.251).
44 A.C. Carter, *A Popular Sketch Historical and Biographical of the Midland Baptist College* (Kingsgate Press, London: 1925) p.5.
45 General Baptist Association Minute Book, June 1819, p.32.
46 *Ibid.*, July 1824, p.30.

47 Thomas Hopley, *First Sermon Class note-book when entering Midland College* (unpublished, 1818-1821).
48 General Baptist Association Minute Book, June 1822 and July 1824.
49 GBES Minute Book, 1 February 1825.
50 *Ibid.*, 25 September 1838.
51 At Horton this arrangement came to an end with the appointment of Acworth who was full-time at the academy.

Chapter Four
From Horton to Rawdon: 1836-1864

Problems at the General Baptist Academy

Following the amicable uniting of the two tiny General Baptist academies in 1838, the resulting Loughborough Academy survived for less than three years under the leadership of its tutor and president, Thomas Stevenson. He resigned on health grounds in June 1841 and died within a few weeks. There were only four students at the time of the amalgamation, rising to eight at the time of Stevenson's death. During Stevenson's short presidency, a new set of rules had been agreed. They were designed, among others things, to try to raise student academic standards, stipulating that every student "should previously have some knowledge of English grammar", and that it be "absolutely essential that he discover a taste for mental culture"[1].

The two years following Stevenson's sudden departure was a period of considerable uncertainty and division over the future course of ministerial training among the General Baptists. As the academy had no premises of its own, the library was "packed up" and the students entrusted separately to the care of four of the Connexion's ministers. The Annual Association in 1841 invited Stevenson's son John to become tutor. John Stevenson had for a short time assisted his father at the academy in Loughborough, but was by 1841 at the Borough Road Church in London. The Association told him that it was "exceedingly desirable" for the academy to be situated in the Midlands[2]. He replied that he was prepared to accept the duties of tutor, but was unwilling, or unable, to leave London. According to A.C. Carter, the historian of the academy, his church refused to sanction his removal[3].

The committee, having canvassed the churches for their opinions, considered the possibility of the institution being divided between the

Midlands and London. They ultimately came to the conclusion, however, that if Stevenson would not return north, another tutor would have to be found. Ultimately, the decision lay in the hands of the annual Association. When it met in the summer of 1842, it came to the opposite view, appointing Stevenson and agreeing to a move to London. Consequently, he moved to Camberwell, his house there becoming the academy's new home.

This proved to be a very short-term arrangement. Within less than a year, Stevenson told the committee he was resigning "on account of a serious failure of his health and spirits"[4]. It is probable that the strength of opinion in the Connexion that the academy really belonged in the Midlands played at least some part in his decision. In 1843, for the third year in succession, the Association had major decisions to make about the future of the academy. It came to the conclusion that in the light of Stevenson's inability to carry on, at least without extra help, it should definitely be established in the Midlands. It also agreed, citing the example of the Horton and Stepney academies, to discontinue the practice of combining the post of tutor with that of the pastorate of a local church. This gave the Association freedom to decide on a location that best suited its needs, without being dependent on a minister already in post. A full-time tutor could also devote himself wholeheartedly to the task of teaching and leadership. Joseph Wallis, the minister of Dan Taylor's old church in East London, was asked to take up the post. He did not share Stevenson's hesitations about leaving London, and a short time later he moved with his wife, who was to act as matron, to premises rented in Leicester, one of the strongholds of General Baptist activity in the Midlands. The house on Humberstone Road could accommodate Wallis and his family, as well as up to twelve students.

There was no doubt that "these repeated misfortunes severely tested the stability of the institution"[5]. One benefit, however, was that they forced the Association to face up to what needed to be done in order to develop an institution capable of training ministers effectively. The rough and ready enthusiasm of men like Dan Taylor had served an earlier generation of students well, but social and ecclesiastical change now demanded a more sophisticated and systematic approach.

At the time of Wallis's appointment, a more liberal and cultured spirit was influencing Nonconformity than had been the case in earlier decades. For Baptists, as for Nonconformity as a whole, chapels were being built on an unprecedented scale, some of them large and elaborate. Denominational unity and pride were increasing, symbolised by such things as the new Baptist Missionary Society offices in Moorgate, opened in 1844. Doctrinal differences between the Particular and General Baptists diminished in importance, both groups meeting together under the banner of the Baptist Union. In 1842 a leading General Baptist, J.G. Pike of Derby, had become president of the Union. Steps taken at Bristol, Horton and Stepney, such as the affiliation of Stepney to the new London University in 1841, were a challenge and a stimulus to the General Baptists to improve their own provision of ministerial education. Nonconformists as a whole were eager to take their place in the new world of Victorian England. They believed that a ministry adequately educated and equipped to grasp the new opportunities was a necessity if this were to happen.

Like virtually all those Nonconformist ministers who had a university degree at that time, Wallis had studied in Scotland[6]. He had been Association secretary and editor of the denominational magazine for some years, so was a well-known figure among General Baptists. Forty-nine students were trained under his tuition, including most notably John Clifford, who entered the academy in 1855. Wallis had a reputation for "amiability" as well as learning[7]. Unfortunately, while he brought an element of stability to the institution, he was not altogether able to fulfil the hopes of the Association. Partly because of his relaxed approach to training ministers, the fourteen years of his presidency were not without controversy. He was criticised for a lack of firmness in his dealing with the students, which led, at times, to criticisms over inadequate personal discipline and academic rigour.

In 1847, following a breakdown in the health of some students, they were earnestly recommended by the committee not to work too late into the evening, and "to take athletic and vigorous exercise, if possible, every day"[8]. The students, it seems, were not entirely satisfied with this proposed solution to their health problems, believing that the cause lay elsewhere. A few weeks afterwards they brought forward a series of complaints about the conduct of the matron, Mrs Wallis. They accused her of being "rude and insulting", of leaving them without adequate food and heat, and neglecting them when they were ill. Wallis himself was implicated in their criticisms.

The committee could not have been expected to side with the students against the president and his wife, so the fact that it urged them to make greater efforts in the care of the students suggests that it had some sympathy with their complaints. It is also notable that the minute book recorded the students' view that the academy would be best served if Mrs Wallis resigned as matron[9]. It was not really surprising, then, that this is what happened soon afterwards. The appointment of a replacement would involve the Wallises moving out of the house, and when it became clear that this was what the committee intended to do, Wallis himself sent a letter of resignation, charging the committee with breach of contract in depriving him of his house. It was able to persuade him to withdraw by offering financial compensation for the loss[10].

Further controversy arose in 1849 when the academy's secretary, Joseph Goadby, expressed his concern about its admission procedures. New students, he wrote, were "allowed to wander in without caution or correction"[11]. In the following year it was decided to institute an entrance examination to ensure competence in a range of subjects, including English grammar, arithmetic, geography, theology, Biblical history and English history.

The academy did not seem able to create any real enthusiasm from General Baptists for its work. In view of its history of frequent moves and periodic uncertainty about the future this was, perhaps, not surprising. Disappointment with Wallis's leadership, especially after his removal from the house in 1847, must have also played its part. In 1848 the committee expressed concern about the lack of sympathy and support[12]. Soon afterwards both the secretary and the treasurer resigned, following a disappointing annual report. In 1856 the *Baptist Repository* described the academy as "defective"[13].

The failure of the academy to make progress was partly because of the limitations imposed by its inevitably small size, given the number of churches it was designed to serve within the New Connexion. It was always likely that it would be the poor relation among Baptist colleges, a status that became more burdensome as its theological distinctiveness diminished over time. General Baptists themselves sometimes preferred to send their ministerial candidates to one of the Particular Baptist colleges, undeterred by differences in doctrine[14]. The whole question of training for ministry, however, was generally controversial among Baptists, quite apart from difficulties faced by particular institutions. Some rejected academic training of any kind, considering such human intervention as a denial of God's sole sovereign right to call and equip ministers of the Christian Church.

Such considerations no doubt influenced those who called for a review of the whole future policy on ministerial education in 1856. The immediate cause was the removal of Stepney College to an impressive mansion close to Regent's Park that year. Some leading figures within the Connexion called for a return of the academy to London to share with them in the new building. Although Joseph Angus, the principal of Stepney, was prepared to consider the proposal, the suggestion came to nothing, and after Wallis's death in 1857 the Association decided to continue its separate existence in the Midlands. William Underwood, who had been trained under Thomas Stevenson at Loughborough, was appointed principal, supported by William Stevenson as classical tutor, and new premises were sought in or near Nottingham. By the start of the 1857-8 session, a property on Sherwood Rise in the city had been secured. Underwood and Stevenson provided capable and stable leadership, though many regarded Underwood as severe and unbending. It was, perhaps, a necessary contrast to Wallis's relaxed attitude.

James Acworth

Between 1836 and 1857, while the General Baptist's academy was struggling for stability under five different principals in five different places[15], James Acworth was giving stability to the Northern Baptist Education Society's academy at Horton. Together with Henry Dowson, Steadman's successor as minister of the Bradford Westgate Church, and secretary of the society from 1840, Acworth provided the academy with the solid basis it needed to become a leading national Baptist institution in the second half of the century.

Acworth was born and raised in Chatham in Kent and trained for the ministry at Bristol. Although he had studied for a while at Glasgow University, and was eventually awarded an MA, he was more a practical businessman than a scholar. He preferred discussing theology with his students to giving formal lectures, and published nothing more than the occasional sermon. Unlike Steadman, he did not attempt to combine responsibility for a church with that of leading the academy, and upon appointment resigned from his pastorate in Leeds. He had successfully led the church from its original premises in the Old Stone Chapel to a new building in South Parade, having built on the work of his predecessor, Thomas Langdon, in establishing the church as a leading institution in the town. A contemporary said of him that his "example of industry and perseverance was more useful" than his teaching[16], and he soon gained a reputation for discipline. From the start he insisted on keeping the academy on a sound financial footing, restricting student admissions to numbers that could be afforded, and even going so far as threatening to resign if it ever got into debt.

To begin with, at least, Acworth relished the opportunity of working in the stimulating environment of mid-century Bradford. Shortly after his appointment he wrote to Edward Steane, co-Secretary of the Baptist Union in London, that the area was "becoming daily more and more interesting from an increase both of population and of wealth"[17]. Bradford was emerging as a major industrial centre, with a strong Nonconformist presence, particularly of Baptists and Congregationalists[18]. Acworth was "a highly esteemed citizen"[19], and became president of the town's Mechanics Institute.

The first few years of Acworth's presidency were relatively uneventful. Shortly after his appointment the "diffident" and "retiring" Francis Clowes was appointed classical tutor[20]. Some improvements to the premises were made. Student numbers continued to grow, reaching thirty, the highest ever, in 1842. The course became more demanding, and was extended to five years in 1843, when Syriac and Chaldee were added to the syllabus. A steady stream of applications meant that the academy could afford to be more selective in the students it accepted and the demands it made of them. At the end of 1842 the resignation of one student was accepted because of his "inability to pursue to the full extent the course of study prescribed in the Institution"[21]. A year later another was excluded because he "refused to complete the term of his studies"[22]. In 1845 several suitable applicants had to be rejected because of lack of accommodation[23]. The annual report that year appealed to the churches to commend high-quality students to the academy. They should be guided "by indications of mental vigour, of clear and ready apprehension, of expansiveness and improvableness, coupled of course with sterling principle, exalted piety, and unquenchable zeal for the glory of Christ, and the salvation of men". The churches were told that what they needed were "characters of lofty aspiration and noble daring"[24].

Following the establishment of London University, discussion took place on the value of establishing links either with it or with one of the Scottish universities, in order to enable students to matriculate. This eventually resulted in Horton joining Stepney in affiliating to London University in 1852. By then the syllabus had broadened to incorporate various branches of mathematics, such as geometry and algebra, and several scientific subjects such as mechanics and optics. Acworth was determined to raise the standards and reputation of the academy as much as possible. By the 1850s, the priorities of Steadman, with his emphasis on evangelistic preaching, and his reluctance to turn away anyone who demonstrated such a gift, had given way to a stricter and more demanding approach to the task of ministerial education.

The search for new premises

It is not surprising that dissatisfaction with the premises at Horton grew. The society's exalted ambitions for its "college", as it was increasingly styled, could hardly be realised in an old weaving shed and warehouse that were being increasingly surrounded by the smoke and dirt of industrial Bradford. From 1853 onwards, Acworth seriously started looking for a new home for the academy.

A possible change of location raised a question that had not exercised the minds of the society since Steadman's appointment back in 1804. Should they consider a move to Lancashire? Leading Baptists on both sides of the Pennines were ready to press their case. Circumstances had changed significantly since the early days of the society's work. Several towns in the north had now become substantial and affluent conurbations. Some had two or more thriving Baptist churches. The number of churches and church members had grown dramatically, especially in the 1830s and 1840s. In the early 1830s the churches of the Lancashire and Yorkshire Association possessed fewer than 4,000 members. Two decades later the figure had risen to over 11,000. Partly because of this growth, and the difficulty of maintaining a sense of fellowship with so many more churches coming into membership, the association decided in 1837 to divide into two along county lines[25]. Friendly relations continued, with regular joint assemblies for several years. The academy received support from both sides of the Pennines, as it did from other parts of the kingdom too, notably Scotland, and Acworth remained a leading and respected figure in both associations after the split. Soon after the creation of the Lancashire and Cheshire Association of Baptised Churches, as it was known, a resolution was passed acknowledging the connection between it and Horton[26]. However, there were some in Lancashire who believed the county needed and deserved its own academy. Others, like Charles M. Birrell of Liverpool, one of the leading Baptist ministers of the day and a keen supporter of the academy, believed that Manchester was the best location for an institution serving the whole Baptist community in the north.

The Accrington Academy

In fact, an academy for training Baptist ministers was established in Accrington for several years in the 1840s. Joseph Harbottle, minister of the church on Blackburn Road in Accrington, had studied at Horton, and for a short time had assisted Steadman in teaching languages there. Under his ministry the Accrington church grew considerably. In 1841, he and David Griffiths, who had also been a student at Horton, began receiving men for training for the Baptist ministry in Harbottle's Accrington home, with the support of several Lancashire churches, including Bacup and Cloughfold, Griffiths' old church. The institution provided training for about ten students during its short life, and closed in 1849.

The failure of the Accrington Academy to last was probably partly due to the theological differences between the two tutors. Harbottle was from the conservative wing of the denomination, holding to strict-communion principles (i.e. refusing admission to communion to any not baptised by immersion as believers), while Griffiths was known for his liberal views on such things as the atonement[27]. Another factor was Griffiths' obscure lecturing style. One of his Cloughfold congregation confessed that "many had to bring their dictionaries with them to the service, his long pauses giving them ample time to turn out the meaning of the long, strange words in which he delighted to embody his robust thoughts"[28]. The students in Accrington found they had to give the closest attention, and "the most strenuous exertion of the mental faculties"[29] to follow his lines of thought. Harbottle, too, was not, apparently, without his eccentricities. Not in favour of clerical attire or the title "Reverend", he looked like "a seafaring friend of the Principal"[30].

Manchester

In spite of the failure at Accrington, there were considerable arguments in favour of a move across the Pennines. In many ways, Manchester was an obvious choice. The town had been incorporated in 1837 under the Municipal Reform Act, and was granted city status in 1853. The conurbation centred on Manchester had emerged as the largest and most important of the industrial areas in the north, with a total population then approaching one million. Its growth was one of the most impressive features of nineteenth-century English social and economic history. The elaborate network of canals throughout Lancashire and Yorkshire that had begun with the Duke of Bridgwater's waterway linking his coal mine at Worsley with Manchester in 1764 was centred on the city. The same applied to the railways, which by the 1840s were rapidly replacing canals as the main means of industrial transport.

The argument that weighed most heavily with the Horton committee was not the economic and industrial importance of Manchester, however, but the advantages it afforded educationally. By 1850 the Wesleyans and the Congregationalists both had colleges in the city, as well as in the West Riding, but it was the presence of Owens' College that was the strongest attraction.

John Owens, a leading Manchester businessman, shared in the ambitions of several of its leading citizens for a university in the city. When he died in 1846 he left a substantial sum of money for the establishment of a university college. Most opportunities for pursuing higher education in England were then under the control of the Established Church. As a Congregationalist, Owens stipulated that there should be no test of religious opinion for students at the college, and that nothing should be taught that would be offensive to anyone's religious views. He nominated trustees from all the leading Protestant religious bodies in Manchester, including the Baptists and the Church of England.

Owens College was duly established, and in 1850 Alexander John Scott, a Scottish Presbyterian then holding the Chair of English Literature at University College London, was appointed the first principal. London University degrees were taught there, and it soon became the leading centre for higher education in the industrial north. The advantages of an association with Owens College for Nonconformist academies like Horton were clear. Aiming to provide an education in arts and science subjects as well as in theology, they were finding the burden of an ever-expanding syllabus increasingly unrealistic. The emergence of the new institution in Manchester seemed to many to be an opportunity too good to miss. The main obstacle was the desire of many Yorkshiremen to keep the academy on their side of the Pennines. Relying as it did on voluntary support, rather than any national or denominational funding, the influence of Horton's local supporters on any decision to move was considerable.

The jubilee celebrations at Horton in 1854 provided the Northern Baptist Education Society with the opportunity of reviewing the past and setting priorities for the future. Benjamin Evans gave an historical sketch of the college, concluding with the assertion that the premises had become totally unfit for the institution's purposes. "Manufactories are rising up in every direction", he said, "and pouring their dark and unhealthy clouds of smoke over them"[31]. The preacher, Benjamin Godwin, who had been the classical tutor at the college under Steadman, outlined the moral and intellectual qualifications required for ministers. The power of acquiring and imparting knowledge, the capability of fixed thought and of bringing inner thoughts out "in a lucid and impressive manner" were necessities, he believed[32]. He also stressed the need for a course of regular study to develop habits and training in thinking. Academic institutions like Horton were required as much as ever, especially in view of the increasing standards of education generally and the rising tide of atheistic and sceptical literature emanating from Germany and elsewhere. Godwin, like Evans, urged a change of location for the college. "The smoke and noise", and the "heterogeneous and annoying buildings" of Bradford now surrounding it, rendered the situation "unendurable"[33]. A third tutor, extra scientific instruments and a museum were also needed.

Godwin also advocated the provision of two kinds of course at the college. He wanted to see the current five-year course restricted to the most academically gifted students, and a less demanding two-year course established for those who had "neither the capacity nor the inclination" for learning Biblical languages and other more serious study[34]. His opinion reflected the views of others who were responsible for ministerial training at about this time. R.W. Dale, principal of the Congregationalists' Airedale College, for example, acknowledged that, while the pursuit of the highest academic achievement was important for some ministerial candidates, it was not appropriate for all. The opening of the Congregational Institute in Nottingham in 1860, running two to three-year courses with a practical and preaching emphasis, was designed to meet the need of less academic students. Spurgeon's Pastors' College, that commenced work in 1856, had a similar approach, welcoming any student who demonstrated preaching ability, regardless of educational background or intellectual ability. Unlike Godwin and Dale, however, Spurgeon viewed academic achievement in itself as being irrelevant for ministry.

In 1855 the college committee learned that £5,000 had been promised towards a new college, and decided that the time had come to leave Horton[35]. Following Godwin's suggestion of a two-track programme of training, it came to the conclusion that instruction would best be given in two distinct locations, one in the Bradford area providing a "sound theological education" and the other in the neighbourhood of Owens' College providing "a more extended system of literary and biblical instruction". The course in Bradford could either lead directly to ministry, or be the foundation for the more advanced study in Manchester[36].

Early in 1856 Portland House, in Victoria Park, Manchester was purchased for £3,500. It was decided to continue using the Horton premises for the Bradford branch of the college. Acworth would continue leading the work at Horton, and Charles Birrell would be asked to preside in Manchester, sharing tutorial duties there with S.G. Green, who had replaced Clowes as classical tutor in 1851[37].

Rawdon College

During the course of the next year this adventurous scheme, and any intention of moving part of the academy to Manchester, was abandoned. The reason for this change of heart is not entirely clear. Officially, the "undesirability of proceeding any further with the project of removing the College from Yorkshire" was given as a reason, which suggests that rivalry between the two counties played at least some part[38]. The college's 1857 annual report states that the churches were unable or unwilling to give financial support to the move. Portland House was put back on the market[39].

The search for a suitable site in the Bradford area began. Robert Milligan, a previous mayor of the town and prominent Congregationalist, had offered a plot of land on very favourable terms some time previously, and agreement was soon reached with him for a 7½-acre woodland site a short distance from his house near the village of Rawdon. Rawdon, the location of one of the oldest Baptist churches in the county, was in the parish of Guiseley, about four miles north of Bradford and six miles north-west of Leeds. The plot was 200 yards from the river Aire and close to the railway line running along the valley, thus, the 1858 annual meeting was told, combining "the benefits of both Town and Country"[40]. It was a beautiful spot, and inspired many poetic tributes, including one by William Medley, tutor for many years, who wrote of "sweet Nature's very own, wooded depths, green winding walks, moss-grown rocks bracken clothed, where anemones and hyacinths find the home they love"[41]. Although only a few miles distant, it was as far removed from the soot and noise of industrial Bradford as could be imagined. The fact that the Congregationalists' Airedale College was very close by was another advantage. For some years friendly relations had existed between the students of Horton and Airedale, and closer proximity offered the prospect of greater co-operation.

Acworth's health was beginning to deteriorate, and he found the uncertainty surrounding the future of the college between 1854 and 1858 difficult. He was not living in the Horton premises, that responsibility having been taken over by a "resident tutor", C. Daniell. In 1857 Acworth offered to resign. Officially this was on health grounds, although disappointment over the scheme for the premises and anxiety over the financial loss incurred in the purchase and sale of Portland House also may have played a part. He was persuaded to carry on until the new building had been completed[42]. A competition was held for its design. This was won by the architects H.J. Paull of Cardiff, and in August 1858 the foundation stone was laid at the annual meetings. The *Bradford Review* reported that Sir Morton Peto, who had agreed to perform the ceremony, had been delayed by storms in the Bay of Biscay following one of his business trips abroad, and was unable to be present. The treasurer, Thomas Aked, deputised for him[43]. The new building was opened with suitable celebrations, including a sermon by the Hon. and Rev. Baptist Noel of London, in September 1859. The generosity of Milligan, Titus Salt and other Yorkshire friends of the college helped ensure that it could start work in its new home free of debt. Shortly afterwards the Horton premises were sold, fifty-four years after they had been originally secured by the society.

Rawdon College was, for over a hundred years, an impressive monument to Victorian Baptists' commitment to the need for an educated ministry. Acworth, speaking at the opening celebrations, suggested a motto of "Esto Perpetua" ("Let it be for ever"), hoping it would continue until the final consummation of Christ's Kingdom[44]. The main college building provided accommodation for a resident tutor and twenty-six students, consisting of a study and bedroom for each, together with library, lecture room, dining room and other ancillary rooms. The main stairs led from the entrance hall to the library, past a large stained-glass window erected in memory of John Mackay, a missionary trained at Horton who had been killed in the Indian mutiny of 1857. The college's "fine gabled frontage" faced southwest, towards the river Aire in the valley below. Along its length was a broad terrace. Paths and drives were laid through the surrounding woodland.

The erection of Rawdon College was important not only in providing accommodation for ministerial training, but also as a sign of Baptists' aspirations for their future ministry. It was a place for quiet reflection and study, shut away in the leafy seclusion of Cragg Wood from the distractions and challenges of nearby Leeds and Bradford. Its stone towers, gables and terrace were eloquent testimony to the fact that the Baptist ministry was advancing, culturally and intellectually, and no longer felt at home among the sweat and dust of the working classes. The character of the rapidly industrialising towns of the West Riding and southern Lancashire had been transformed since Steadman arrived in 1805. Capitalism had brought spectacular growth in population and wealth, its success symbolised by the building of Manchester Free Trade

The main entrance to Rawdon College

Hall and Leeds Town Hall, both opened in 1853. The leading figures among the entrepreneurs who had benefited most from these changes, and helped shape them, were often Nonconformists. They exercised their new power, and expressed their new prestige, through the institutions they created and the buildings they erected. The denominational colleges were among their most imposing structures. The Congregationalists' Manchester College with its arcades and ninety-two-foot tower, which was opened in 1843, and the new Airedale College (1877) were among the most notable of these. Baptists could not match the Congregationalists for wealth, but Rawdon was the first and best venture of this kind.

The move to Rawdon also expressed other changes in the attitudes of Baptists. It was increasingly clear that most ordinary working people, whose confidence and influence grew as the century progressed, especially in the north of England, felt alienated from organised religion of all kinds. The 1851 national census shocked many by showing that only half the population nationally were church attenders. The poor and working classes were those least likely to darken the doors of a place of worship. Among the main Nonconformist denominations, the Baptists and the Primitive Methodists tended to draw their congregations more from the working classes than the Congregationalists and the Wesleyans. The move from Horton to Rawdon could be seen as a sign that Baptists were not really interested in maintaining this connection. It is noteworthy that one of the options rejected by the move was the retention of Horton as a place for a shorter and less academic course. Such an option could have provided training for those with a closer affinity with the working classes.

The *Freeman*, a weekly newspaper read by many Baptists, was sent a picture of the new college at Rawdon during its construction. The attention of the readers was drawn to an apparently minor detail, but one that is suggestive of the kinds of tensions and changes underlying the move:

> We observe that in the foreground of the picture several figures are represented as attired in not very elegant black gowns: we suppose that these are put in merely for artistic reasons: we hope the Committee at Bradford do not intend to follow the example which has too frequently

been set them, by "apeing" a fashion, which, however proper in older institutions, in a modern college is simply absurd.[45]

Rawdon symbolised the seriousness with which Baptists wanted their ministry to be regarded, not least academically. In the long run, however, it meant academic and social isolation. Apart from Owens' College, institutions for adult training and education were springing up in many of the larger northern towns and cities. The new building was too distant from any of them for students easily to take advantage of their courses. Some sharing with the Congregationalists at Airedale, both for students and tutors, would be possible, but this was of only limited value. Rawdon continued the affiliation to London University that had been established at Horton, and prepared its more able students for examinations offered there[46], but this was no real substitute for the educational stimulus available in places like Leeds or Manchester.

Acworth's resignation

The first three years at Rawdon were fairly uneventful. Acworth continued as president until the end of 1862, when he once more tendered his resignation to the committee, saying that the time had come for him to retire. He was sixty-four. A few months later the classical tutor Samuel Green accepted the post of president and theological tutor. Green and his wife were at the time of his appointment resident at the college, having taken over responsibility for its domestic affairs from Daniell.

The 1863 annual meetings gave the friends and subscribers of the college the opportunity to pay generous tribute to Acworth's achievements after a presidency of twenty-eight years. His status among Baptists nationally was shown by his having served as president of the Baptist Union no less than four times[47]. In his response, Acworth said that he was withdrawing because the institution was "in its most palmy state". He went on, "Happily our vessel is at this moment in admirable trim. …We have abundant reason, brethren, to congratulate one another"[48]. Twelve months after Acworth's retirement and Green's appointment, the college secretary, Henry Dowson, also resigned. For twenty-three years, alongside his ministry as Steadman's successor at Westgate, he had worked with Acworth, and much of the credit for the achievements of that period belonged to him. In his letter of resignation, he wrote that he was compelled "by the pressure of manifold engagements" to take this step[49]. He was replaced by J.P Chown, a fellow minister in Bradford. The withdrawal of both Acworth and Dowson, so soon after the move to Rawdon, meant that the work of the society was entering an entirely new phase. The academy, with its reminders of eighteenth-century Dissent, had disappeared, its place having been taken by a college that was not only proud of its Nonconformist heritage, but also ready to take its rightful place in the social and ecclesiastical life of Victorian England.

Chilwell

Possibly inspired by the example of Rawdon, the General Baptist College in Nottingham also moved to new premises out of town in 1862. Having considered the possibility of purchasing the house rented in Sherwood Rise since its move to Nottingham five years earlier, the committee decided instead to buy premises in Chilwell, a village three or four miles to the south. They had been used previously by a leading Nottingham school, and were situated in eight acres of ground. It was later described as a "collegiate paradise", with opportunities for "afternoon walks through leafy lanes and golden cornfields, or along the banks of the silvery Trent"[50]. The parallels with Rawdon are obvious.

The principal, William Underwood, who was regarded by many as a severe and unapproachable figure, was assisted by his sister as matron and William Stevenson, tutor for non-theological subjects. Chilwell was an attractive place for young men to pursue their studies, but naturally it was not always a paradise. They were not allowed to smoke on the premises, and were expected to provide their own coals, firewood, study lights, soap and towels[51]. In July 1864 a special committee meeting had to be called to consider the case of a student who had unwisely allowed the female servant of the college to visit him in his study. In his defence he told the committee that he was "honourably engaged" to her, but confessed his "indiscretion" in doing this. By a narrow margin the committee, while exonerating him from any charge of immorality, felt obliged to ask him to retire from the college[52].

The move to Chilwell, where the college remained for twenty years, marked the start of a period of stability and relative prosperity. This must have been a welcome change after the almost constant uncertainty about its future since the retirement of Dan Taylor nearly fifty years before. The summer of 1863, when Acworth was congratulating the supporters of Rawdon for what they had achieved, was also a time when the General Baptists had reason to feel pleased with themselves. Academic standards were rising, student discipline was being maintained and leadership was in capable hands. Prospects for the future seemed good.

---

1   GBES Minute Book, 28 April 1840.
2   Minutes of the General Baptist Association, 29 June – 2 July 1841.
3   A.C. Carter, *A Popular Sketch Historical and Biographical of the Midland Baptist College* (Kingsgate Press, London, 1925) p.12.
4   GBES Minute Book, 23 May 1843.
5   Carter, p.13.
6   It was to be many years before divinity degrees were available from London University.
7   Carter, p.14.
8   GBES Minute Book, 27 April 1847.
9   *Ibid.*, 8 June 1847.
10 *Ibid.*, 15-22 July 1847.
11 *Ibid.*, 5 April 1849.
12 *Ibid.*, 2 May 1848.
13 Cited in Frank Rinaldi, *The Tribe of Dan* (PhD thesis, Glasgow) p.214.
14 In 1831 J.G. Pike sent his son to Stepney College, and in 1863 Joseph Goadby's son Frederick also preferred Regent's Park to the General Baptist College.
15 Jarrom in Wisbech, Thomas Stevenson in Loughborough, John Stevenson in London, Wallis in Leicester and Underwood in Nottingham.
16 Henry Kelsall of Rochdale, speaking at the annual meetings in 1863 (*Bradford Review*, 27 June 1863).
17 Correspondence of Edward Steane (Angus library), letter dated 29 August 1836.
18 The first two mayors of Bradford, Robert Milligan (1847-8) and Titus Salt (1848-9) were Congregationalists. They both gave support to Acworth in his work at Horton and Rawdon.
19 William Medley, *Rawdon Baptist College Centenary Memorial* (Kingsgate Press, London: 1904) p.27.
20 *Ibid.*, p.23.
21 Horton College Minute Book, 21 December 1842.

From Horton to Rawdon:1836-1864 77

22 *Ibid.*, 20 December 1843.
23 *The Church*, July 1845.
24 Annual Report of the NBES for 1845, p.11.
25 In fact the division did not occur quite as neatly as this. The churches of the North and East Ridings had already formed their own Associations and did not rejoin the Yorkshire Association until 1847.
26 Records of the Lancashire and Cheshire Association of Baptised Churches, 5-6 June 1838.
27 A difference of opinion between the two men on the atonement in the 1850s was one of the factors leading to the formation of a breakaway association in the north west in 1859.
28 Abel Jones Parry, cited in James Edward Watson, *The Educational Activities of Baptists in England during the 18th and 19th Centuries, with Particular Reference to the North-West* (University of Liverpool MA, 1947) p.108.
29 Robert J.V. Wylie, *The Baptist Churches of Accrington and District* (W. Shuttleworth: Accrington, 1923) p.128. The memoir of Griffiths in the 1863 *Baptist Handbook* described his style as "often obscure in the estimation of common hearers". Given the usual convention of speaking well of people on such occasions, this can probably be taken to mean that he was virtually incomprehensible.
30 Wylie, p.131.
31 Rev. B. Evans, *Historical Sketch*. In *The Jubilee Memorial of Horton College Bradford* (J. Heaton and Son: Leeds, 1854), p.68.
32 Sermon by Rev. B. Godwin DD at the Jubilee Service of Horton College on 2 August 1854. In *The Jubilee Memorial of Horton College*, p.7.
33 *Ibid.*, p.20.
34 *Ibid.*, p.22.
35 Horton College Minute Book, 1 August 1855.
36 *Ibid.*, 21 August and 2 October 1855.
37 *Ibid.*, 19 February and 12 March 1856. It is clear from these minutes that Birrell was intended to be the senior tutor of the college. His salary was fixed at £300, plus residence in Manchester, while Acworth's was £250.
38 *Ibid.*, 6 August 1856. John Barrett remarks that the reasons for this change in plans are "wrapped in obscurity" (John O. Barrett, *Rawdon College (Northern Baptist Education Society) 1804-1954: A Short History* (Carey Kingsgate Press: London, 1954) p.23.
39 Horton College Annual Report, 1857, p.11.
40 Horton College Annual Report, 1858, p.11.
41 William Medley, *Rawdon Baptist College Centenary Memorial* (Kingsgate Press: London, 1904) p.7.
42 *Ibid.*, 4 August 1857.
43 Bradford Review, 5 August 1858.
44 J.D. Rowland, *Esto Perpetua* (in the *Rawdon College Magazine*, No.10 (1959), pp.18-20).

45 *Freeman*, 11 May 1859.
46 At this stage, London University did not offer degrees in divinity or theology.
47 Acworth was President of the Baptist Union in 1840, 1856 and 1859 as well as 1861.
48 *Bradford Review*, 27 June 1863.
49 Rawdon College Report, 1864, p.18. Subsequent events raised questions over whether there were other reasons for Dowson's resignation, but these belong to a subsequent part of the story.
50 A.C. Carter, pp.19-20.
51 *Rules for the Government of the Baptist College Chilwell*, in the Minute Book of Nottingham Baptist College, 1862 annual meeting.
52 Minute Book of Nottingham Baptist College, 5 July 1864.

Chapter Five
The Creation of Manchester Baptist College

Baptism and Communion

As an institution, Manchester Baptist College had its origin in 1866 when the training of ministers started at Chamber Hall in Bury. Two fundamental factors lay behind the formation of this second Baptist theological college in the north of England. One was doctrinal. The other was related to rivalry between Yorkshire and Lancashire and the desire of Lancashire Baptists to have a college of their own.

The doctrinal issue was not limited to Lancashire or the north. Ever since the Evangelical Revival had begun to have an impact on the Baptist denomination at the end of the eighteenth century, some had expressed concern about the dilution of Baptist principles. This related in particular to church polity and discipline, central to which was baptism. Changes in practice had resulted from the widespread evangelistic activity that had been such a feature of Baptist life in the forty years or so around the turn of the century. It frequently involved co-operation with other Nonconformists, especially the Independents, and occasionally with the Church of England. The resulting church growth had brought into their churches large numbers of new people with no knowledge of Baptist history and principles. In many people's minds, the ready response to the preaching of the Gospel had relegated previously held convictions over such things as church membership, baptism and communion to a secondary position. In the minds of others, however, this amounted to an abandonment of vital and long-cherished principles.

By the 1820s, the question around which controversy was particularly intense was whether or not to open fellowship at the communion table to people who had not been baptised by immersion as believers. Infant baptism was regarded almost universally by Baptists as unscriptural and therefore invalid, although the strength with which this opinion was held varied. Robert Hall of Cambridge, Leicester and Bristol, and Joseph Kinghorn of Norwich, two of the country's leading Baptist ministers, were the most prominent antagonists in this debate. Hall maintained that faith alone was needed for communion. Baptism, he argued, was no more an indispensable condition for communion than it was for salvation. Kinghorn, on the other hand, pleaded for a proper adherence to Scriptural discipline and order at the table, which required that baptism preceded communion.

Hall carried many Baptists with him, and the practice of open communion was fairly widespread by the 1830s. However, a significant minority of churches continued to adhere to strict, or closed Baptist principles. The issue rarely disrupted fellowship among Baptists in a serious way, although there were a number of church splits, including one affecting Thomas Littlewood's church in Rochdale as early as 1809. It was brought into sharper focus when Christians from different traditions sought to express their unity through inter-denominational societies such as the Evangelical Alliance, founded in 1846.

Sympathy with the strict Baptist position was particularly evident among the Baptists of Lancashire. This was partly because of the influence of the ultra-Calvinist William Gadsby, minister at Back Lane Baptist Chapel in Manchester, who opposed not only open communion but also co-operation in mission and association between churches of any kind[1]. Gadsby's converts and sympathisers included John Kershaw of Rochdale, and their views were disseminated through their monthly paper, the *Gospel Standard*, founded in 1835. Although most of them would have nothing to do with their fellow Baptists in the Lancashire and Yorkshire Association, they kept the fire of old-style Calvinism burning in the area. There was a range of views among strict Baptists over the communion question, ranging from the Gadsbyites at one end of the spectrum, through those who formed themselves into Strict Baptist Associations, as happened in London and East Anglia, to those at the other end of the spectrum who were quite prepared to work together with open-communion Baptists. A strict-communion policy and conservatism in doctrine did not necessarily go together, as Charles Spurgeon, who practised open communion, showed. The Manchester College was founded by Baptists who were both strict over communion and doctrinally conservative, but who, for the most part, did not want to separate themselves from the main stream of denominational life.

The second factor that led to the creation of the college had to do with geography as much as anything else. Many Lancashire Baptists had been ambitious for an institution for training ministers on their side of the Pennines from the very early years of the nineteenth century. This was strengthened when the Lancashire and Yorkshire Association divided into two separate county associations in 1837. The short-lived Accrington academy under Griffiths and Harbottle in the 1840s was an attempt to satisfy this desire. For the most part, however, support for the academy at Horton remained strong, and Acworth commanded as much respect in Lancashire after the division of the association as he had before.

The plans of the Northern Education Society to establish a centre in Manchester alongside Horton, and its purchase of Portland House in the city in 1856, raised hopes and expectations, and when these collapsed soon afterwards, the disappointment among the Lancashire Baptists must have been considerable[2]. It seemed to many of them that the Baptists, like the Wesleyans and the Congregationalists, should have a training establishment in or near the city. The "Manchester Men", an elite of merchants, manufacturers and bankers, were keen to demonstrate the city's cultural prowess, and were creating magnificent civic buildings and prestigious societies. Educational establishments were multiplying, culminating with the foundation of Owens College in 1851. The Nonconformist denominations, in whose places of worship many of these businessmen worshipped on Sundays, were an integral part of the city's advance. Baptists had not prospered in the city as much as other Nonconformists, partly, no doubt, handicapped by Gadsby's reputation. They were strong in several other towns in southern Lancashire, however, and it is not surprising that they felt the way they did.

The Baptist Evangelical Society

During the annual London meetings of the Baptist Union in April 1841, a meeting was arranged of ministers concerned about the decline in church discipline in the denomination. For the previous three years, a journal called *The Primitive Communionist* had been promoting strict-communion practice among Baptists. This was re-launched in 1841 under the title *The Primitive Church Magazine,* "with a view to stem the tide of denominational decadence". It was decided to organise an annual meeting for the purpose of discussing how best to achieve this objective.

Ministerial training was a live issue within the denomination, and the strict communionists soon turned their attention to the encouragement of their views among those who were preparing themselves for ministry. The academy or college system was regarded by many as defective because it was felt to lead to an undue emphasis on academic qualifications and hindered the spiritual development of students. Perhaps equally important was the fact that none of the existing Particular Baptist colleges was committed to strict-communion principles. In 1844 the Baptist Theological Education Society was created to look at alternative approaches. Its preferred policy was to place two or three students with a minister, who would supervise their training by means of a combination of Scriptural studies and practical experience. *The Primitive Church Magazine* feared that the colleges were not likely to supply the kind of ministers who relied on the power and Spirit of God rather than "human science". "The pursuit of human learning, and its honours", it said, "have so thrown into the shade the teaching of the Spirit ... that hope turns to the gifts and workings of the Spirit in others". "A learned nation, when arrived to its highest pitch of human science, is just become ripe for slavery, and doomed to perpetual bondage"[3].

One of the remarkable things about such language, which seems to represent the very attitudes Fawcett, Steadman and Acworth struggled against, is how many of the ministers behind the movement had themselves been college trained. Some were quite heavily involved in one or other of the existing colleges. As well as several who had been trained at Stepney, Henry Dowson of Bradford, Benjamin Evans of Scarborough and Thomas Dawson of Bacup and Liverpool had all been to Horton. Dowson and Evans were enthusiastic supporters of Horton, Dowson being the college secretary. They cannot, then, have objected to college training in principle.

The Creation of Manchester Baptist College

In 1845 a new body calling itself the Strict Baptist Convention was formed. The title "convention" was a new one for English Baptists, although it was familiar to their American counterparts. In America, Baptists had co-operated in missionary work under the General (or Triennial) Convention since 1814, and many of the churches in the southern States joined together to form the Southern Baptist Convention, also in 1845. The idea of a convention differed from that of a society in that it was normally made up of churches rather than individuals. In this sense it was similar to an association or the Union. The leaders of the Strict Baptist Convention were at pains to emphasise, however, that there was no need for churches that supported it to abandon their existing association commitments. A London Strict Baptist Association came into existence at about this time, but did not survive for more than a few years.

The convention assumed responsibility for the movement's work in ministerial education. It also developed an interest in missionary work on the European continent. Support was given to the German Baptist pioneer, Johann Gerhard Oncken, for his work in Denmark. Later this interest broadened to include support for Baptist causes in Belgium and Saxony.

In consequence of strong support for the convention in the north of England, and the practical difficulties of travelling to London for meetings, a northern branch was set up in 1847. Joseph Harvey, the minister of the church in Bury, and Joseph Harbottle of Accrington, among others, joined Dowson, Evans and Dawson in supporting it. Another important recruit was the wealthy Huddersfield businessman, William Shaw. During the next fifteen years or so, the northern branch proved more durable and vigorous than the parent body in London, and gradually took over responsibility for its educational, missionary and publishing activities. Harvey became the convention's most prominent advocate, travelling the country on its behalf, raising money and stimulating interest in its activities.

In 1850 the convention's supporters decided that the name of their organisation was hindering its work, as it was associated in some people's minds with Chartism and the French revolutionary Convention. They agreed to rename themselves the Strict Baptist Society. This revised name, however, did not itself prove acceptable for long. If "convention" had unfortunate connotations, so, for some, did "strict". Support for the society's educational work was being increasingly received from people who did not subscribe to its strict-communion stance, and who wanted to distance themselves from the more rigid Strict Baptists. In recognition of this the society changed its name again, to the Baptist Evangelical Society, in 1856.

This second change of name also suggested that the organisation had broader interests than just communion practice. The term "evangelical" was then associated with preserving the principles of the Protestant Reformation, and resistance to what was perceived as a return to ritualism and priestcraft within the Church of England. It did not denote a move by the society away from its commitment to strict communion, but it did reflect a desire to encourage wider sympathy and support within the denomination.

Tension over communion and other doctrinal issues among Lancashire Baptists came to a head in the late 1850s. In 1857, Charles Williams, the liberal-minded minister of Blackburn Road, Accrington, outraged conservatives by a sermon on the atonement at the association's annual meetings. A controversial letter from David Griffiths, theological tutor at the short-lived academy in Accrington in the 1840s, was also circulated among the churches. Joseph Harbottle, a prominent supporter of the society, fiercely opposed the views expressed by Williams and Griffiths. When the association failed to take a stand against them, he and several other ministers took their churches out of membership. In 1860, thirteen dissenting churches formed a new and rival body, the North Western Association, with the support of the society. The new association was theologically conservative and committed to strict-communion principles[4].

Yorkshire Baptists did not suffer the controversies that were damaging their sister association west of the Pennines. For most, the erection of Rawdon College and the appointment three years later of the academically inclined S.G. Green as principal, with all that those developments implied in terms of the pursuit of intellectual and cultural respectability, were welcomed. They did nothing, however, to reassure the seceders in Lancashire. The strict communionists there were also deeply concerned about the judgement given in London by the Master of the Rolls in the St Mary's Baptist Church case in May 1860. St Mary's, in Norwich, was one of the leading churches in the country. A legal challenge had been brought by several of the church's trustees against the minister, G.P. Gould, who had instituted an open-communion policy, contrary to previous practice. The Master of the Rolls decided in favour of Gould. The tide seemed to be turning against the strict communionists, but there were some, in the north west at least, who were determined not to relinquish their position without a fight.

Chamber Hall

In the 1860s the Evangelical Society's involvement with ministerial training developed to such an extent that its other interests virtually disappeared. Applications were regularly received for training from young men and, although only one or two were accepted for training each year, it was regarded as the most important and strategic matter facing the society. There was a desire to expand the work and to win greater support for it within the denomination. The need for a more systematic approach to the task, rather than relying on individual ministers such as Thomas Dawson or Joseph Harbottle for training, was increasingly seen as important. After 1861, the ministry of Dawson in Liverpool was unsettled and dogged by controversy. The society continued to place men under his tuition until 1866, but some people, at least, were dissatisfied with this arrangement[5].

In the summer of 1864 Henry Dowson resigned as the secretary of Rawdon College, after twenty-four years of service. This immediately led to serious and lengthy correspondence between Dowson and Joseph Harvey about the society's future plans and the part Dowson might play in them. At the society's meeting in December 1864 the officers suggested that a "Theological College or Institution" be established on strict Baptist lines, and they were given authority to talk to Dowson about it. Over the next eighteen months plans were agreed for the constitution and conduct of such a college, money was raised from the society's supporters and premises were secured. In 1866 Dowson resigned from the Rawdon committee, and in October of that year a

Baptist Theological Institution was opened at Chamber Hall in the town of Bury under his presidency. Bury is about ten miles north of Manchester. The Hall was situated in extensive grounds on the banks of the river Irwell. Its spacious rooms were contained in two linked buildings, one a house dating back to the early seventeenth century and the other an eighteenth-century addition. It had been the home of the Peel family, and reputedly the birthplace of Sir Robert Peel.

The opening of Chamber Hall represented a radical change in the society's policy on ministerial training. It was not merely "extending and enlarging" its educational work, as it claimed, but, in effect, deserting the principles that had guided it up until that point. In spite of the element of ambivalence that existed because of its supporters' links with colleges, there had from the start been suspicion, if not downright hostility, towards the college system of ministerial training as "detrimental to piety and usefulness"[6.]

The reason for the change of heart, apparently in the space of just a few months in 1864, is not entirely clear. The committee was naturally enthusiastic about the possibility of Dowson's direct involvement in ministerial training under their auspices, in spite of the clash between the Society's antipathy towards college training and his experience of its benefits under Steadman and Acworth. As a member of the committee himself for several years, he was known and trusted. Discussion between Dowson and Joseph Harvey, representing the committee, went on for a considerable period. The fact that it was in private reflects its sensitivity, both for Dowson personally and for the society. In July 1865, a year after Dowson's resignation as secretary of Rawdon, a subcommittee was appointed by the society "for the new educational scheme"[7]. In May 1866 the annual meeting resolved that "it deeply feels the necessity of more extensive operations" in the education of young men for the work of the ministry, and the fact that a search for premises was being undertaken was first publicly disclosed[8].

In September 1866 *The Primitive Church Magazine*, now jointly edited by John Howe of Waterbarn and Edward Parker of Farsley, revealed to its readers that Chamber Hall had been leased and that Dowson was about to start work as president. The institution, it said, would provide a "thoroughly English, theological, pastoral and denominational education" for young men recommended for the ministry, and was designed specifically to meet the needs of churches of a strict-communion stance. Students would also be employed in Christian effort, "preaching the Gospel, holding cottage meetings and visitation in the town and neighbourhood". The object was "not to send forth into the great harvest-field men of classical or high literary attainments, but sound divines, acceptable preachers and able ministers of the Gospel of Christ"[9.]

Chamber Hall, the first home of the theological institution established by the Baptist Evangelical Society in 1866

A sign of the seriousness with which the project was viewed was the abandonment of the society's missionary activities. In 1865, support for the Danish mission came to an end when the missionary involved emigrated to America. There was no hint of a replacement. The reason officially given for this withdrawal was because "an important project is contemplated which will require all the attention of the resources of the Society", an obvious, if rather mysterious, reference to the educational scheme being discussed with Dowson[10]. Once Chamber Hall had been opened, the Saxony Mission was also disbanded, responsibility for missionary Moritz Geissler's support being transferred to the General German Mission led by Oncken[11] The speed with which this happened is striking. Frequently, and as late as the annual meeting in May 1866, the fate of the persecuted Baptists in that part of Germany at the hands of the Lutheran authorities was a major concern of the society.

Charles Rignal, in his history of the Manchester College, suggested that the policy on ministerial training changed because the earlier apprenticeship system had failed to produce the number and quality of men the churches needed and demanded[12]. It is difficult to say whether this was because of the system itself, or the ability of the tutors, or diminishing enthusiasm in the society once the prospect of having its own college became realistic, or for other reasons. Several notable ministers, including Edward Parker, who went on to become principal of Manchester College, came through the older method of training. Rignal also suggested that there were economic advantages in having students in one place, rather than scattered among a number of tutors, although this is far from self-evident.

The strict-communion stance of the new college at Chamber Hall was its most obvious distinguishing feature, but whether it was the main factor behind its creation is open to question. Communion practice varied within the denomination, and for most churches was not a reason for separation, either over ministerial training, association membership or co-operation in other ways. The fact that Dowson himself had been prepared to devote considerable time and energy to a college that was neutral on the communion issue indicates that it was not of paramount importance to him personally. The formation of the conservative North Western Association in 1860 no doubt gave impetus to the new venture, and anxieties about the direction Rawdon might be heading under its new principal Green may also have had a part to play. Just as important was probably the continuing growth of the Baptist cause in Lancashire[13]. The society drew support from throughout the north, but many of its most enthusiastic advocates came from the county. For them, geography was important as well as doctrine, as was the case on the other side of the Pennines too.

Whatever the reasons were for the change of policy over ministerial training, the opening of Chamber Hall demonstrated the desire of the society to expand its work in this area, and was an expression of its confidence that this could happen.

Henry Dowson

A crucial factor in the successful establishment of the college at Chamber Hall was the recruitment of Henry Dowson. Without him, it is unlikely that the project would ever have got off the ground. A keen supporter of the doctrinal and ecclesiological stance of the Evangelical Society, he also brought with him a wide range of experience, gained over thirty years of ministry at the Westgate church in Bradford, including the twenty-four also as secretary of Horton. He knew the churches of the north as well as anyone.

Dowson was born in Nottingham in 1812. His family had long been associated with Hamsterley Baptist Church in the north east. Apprenticed in his father's printing business as a young man, he entered Horton as a student under Steadman and Godwin in 1832. After a short period studying at Edinburgh University he became Steadman's assistant at Westgate, taking over as pastor when he retired soon after. His length of service in Bradford demonstrated a stability and constancy of character that would provide a solid foundation for the new work in Lancashire. He was remembered for a "ponderous and dignified" personal style, a "rock-like steadiness" in doctrine and "the absolute subordination" of every other pursuit to the task of being a Christian minister[14].

Any assessment of Dowson's personal attitude towards the events in which he was caught up between 1864 and 1866 is bound to be largely speculative. Given his strict-communion views and conservatism, it is difficult to imagine that he was entirely comfortable with the developments at Rawdon in the 1850s and 60s, and in particular with the appointment of Green as principal. Green, a Cornishman trained at Stepney and possessing a degree from London University, had been classical tutor at Horton since 1851. He was known for his "broad and catholic sympathies", and his opposition to "unprogressive sectarianism"[15]. His published work shows an interest in hymnology and

Henry Dowson (1812-1885), secretary of Horton Academy and Rawdon College, minister of Westgate Baptist Church, Bradford, and first president of Manchester Baptist College

work with children, activities that did not naturally fit with Dowson's rather formal and traditional style. There is, however, no evidence of personal friction between the two men, and Dowson continued as college secretary for a year after Green's appointment. When Dowson resigned in 1864 he assured the college's supporters of his continuing support, and he remained on the committee for a further two years.

It has been suggested that Dowson harboured hopes of the presidency of Rawdon himself, but it seems safest to assume, in the absence of any evidence to the contrary, that his resignation had nothing to do with any disappointment over this, nor with the conversations that subsequently took place with the Evangelical Society. He was, apparently, absent because of sickness when the possibility of a new college was first raised. We should probably take the reason given for his resignation in

Rawdon College's 1864 annual report at face value, that he was compelled to take the step "by the pressures of manifold engagements"[16]. No doubt the demands of church and college were burdensome at times, especially now that the latter had moved out of Bradford.

Training began at Chamber Hall in the autumn of 1866, under the direction of Dowson, the society having secured a five-year lease on the property. When it opened there were five students, rising to ten by the close of the first session. Of the ten, it is interesting to note that only one came from Lancashire. Of the rest, one was from Paris and another from Hamburg[17]. After the opening, the Baptist Evangelical Society disappeared. It held its last meeting in November 1866 and transferred all its business to the new organisation.

In his inaugural address, Dowson defended the creation of "a collegiate institution" on the grounds of the need for a properly educated ministry, and outlined the principles that would guide its work. He acknowledged that there were still objections to this method of training and described how these would be met. He reassured those who believed it was harmful for the development of religious feeling and Christian friendship for young men to be "constantly associated under the same roof" that the "collegiate family", as he called it, would be divided up, some of the students being accommodated in the houses of nearby Christian families. Those who objected to students spending time on "classical, mathematical and secular studies" were told that these would be unnecessary. He said,

> The young men whom the churches call to the work of the ministry, and whom God qualifies by His grace, are for the most part such as have had few advantages of previous education. To take them from the loom, the plough, the shop, or the counting house, unaccustomed to habits of study and only imperfectly acquainted with their own language, and to put before them Latin, Greek, and Hebrew, and to expect them to become proficient in these difficult languages, is in nineteen cases out of twenty, simply an absurdity[18].

Dowson announced that integral to the three-year course of training would be opportunities for town missionary work and preaching. "We propose that our young men should use their materials as they acquire them", he said. He went on to affirm the institution's commitment to the Calvinistic confession of faith adopted by Baptists at the 1689 General Assembly, and to strict communion, and concluded with an exhortation to seek revival. "But this revival must begin in the pulpit", he said. "And a revived ministry is not a ministry which brings into the proclamation of its messages novel doctrines or a new gospel, but which throws around old and immutable truths the freshness which is connected with earnest zeal and steadfast faith".

The curriculum of the institution included theology, pastoral relations and duties, English literature, composition and elocution, church history, general history, geography, natural philosophy, logic and mental science. Latin was taught on a voluntary basis, in order to help with a better understanding of English. From the start, the intention was to encourage more able students to take advantages of courses available at other institutions in Manchester and, where appropriate, to prosecute their studies "at one of our Scottish or London Universities"[19].

Whatever the original intentions might have been, classical languages soon began to find a regular place in the curriculum. Within five years there were classes in Latin, Greek and Hebrew, the more advanced ones being taken at Owens College. In 1870 James Webb joined Dowson on the tutorial staff, initially with primary responsibility for teaching "general literature", although Latin and Greek soon became his main duty. Webb and Dowson had been students together at the Horton Academy.

Brighton Grove

The five-year lease on Chamber Hall ran out in 1871. Its inadequacies, both in terms of its age and the facilities it offered, had by then become obvious, and the committee's attention turned to securing accommodation more suited for its purpose, preferably as the owner rather than the tenant. The lease on Chamber Hall was renewed on an annual basis until new premises could be found. There would be advantages in moving nearer to Manchester, mainly because of the courses run by Owens' College, and the search was mainly aimed in that direction. In October 1871 a site was purchased in Brighton Grove, Rusholme, on the outskirts of the city.

The financial challenge of building new premises was large, but the committee, led by William Shaw, promised to raise about half the expected cost. Architects were appointed, and plans for the new building drawn up. The go-ahead was given for an impressive structure, including a seventy-foot tower, various ornamental brick and ironwork features, and accommodation for the president and about twenty-four students. Its outward appearance and situation could not match the grandeur of Rawdon, but there were several similarities between the two buildings. The student accommodation provided was much the same, although the Rawdon students had the advantage of a study and a bedroom each. They were both in secluded settings, away from the distractions and noise of the city. They were both decorated with elaborate architectural features, as if to demonstrate the cultural sophistication and self-confidence of the occupants. The accommodation at Brighton Grove was substantially greater than was currently needed, but the committee knew that the students of Owens' College would take up any empty rooms. It seems that the principle of students being domiciled out was to be quickly abandoned once sufficient accommodation in the main building was available.

In October 1872 the autumn Baptist Assembly was held in Manchester, and this proved too good an opportunity to miss for promoting the interests of the institution. A stone-laying ceremony at Brighton Grove was arranged during the meetings, and Charles Spurgeon was invited to be the chief speaker. This guaranteed a large gathering of Baptists for the occasion. The choice of Spurgeon was interesting. He was well known as advocating and practising an open-communion policy at the Metropolitan Tabernacle, a position he made no attempt to disguise in his address. Although the strict communionists in his audience claimed that open communion was no more Scriptural than infant baptism, it was obviously not an issue that prevented them making common cause with Spurgeon when it suited them. The combination of his popularity, Calvinistic theology and position as president of his own college in London proved more compelling than his views on communion. The stone laying itself was performed by William Shaw, in recognition of his financial generosity[20].

Fund raising for the new building extended to America and Canada, where there was considerable sympathy for the strict Baptist position. John Howe was dispatched across the Atlantic in 1873 to solicit help. In September 1874 the premises were formally opened. Dowson reiterated the advantages of the Brighton Grove site, combining proximity to the city with the advantages of the countryside, and being conveniently close to Owens College. He urged his audience to join him in resisting the "loose doctrine, necessarily connected with laxity in Church government and polity" that was spreading on every hand. He claimed that there was not a Baptist church within miles of Brighton Grove practising orderly communion[21], and it was probably for that reason that one was formed there, meeting each Sunday in the lecture room.

The 1874-5 session commenced with twelve ministerial students resident in the building, living alongside a similar number from Owens College. Dowson and Webb undertook most of the teaching, sending those students who could benefit from them the short distance down the road to attend courses at Owens College[22]. Although there was still hesitancy on the part of some people in calling the institution a college, it was increasingly referred to in that way, and within a few years Manchester Baptist College was its accepted name[23].

The rapid changes in the thinking and policy of the strict Baptists that had led to the formation of the institution in 1866 continued in the years that followed. Apart from its official commitment to strict communion and the 1689 Baptist Confession, it was virtually indistinguishable from Rawdon in the way it conducted its training. Opposition to accommodating and training students in a college setting had quickly evaporated, as had resistance to the inclusion of classical languages in the curriculum.

Of the colleges at Chilwell, Rawdon and Manchester, Manchester's situation had most to commend it from an educational point of view. The city itself provided many social and cultural opportunities, and its other colleges constituted a stimulating academic environment. Among Nonconformists, the Methodists, who had been training ministers in the city since 1842, opened two new colleges in 1872 and 1881, and the

Congregationalists had been running a college in Manchester since 1843. All three Baptist colleges, even in the 1870s, were beginning to feel handicapped by their small size. Manchester was able to compensate for this in ways not open to the other two.

The formation of the Manchester College had an inevitable impact on Rawdon. It could no longer claim the allegiance of Baptists throughout the north, and its support base was inevitably eroded. Some of those involved with the Evangelical Society did not support Rawdon anyway, but many did, and the loss of influential ministers like Dowson and Benjamin Evans in Scarborough was damaging. If the vigour shown by Fawcett, Steadman and Acworth to maintain Baptist unity throughout the north in support of the task of ministerial education had continued, or if the 1850s scheme for a two-centred academy had succeeded, matters might have turned out very differently.

However, divisions of this kind in church life have generally accompanied Baptist growth, and at least there was no destructive acrimony between the two colleges. Growth in numbers and wealth meant that there were sufficient resources to maintain two colleges in the north, as did other Nonconformist denominations. More damaging may well have been the effect Manchester's formation had on the way the two colleges were viewed. Manchester's doctrinal stance naturally tended to polarise opinion between conservatives and liberals. Rawdon soon began to gain a reputation for theological liberalism, which was in some respects self-fulfilling as the more conservative churches and students were drawn towards Manchester. Those who founded Manchester claimed that they were responding to liberal tendencies that already existed, but they also contributed towards an unfortunate institutionalisation of theological differences among northern Baptists. The consequences of this remained apparent for years afterwards, hindering later efforts to bring the colleges together.

By the mid-1870s, the three Baptist colleges had emerged from their development stage. They were all housed in their own premises, in two cases purpose built. Good quality ministerial education was widely valued and academic standards were rising. The future was, in many ways, full of hope. The president, committee and subscribers of the Manchester College had good reason to congratulate themselves on what they had achieved. John Lea was surely wrong in his negative assessment of the opening of the college at Brighton Grove. His judgement that "the Baptists of Victorian Lancashire displayed no determination to improve their inadequate ministry" is harsh, and shows little appreciation of the difficulties that had to be overcome[24].

As the general educational level in the country rose, however, the challenge facing the colleges increased. Already there had been talk in the Baptist Union about improving standards through a greater degree of co-operation between the colleges. Affiliation to London University helped to some extent, but did not solve the problem of providing a good theological education. Responding to this challenge was the main feature of the next twenty years.

---

1   Gadsby regarded Andrew Fuller, whose moderate and evangelistic Calvinistic theology was so important in the creation of the Baptist Missionary Society, as "the greatest enemy the church of God ever had" (J. Gadsby, *A Memoir of the late Mr. William Gadsby (2nd edition)* (Manchester: 1847) p.27.
2   The Lancashire and Cheshire Association recorded its "unfeigned pleasure" at news of the proposed Manchester branch of Horton College in 1856, and urged the churches to support such an endeavour (*Records of the Lancashire and Cheshire Association of Baptised Churches*, 15 May 1856: Rylands Library, NBC MS.80).
3   *The Primitive Church Magazine*, February 1847 (pp.47-8) and March 1847 (p.74).
4   Not all the churches in the new association had been members of the Lancashire Association. Those who resigned amounted to about one-fifth of the total. Ian Sellers points out that personal relationships may have played at least some part in the split. Harbottle had been Griffiths' colleague at the Accrington Academy, and theological tensions there probably contributed to its demise in 1849. He was also Williams's predecessor in Accrington, and possibly felt aggrieved at the change of theological emphasis taking place in his old church (see Ian Sellers, *Our Heritage: The Baptists of Yorkshire, Lancashire and Cheshire 1647-1987* (Yorkshire Baptist Association and Lancashire and Cheshire Association: Leeds, 1987) p.42.
5   See Ian Sellers, "Thomas Dawson of Liverpool" (*BQ* vol. 19 no. 8 (October 1962) p.361) and the Minute Book of the Northern Branch of the Baptist Evangelical Society for 1864-66.
6   Charles Rignal, *Manchester Baptist College 1866-1916* (William Byles and Sons Ltd.: Bradford, 1916) p.24.
7   Minute Book of the Northern Branch of the Baptist Evangelical Society, 5 July 1865.
8   *Ibid.*, 9 May 1866.

9   *The Primitive Church Magazine*, vol. 23 no. 273 (September 1866) pp.208-9.
10 *Ibid.*, 5 July 1865.
11 *Ibid.* 24 October and 21 November 1866.
12 Rignal, p.24.
13 The number of churches in the Lancashire and Cheshire Association rose from 41 in 1861 to 54 in 1866, with total membership figures rising by over 27% in the same period (Sellers, *Our Heritage*, p.169). This was quite apart from the churches in the North Western Association, also growing during that period.
14 *Baptist Handbook* 1886, pp.113-4.
15 *Baptist Handbook* 1906, p.439.
16 *Rawdon College Report* 1864, p.18.
17 Rignal, p.45.
18 Dowson's address was published as a pamphlet and is bound with the College Report for 1867 (Manchester College Reports 1866-1877). It was also reported in detail in *The Primitive Church Magazine* vol. 23 no.275 (November 1866) pp.257-8.
19 *The Primitive Church Magazine* vol.23 no.273 (September 1866) p.208.
20 The foundation stone, now repositioned, is still to be seen at Luther King House.
21 *Proceedings in connection with the opening of the College, Brighton Grove, Manchester*, p.3 (pasted in the front of the College Minute Book for 1874-1899).
22 Owens' College opened its new premises on Oxford Road, between Brighton Grove and the city centre, in 1873.
23 The change did not officially take place until 1884, when the Baptist Theological Institution was renamed Manchester Baptist College.
24 John Lea, "Baptists in Lancashire 1837-1887: a Study of Mid-Victorian Dissent" (University of Liverpool *PhD* thesis, 1970) pp.128 and 131.

Chapter Six
Raising Standards:
the 1870s and 1880s

The foundation of the college in Manchester meant that from 1866 there were three Baptist colleges in the north and midlands. This remained the case for over fifty years. They were small institutions, each normally having two full-time tutors and between twelve and twenty-five students. From time to time they all struggled financially. However, this was the period of Nonconformity's greatest strength, and on the whole they enjoyed relative security and improving standards. Each institution owned its own premises, and in the case of Manchester (from 1874) and Rawdon these were purpose-built. As the importance of ministerial training became more widely recognised, the standing of the colleges within the denomination rose. In 1873 they were given the right to become members of the Baptist Union, a privilege previously granted only to churches. Their principals often became leading national Baptist figures. Academic standards, both for admission and of the training itself, were steadily raised. There were setbacks from time to time, naturally, but the general picture was an encouraging one. Until the late 1880s, when the college at Nottingham began its slow decline, struggling for support especially after the disappearance of the General Baptist Association in 1891, all three institutions shared in the growing prosperity of Victorian society in general, and the advance of Baptist fortunes in particular.

The 1870 Education Act

The passing of W.E. Forster's Education Act in 1870 was a major national event, and provided the background to the colleges' developments during the closing decades of the century. It was the Liberal Government's response to growing national concern about the widespread illiteracy that resulted from inadequate and uneven provision of education at the elementary level. Its main aim was to provide schooling of a minimum standard for all children up to the age of twelve. Before it was passed this was mainly done either by Church of England or private schools, and was often dependent on parents' ability to pay. The Act allowed for the election of School Boards in areas where there was insufficient existing provision. These Boards were empowered to build new schools and could, if they saw fit, compel attendance. Its effect was only gradually felt, but within five or six years virtually all five to twelve-year-olds were on a school register, and in 1880 attendance was made compulsory by national legislation. It was a particularly important development for Nonconformists because of the previous dominance of the Established Church. The new Board Schools were required to be non-sectarian in character.

The 1870 Act was a central part of the general development of education in mid-Victorian England. Once the challenge of elementary schooling had been faced, the demand increased to improve secondary and higher education as well. The universities of Oxford and Cambridge, with their enormous wealth and ancient privileges, came under increasing scrutiny. In 1871 their religious tests were abolished, except for degrees in divinity, and this enabled non-Anglicans to benefit from the education they provided.

Cambridge, Oxford and London Universities all ran university extension classes in various towns and cities from the 1870s onwards. University colleges were established, and proposals for the creation of provincial universities put forward. *The Baptist* approved of these developments, and hoped that the denominational colleges would be able to take advantage of the new opportunities[1]. In 1884 the first of the modern provincial universities was created, a federal institution, Victoria University, bringing together Owens College and Manchester with colleges in Leeds and Liverpool[2].

Many of the new School Boards expanded their activity into non-elementary education. In the field of secondary education, provision for boys was made by public and grammar schools, as long as their families could afford it. There was very little provision for girls. The situation in higher education was worse. From the 1870s onwards, however, public schools for girls began to multiply, and the creation of Girton College in 1869, Newnham College in 1871 and Lady Margaret Hall in 1878 made some inroads for female students into the field of higher education[3].

These changes affected Baptist colleges in several ways. Gradually, the academic standards of incoming students rose. This freed the tutors from spending time on basic skills. Also, as education generally improved, in Baptist congregations as elsewhere, more was demanded of preachers, especially in the larger city churches, and therefore of those who trained them. Preaching was regarded as the chief task of ministers, in Baptist circles at least, and if they were to deliver acceptable sermons to graduates, they needed an equivalent level of education themselves, or so it was thought. There were, no doubt, elements of snobbery and self-seeking in this, but also a sincere desire to provide ministers with the highest level of education and training possible. In most people's minds, academic standards in the colleges were important, for the reputation of the colleges and tutors and the benefit of students, churches and the denomination as a whole[4].

It was not only in the field of education that English society was changing. The 1867 Reform Act had enfranchised a large number of male householders for the first time, and it led the way to further constitutional and political change. The process of urbanisation, already quite advanced in parts of the north, particularly around Manchester and Liverpool, accelerated rapidly in the 1870s[5]. The expansion of Britain's colonial activity, symbolised by the opening of the Suez Canal in 1869 and the declaration of Queen Victoria as Empress of India in 1876, created a greater awareness of the country's global influence and responsibilities. Intellectually, the advance of science was regularly throwing up revolutionary new ideas in such fields as biology and geology. Thoughtful Christian believers wrestled with the increasing tide of biblical criticism, emanating mainly from Germany, as a result of which many old certainties were coming under question.

The historian Robert Ensor described 1870 as a "watershed in English life". Ways of thinking that had typified the early Victorian period, through the works of such people as John Stuart Mill and Thomas Carlyle, were being eclipsed by a new style of humanism represented by Matthew Arnold and T.H Huxley[6]. The Anglican, and largely evangelical Protestant orthodoxy that had, until then, permeated most sections of English society was being assailed from many sides. The changing scene presented Baptists, like all Nonconformists, with new opportunities, as doors previously closed to them were opened. The Civil Service, for example, was from 1870 open to all through competitive examinations. It also presented them with intellectual and evangelistic challenges, as they sought to adapt to new ways of thinking and living. The role of the colleges in this process of adaptation was crucial.

S.G. Green

The thirteen-year presidency of S.G. Green at Rawdon does not seem to have been a great success. Born in Cornwall as a son of the manse, he had entered Stepney College at the age of eighteen and was a graduate of London University. He had been appointed classical tutor at Horton in 1851 after two fairly short pastorates in High Wycombe and Taunton. During his ministry in Taunton the church had started practising open communion. When Rawdon was opened he had been appointed resident tutor, with Acworth living away from the premises, and he took over as president in 1863. An expert hymnologist and known as a preacher to children, he was also an artist, publishing several volumes of drawings. He was noted for his refined scholarship and had a reputation for being more liberal than conservative theologically. John Barrett described his time in office as "lean years",

Rawson College Library

attributing the problems he faced to his insistence on raising the educational standards for admission[7].

A fascinating insight into Green's character, his relationship with his predecessor Acworth, and life at Rawdon at the time was provided by a romantic novel published in the 1890s by Green's daughter, Lily Watson. *The Vicar of Langthwaite* has so many parallels with events and personalities at the college that it is tempting to think of it as a reliable historical description. Most of the first half of the story is set in the "wood embosomed" Northminster Theological College in the north of England. A college for Dissenters, it has "Gothic pinnacles and gabled fronts" and a stained-glass window in the entrance hall. It is the home for about thirty students undergoing a five-year course of training. Each student has a little study with a bedroom above, plainly furnished. There was, Watson tells us, "no monastic gloom or seclusion in the life, and the outbursts of noise and laughter that came from the public rooms after class hours would rather have shocked some of the stricter members of the committee". The students enjoyed boating, cricket and football. Their "most dreaded" occasion was the sermon class.

At the start of the book, the college's puritanical principal, Septimus Yorke, clearly modelled on James Acworth, is about to retire. "Huge, sinewy, and loosely knit, his frame denoted great physical strength ... He looked as if he had been fighting all his life", writes the author. "Young men who were troubled by religious doubts did not feel drawn to confide in Dr. Yorke". On the other hand, the classical professor and Yorke's successor, Philip Hawthorne, is "a man of gentle, scholarly mien and quiet demeanour, with prematurely bowed shoulders", who abhors fighting. He is a cultured man, interested in music and keen to soften the discipline of the house. Accused by the local "Squire Rhodes" of not being theologically sound, he is eager to have good relations with people of every religious opinion, "Churchmen as well as Dissenters".

Hawthorne's sister Priscilla is appointed matron of the college, and the author demonstrates the kind of insight into the nature and importance of this role that is rarely found in official records. Priscilla was to be "mistress of a large establishment, handling finances with thrift and energy, dispensing patronage to tradesmen". "The self-denying part of providing a household environment for unpractical people is deserving of higher esteem than it usually receives", she writes. Yorke remains nearby after his retirement, and there are arguments between him and Hawthorne over the latter's leadership of the college[8].

Even though the book is fiction, and the author's primary interest romantic, its value is considerable. It brings an element of imagination and feeling into a story which is often told only by means of official reports and minutes. It is also valuable because it is written by a woman.

In 1864 William Skae of Edinburgh took over Green's old position as classical and mathematical tutor[9]. This took place shortly after Dowson's resignation as college secretary. The range of classes taught by Green and Skae was remarkable. Among Green's responsibilities were theology, pastoral theology, church history, New Testament Greek, Hebrew, philosophy and preaching. Skae undertook English, Greek, Latin and mathematics. Several of the subjects involved more than one class for different standards of student.

Skae's work soon came under criticism. He was accused of an "inaptitude for the work of teaching and conducting a class, and an eccentricity of manner which affected his influence with the students"[10]. Within five years, and after considerable heart-searching, his work was condemned as "not satisfactory", and he was dismissed[11]. It was not only Skae's conduct that caused anxiety, however. Green's fragile health, the state of college finances and the domestic management of the house also gave rise to "long and anxious conversation"[12]. Green, supported by his wife, found the combined responsibility of presidency, teaching, fund-raising and domestic management very arduous. His interests were primarily academic, and he seemed to be only really happy in "the blest retirement of his study"[13]. It became obvious to the committee that he needed an extended break, and early in 1869 he was given six months leave[14]. He was apparently able to achieve a restoration of health, and went on to lead the college for another seven years.

For a few months the college was left without any tutorial provision, Green being in Torquay on sick leave and Skae having been dismissed. In May, William Medley of Liverpool accepted an invitation to take Skae's place. Although Medley had no pastoral experience, he was familiar with Baptist church life in the north. His great-grandfather, Samuel Medley, was the Baptist minister who had helped John Fawcett to establish the Horton academy sixty-five years before. William Medley had been educated at

Regent's Park College, gaining an MA from London University, and at Gottingen. He proved to have the qualities Rawdon required, combining a patient and painstaking approach to teaching with a lively sense of fun, and enjoyed a happy association with the college as tutor for thirty-nine years. He was remembered by his students as "one of those few men whose jokes lost nothing of their point or quality by the manifest enjoyment he had in them himself"[15].

In 1869 an application to study at the college from a married man was rejected because it was not possible for satisfactory arrangements to be made for his wife and family. Whether it was primarily a matter of principle, or of the practicalities of providing accommodation, is not clear[16]. Eleven years later James Moffatt Logan was admitted as a student in spite of the fact that he was married. It was an issue that was destined to return in the years ahead. Later in 1869 the decision was made to drop the names of three men trained at the college from the list of ex-students because they had abandoned the Baptist denomination. Two had become pastors of Unitarian churches and another had connected himself with the Church of England[17].

From the early 1870s onwards relationships between the six Baptist colleges in England were frequently discussed in the denomination. Green was eager to promote closer co-operation, and made a plea for this at the 1871 spring annual meetings of the Baptist Union. The authorities at Bury had no interest in any such scheme, having established their college at Chamber Hall five years earlier precisely because they were unhappy with existing college provision. At Chilwell, the committee was no more enthusiastic, regarding the proposal as inappropriate and untimely[18]. Rawdon was predictably more positive, and for a while held conversations with Bristol and Regent's Park about co-ordinating training. These centred on the possibility of providing preparatory training for candidates who were not ready for the advanced theological training needed for ministry. No practical way of achieving this could be agreed, however, and by the end of 1873 the matter was dropped.

Thomas Rooke and an Organised Student Disturbance

At the college's 1876 annual meeting, Green announced his resignation in order to become editorial secretary of the Religious Tract Society. William Medley was first approached to take over as principal, but refused. While the search for a successor was going on, a deputation was sent across the Pennines to investigate the possibility of the two northern colleges co-operating. The Lancashire college had by then opened its new premises in Manchester. The Rawdon Minute Book recorded that "feelings of cordial mutual respect with a desire to co-operate as far as practical were expressed, but it was found that no further action is at present possible"[19]. By the end of 1876, Thomas George Rooke of Frome in Somerset had accepted the presidency. He commenced his duties early in 1877.

Rooke was the son of a London solicitor and had trained for a career at the bar. After a trip to the Middle East as a young man, during which he was imprisoned by Arabs, he had decided to abandon the law and entered Regent's Park College for training as a Baptist minister. Like Green, he came to Rawdon from Somerset. Frome, where he had been pastor since 1863, was his only ministry. Also like Green, he did not enjoy good health. Of "slight, lithe and delicate frame", he suffered "continual physical infirmities"[20]. Less of a scholar than his predecessor, his main area of academic expertise was oriental languages. According to Medley, he emphasised the "power and originality of thought" and introduced to the college "an air of larger freedom"[21] This liberal approach to the teaching of theology did not endear him to the conservatives in the denomination like C.H. Spurgeon, who grew increasingly concerned about Rawdon's influence on the new generation of ministers as the 1880s progressed[22].

A feature of Rooke's presidency was unhappiness in the student body. Before Rooke was appointed, the domestic affairs of the college had been placed in the hands of a matron, rather than leaving it to the president and his wife. Whether it was this arrangement, differences between Green and Rooke over student discipline, or other factors is unclear, but there is no doubt that the relationship between Rooke and the students was a difficult one. After several unsettled months in the spring and summer of 1878, new rules for the discipline and order of the house were imposed. These events are recorded in some detail in the college minute books, giving a fascinating picture of college life at that time[23].

There were about twenty students in residence. On 3 April Rooke was disturbed by five of them "forcing a bedroom door and throwing pailsful of water upon the contents of the room". According to Rooke, upon seeing him the assailants "took to flight". Soon afterwards "an organised disturbance" took place, involving "the most discordant noise conducted in different studies". Having asserted his authority and calmed the situation down, Rooke called a special meeting of the Finance and House Committee, which met a week later. The matron, Mrs Yeadon, was dismissed, and the students concerned were asked to appear before the committee. One defended their behaviour as "only fun and frolic", justifying the consequent noise as "a protest against the claim of the President to interfere with their freedom of action". Another expressed indignation at Rooke's interruption of their "innocent diversions". The senior student admitted to leading the noisy disturbance, saying he would do the same again in similar circumstances.

The main college committee, at a meeting soon afterwards, heard that nine students were being interviewed about their part in the affair. The student body had by then agreed to "submit to the ruling of the President", and expressed regret for their conduct. The committee endorsed Rooke's response to the disturbance. This, however, obviously was not the end of the matter, however. Two months later the eighty-year-old Acworth wrote a letter of complaint, "reprobating very strongly the conduct of some of the students". An investigation was carried out, and by the time it had been completed three students had left the college without finishing their courses, two to continue their studies elsewhere, and a new set of rules had been agreed. This covered such matters as meal-times, college prayers and the general conduct of the students. "Unnecessary noise" was to be avoided at all times in the corridors, and quietness was to be observed in all parts of the house after 10.30 p.m.

Trouble broke out again a few years later. This time it prompted a letter of resignation from Rooke, but he was persuaded to withdraw it. This time, four students were asked to leave. Two college officers, the secretary and the finance secretary, resigned over the affair, which suggests that the problems were more than just student misconduct. The committee expressed their "fervent desire that nothing which has transpired will lead to anything so disastrous to this institution as the resignation of the President"[24]. There is no direct evidence of any involvement by Medley in any of these unfortunate events, but a special committee meeting in 1884 referred to reports of "antagonism" between the tutors. It is impossible now to come to any definite conclusion about the causes of these disruptions, but they illustrate the difficulties that could arise within a community of mainly young men living and working in such close proximity. For a while, Rawdon was not a happy place.

Wider Links: the *Senaticus Academicus*

During Rooke's presidency, a partnership was established with the Leeds School of Medicine, by which one or two Rawdon students each year undertook medical training. This link became an important and long-standing feature at the college. The students involved were among those preparing for work overseas with the Baptist Missionary Society. At the beginning of 1878 there were already thirty-two Rawdon students serving overseas, and an element of medical training enabled the college to offer a more complete course for such men. Qualified doctors were not yet accepted by the society as medical missionaries, but short courses in medicine and surgery were regarded from about this time as useful additions to the training of missionaries, whose primary task was preaching[25].

The opening up of Oxford and Cambridge to non-Anglicans and the beginning of university extension courses in the 1870s stimulated colleges like Rawdon to think about the opportunities this gave their own students. London degrees had been available for several years, but now there were other possibilities. Degree courses in theology or divinity were still only available for Nonconformists in Scotland, but the benefit of ministers having an arts degree from an English university was nevertheless attractive. Several of the subjects that could be covered, like philosophy and Biblical languages, were central to the courses that theological colleges ran. In 1879 a sub-committee was appointed at Rawdon to look at possible relations with the universities. It concluded that training at Oxford or Cambridge would be highly advantageous, and it was decided to contact other colleges to find out what was happening elsewhere[26]. Nothing systematic seems to have come of this.

Two other developments in higher education were also important. One was the establishment of the *Senaticus Academicus* in 1879; the other was the formation of the Federal Victoria University in 1880. For about twenty years, the *Senaticus Academicus* was the main way that English Nonconformist colleges guaranteed high academic standards for their students of theology. Divinity degrees were only obtainable after 1898 when London University began to offer BDs and DDs. The *Senaticus Academicus* attempted to fill this gap, and although its standards were probably not as high as that offered by the Scottish universities, it made a valuable contribution to theological education, setting standard examinations for participating colleges and offering associateships and fellowships. Almost from the start the Baptist colleges recognised its value, and in 1881 Rawdon became the first to apply for membership. Rooke was no doubt conscious of the high standards set by Airedale College and its president, Andrew Fairbairn. Fairbairn, himself an outstanding theologian, was determined to establish Airedale as a centre of excellence in theological education. By 1884 he would only admit students who had already graduated in an arts subject. He actually rejected the *Senaticus Academicus* examinations as being of too low a standard, preferring to take advantage of courses offered at universities in his native Scotland[27].

The creation of the Federal Victoria University, which brought colleges in Liverpool, Manchester and Leeds together into one institution for higher education, highlighted the disadvantages of Rawdon's location. Although only a few miles from Leeds, it was too far away to enable students to benefit easily from the courses being taught there[28]. In 1882 serious consideration was given to moving the college to Leeds. A year later, after a consultation with supporters, the committee went so far as to appoint a sub-committee to "watch for a favourable opportunity of selling the present site"[29]. No such opportunity presented itself, however, before other possibilities for securing the college's future came under consideration.

In the summer of 1890 Rooke's health broke down. In September, unable to teach or attend meetings, and facing the possibility of a long period of convalescence, he offered his resignation. This was not accepted, and temporary teaching arrangements were put in place. However, Rooke did not recover, and died before the end of the year. The challenge of finding a successor was made more difficult by the news that two other key men were leaving. W.T. Whitley, Rooke's nephew and the minister of the church in Bridlington, had been covering much of Rooke's tutorial work during his final illness, and seemed destined to join the tutorial staff. He and George Hill, the college secretary, both announced early in 1891 that they had accepted an invitation to help establish a Baptist college in Melbourne, Australia.

During the first half of 1891 the college's future was urgently debated. A conference with the college at Nottingham was suggested, with a view to possible amalgamation, but this was not approved by the committee[30]. Informal conversations about amalgamating with the Manchester College also took place. In the meantime, Thomas Vincent Tymms, the minister of Downs Chapel in Clapton, was invited to be principal, and J.T. Marshall, tutor at the Manchester College, to become a third tutor[31]. Marshall was unwilling to leave Manchester, but Tymms accepted. By September 1891 he had joined Medley and assumed his duties at the college.

Tymms was the third successive Rawdon president to have been trained at Regent's Park College. He was, like his two predecessors, from the south. In Clapton, he had gained a reputation as an able apologist and a preacher. His *Mystery of God*, published in 1885, one of his several books on theological themes, led to him receiving an honorary DD from the University of St Andrews. He was a well-known figure in denominational affairs, serving on Union and Missionary Society committees, and was eager to continue his links with those bodies.

The challenge of leading Rawdon was an important and strategic one. Talk of amalgamation was in the air, as a response to the inability of small institutions to provide an adequate standard of education at a sufficiently high level[32]. The training of ministers was a matter of vital concern for Baptists throughout the country, and as the Baptist Union's role in denominational life increased, the recognition, support and deployment of ministers were being increasingly discussed at national level. In the increasingly complex industrialised society of late Victorian England, Rawdon had to play its part as Baptists sought the most effective way of training their ministers. As Green had recognised, it seemed that the answer would lie in co-operating with others, either Baptist colleges elsewhere or other educational institutions.

Thomas Goadby

The General Baptist college in the village of Chilwell had fewer students than Rawdon. In 1864 there were just eleven. There were, as at Rawdon, two tutors, the principal, William Underwood, and William Stevenson, both themselves trained for the ministry at the same institution. Unlike Rawdon, the direction of the college was ultimately in the hands of the denominational authorities, in this case the annual Association of the General Baptist New Connexion, to which the committee and tutors were answerable.

At the end of the 1872/3 session Underwood resigned as principal. Stevenson placed his resignation in the hands of the committee as well, in order to give it a free hand in appointing a successor. At the 1873 annual meetings the Association turned to Thomas Goadby, the minister of the Osmaston Road church in Derby, to succeed Underwood. The Goadby family was well known in General Baptist circles. Two of Thomas's four brothers were ministers in the denomination, and a third had died as a missionary with the General Baptist Mission in Orissa in 1868. His father Joseph had been a leading minister of the Connexion in Leicester and Loughborough, and was for many years himself secretary of the academy. An uncle had served with the Mission in India. His grandfather, another Joseph, had been one of Dan Taylor's first students in the London academy, going on to be minister of the General Baptist church in Ashby de la Zouch[33].

Goadby had studied at the academy in its Leicester days and at Glasgow University. Like most Baptist ministers of his generation, acquiring a good theological education involved a lot of commitment and self-discipline. As a young apprentice grocer in Leicester, before entering the academy, he had risen at 5 a.m. to study Greek and Latin, and continued to follow the same routine in later life[34]. Like Green, his counterpart at Rawdon, he was known as a man of culture, with considerable intellectual ability. He was also a bit of an eccentric. Walking to a preaching appointment, "he moved along as in a state of subdued rapture, and would recite from time to time with much animation appropriate lines from the great poets"[35].

During the summer vacations Goadby travelled to study in Germany, familiarising himself with the new theological thinking there and translating the works of the theologian Ewald into English. An advocate of incorporating the discoveries and ideas of science into modern theology, his openness to new ways of thinking was regarded by some people as heretical[36]. He was remembered by his students as "a true, sunny hearted, and altogether luminous man of culture", "deeply religious yet entirely free from the conventionalisms of religion"[37]. Before his five-year ministry in Derby he had spent brief periods serving churches in Massachusetts, Coventry and London. He was forty-three when he moved to Chilwell. The Association wanted Stevenson to continue as classical tutor, but he was unwilling to do so, and Charles Clarke of Ashby was appointed to this post in 1874.

Goadby's time as president, which marked the high point of the college's fortunes, got off to a good start with news of a substantial legacy in the year he was appointed. Robert Pegg, a Derby businessman, left £2,000 to the college, and this was used to fund two student scholarships. In 1877 the Association agreed to improvements being made to the Chilwell property, and by 1880 there was accommodation for fifteen students[38]. A wide range of subjects was taught. As well as the usual theological and biblical studies, which included Hebrew and Greek, these covered French, classical Greek and Latin, German, natural philosophy, algebra and geometry[39].

Back to Nottingham

It was a sign of changing times when from 1879 the traditional annual sermon was replaced by a "soirée". This involved a tea, held in the college dining room, "tastefully decorated" by the students, a series of short addresses, "musical intervals" by a choir and opportunity to walk in the college gardens, and was apparently regarded as a great success[40]. Within two years of this innovation, a more significant change was being contemplated. Goadby was keen for his students to take advantage of the new courses being offered in Nottingham by lecturers from Cambridge University, especially those in science and classics. These began in 1873, leading eight years later to the creation of a University College, a municipal project designed largely to keep the town at the forefront of industry and technology.

Goadby urged the Association to move the college back into Nottingham, in order to take full advantage of the new opportunities, and at the annual meetings in 1881 the decision was taken to do this. Two years later the Chilwell premises were sold. "Sandy Knoll", on Forest Row, close to the University College and across the road from the Congregational Institute, became the college's new home. The house, like the Chilwell building, previously housed a school. It was large enough to accommodate fourteen students, a matron and servants, as well as a library, a dining room and a lecture room. Sufficient land was attached to it for the erection of a house for the principal. By 1888, Goadby was able to report that "the advantages of our connection with University College may now be considered fully established"[41]

The move back to Nottingham, after a twenty-one-year sojourn in Chilwell, had significant consequences. One immediate result was the decision to dispense with the services of the second tutor, Clarke, as the subjects taught by him were being covered by university classes. Goadby, too, was apparently able to reduce his teaching load, and devote more time to reading and writing[42]. This reduction in the number of tutors may have been a logical step, but it meant that the college depended a great deal on Goadby, a vulnerability that was destined to become apparent a few years later.

Its position in Forest Row enabled the college not only to take advantage of classes at the University College, but also to develop a close relationship with the Congregational Institute. Co-operation between the two bodies, in teaching, social activity and the supply of students for preaching was to be an important feature of the college's life for the next thirty years. The institute had been established in the early 1860s to provide a more practical ministerial training than was available at other Congregational colleges.

In Chilwell, the situation had been similar to that at Rawdon. In both cases, a move had been made to the quiet seclusion of a rural location, away from the noise and distractions of the town, a generation or so earlier. By the early 1880s, with Leeds and Nottingham becoming centres for higher education, both colleges could see the educational advantages of an urban setting and wanted to move back. Because of Goadby's enthusiasm, the ability of the Association to take a strategic decision fairly quickly and the lack of attachment to the Chilwell premises, the General Baptists were able to do something about it. Rawdon, on the other hand, with a committee deeply attached to the existing premises, found it harder to grasp the nettle, and in the end abandoned the idea. The formation of the *Senaticus Academicus* and the improvement of transport links with Leeds helped to offset the disadvantages of Rawdon's site, however, and being a somewhat larger institution it was better able to cope with them. There were, of course, disadvantages in moving back into the town. The pleasant environment at Chilwell was a benefit for those who lived and studied there. There was little doubt, however, that for educational and social reasons, and for communications links with the rest of the country, Nottingham was the better situation.

Thomas Witton Davies

In March 1889, Goadby was found dead in his study. He was sixty. William Stevenson, who had been a tutor until Goadby's appointment fifteen years earlier, was asked to act as president until a successor was found. The issue was complicated by discussions going on between the General Baptists and the Baptist Union about amalgamation. These had reached a critical stage and, if successful, would profoundly affect the college.

There was a move to try and persuade John Clifford of the prestigious Westbourne Park Baptist Church in London, and one of the most prominent ministers in the denomination, to take over the presidency, but the suggestion that a petition to this effect be organised was turned down by the college committee[43]. Instead, it decided to continue with the temporary arrangements under Stevenson for the following twelve months.

A second blow came with the news of the unexpected death of Thomas Marshall, the college treasurer. As if this were not enough, in this "year of gloom"[44], in July Stevenson himself also died, only a matter of weeks after taking up his responsibilities as acting-principal. As an emergency measure, a syndicate of five ministers was formed to undertake tutorial work during the 1889/90 session.

The college struggled on for the next two years, facing an uncertain future. As a decision on denominational amalgamation had still not been made, the search for a new president was further postponed in the spring of 1890. Later that year, at least two possible candidates were approached but declined. In June 1891 the long-awaited announcement that the New Connexion's General Baptist Association was going to unite with the Baptist Union was made[45].

Bringing to an end the institutional distinction between General and Particular Baptists was a natural consequence of the disappearance of any significant doctrinal or ecclesiological differences between them. However, it involved many adjustments for General Baptists and their churches, particularly in the east midlands, where they were strongest. In other parts of the country they were simply absorbed into existing Baptist associations, in which they were very often already involved. The Association and Missionary Society were soon integrated into the Baptist Union and the BMS. In the east midlands, however, the preponderance of General Baptist churches meant that the solution had to be different. An entirely new Baptist association was formed, comprising the Midland Conference of General Baptist Churches and the two existing east midlands Baptist associations.

As far as the college at Nottingham was concerned, it was renamed Midland Baptist College and given a new constitution. The hope was that it would serve all the Baptist churches of the midlands area. It would be governed by a council consisting of representatives of the two new associations in the midlands[46], the Baptist Union Council and other people elected at the college's annual meeting. A new office of warden was created, an annual appointment whose main responsibilities were to preside and preach at the annual meetings.

The first general meeting of the college's subscribers was held in July 1891. Representatives on the new council were elected, and Clifford, who presided, was appointed the first warden. He appealed to the churches of the midlands for their support. The first major decision of the new council was to invite Thomas Witton Davies to be president. Born in Monmouthshire in 1851, Davies was classical tutor at the Haverfordwest College. He had been trained for the ministry at Regent's Park College and served briefly as minister of the Merthyr church in South Wales. He accepted the invitation, and commenced work in Nottingham at the beginning of 1892. He stated at the start that his interests were primarily "literary and scholastic" and that, as far as possible, he wanted to be relieved of responsibility for the college's management[47]. His particular academic expertise was in Hebrew and other Semitic languages.

For the first time since Goadby's death nearly three years before, the college could face the future with some confidence. Davies was a man of considerable academic ability, and this soon won him a respected place as a lecturer in the University College. Midland College was by now a member of the *Senaticus Academicus*, the decision to join having been taken since Goadby's death. The course was extended to five years, and a commitment was made to appoint a second tutor as soon as money was available.

However, severe obstacles had to be overcome if the college was to make a success of this new opportunity. The uncertainty since Goadby's death had resulted in a drop in the number of students, so that when Davies was appointed there were just seven. The disappearance of the General Baptist Association meant that it no longer had the status of an official denominational institution. While some old loyalties would no doubt continue, it could no longer rely on a supply of ministerial candidates from General Baptist churches, and would be more exposed to competition from the other five English colleges. A lot depended on how enthusiastically the churches of the midlands would throw in their lot with the new body. Historical ties and the loyalty of ministers to the college where they were trained meant that changing college allegiance could not be expected to happen immediately. For Midland College to emerge from its low state and establish itself within the new national Baptist scene would be a tough challenge.

It is surprising that the question of closing the Nottingham college does not seem to have been seriously addressed at this time, either by the denominational or college authorities. After all, talk about co-operation, and even amalgamation, had been going on for a while, and many had come to the conclusion that six English colleges were too many. Even if the number of ministers receiving college training continued to rise, it was hard to justify keeping the situation as it was, either financially or educationally[48]. However, more was involved than just the efficient provision of training, as those who advocated reform constantly discovered. Tradition and personal loyalties were factors that could not be ignored. Allowing the college to disappear, to unite with Rawdon, or fundamentally to change its character, would have been a hard pill for the General Baptists to swallow, and may have made the prospects of denominational amalgamation even more difficult than they already were. Another factor which helped ensure the survival of Midland was the negotiations going on at the time between Rawdon and Manchester about establishing a united northern college at Manchester. These came to nothing, but Clifford believed that this step would be taken and, if it had, the case for closing Nottingham would have lost much of its force.

For good or ill, the commitment was made to continue at Nottingham. John Clifford's support was crucial, as was Davies' ability to provide the right leadership qualities. The next few years, it seemed, were likely to be critical.

Edward Parker

Manchester College tended to be more theologically conservative than either Rawdon or Nottingham, although this was sometimes as much a question of appearance and reputation as reality. It was also conservative in other ways. While both Rawdon and Nottingham recruited tutors trained at other colleges, Manchester preferred men trained within its own tradition.

A theological conservatism was demonstrated by the speeches at the official opening of the Brighton Grove premises in September 1874. Edward Parker was keen to affirm the continuity between the old Strict Baptist Society and the new institution, and Thomas Dawson criticised contemporary liberal trends in theology. Those who looked to science as the way of discovering truth, he said, were looking in the wrong place[49]. The college was still in the process of carving out a position for itself within the denomination, and it is hard to avoid the conclusion that Samuel Green at Rawdon, and the newly appointed Thomas Goadby at Chilwell, were in their sights as they made these remarks.

Support for Manchester did not come solely, or even predominantly, from Lancashire Baptists. Many in West Yorkshire identified more readily with its stance than with that of Rawdon, and its greatest benefactor, William Shaw, was a Yorkshireman. Bradford in particular had a prominent position among the towns from which gifts came to support the new venture across the Pennines.

Dowson continued as president for three years after the opening of Brighton Grove. During that time the North Western Association, formed in 1860 in protest against perceived liberal tendencies in the Lancashire and Cheshire Association, disbanded, and most of its churches rejoined the larger group. It had not succeeded in winning support from more than a handful of churches. Its disappearance enabled the college, which had been closely associated with it, to win more general acceptance as part of the mainstream of Baptist life in the north west.

In 1877 Dowson retired, and his place was taken by Edward Parker. No real change was signified by this hand-over of leadership. Parker, an enthusiastic strict communionist, had been trained under the auspices of the Evangelical Society by Thomas Dawson, and had gone on to become the joint secretary, with John Howe, of its northern branch. He had helped edit the *Primitive Church Magazine* and had been appointed college secretary at Bury when the college there opened in 1866. When he became president at Manchester he was a figure of some prominence among Yorkshire Baptists, having been minister of the church at Farsley, near Leeds, since 1859. A new chapel, with a splendid organ, had been erected at Farsley during his ministry. Dowson continued to lecture part-time at the college alongside Parker until 1880.

Manchester College, opened in 1874 at Brighton Grove

Although Parker shared the same views as Dowson, and continued to lead the college along much the same lines, changes inevitably took place. The assistant tutor, James Webb, also resigned in 1877. Webb had been appointed tutor for "general literature", but had increasingly taken on responsibility for teaching classics, as Latin, Greek and Hebrew became integral parts of the curriculum. His replacement was John Turner Marshall, who was designated classical tutor. Marshall, like Parker, was well known at the college, having been a post-graduate student there since 1875. Originally trained as a lay student at Rawdon, he held an MA degree from London University. His special area of expertise was in Hebrew and Old Testament studies. He had no ministerial experience, having devoted himself to academic work prior to his appointment. Given the Evangelical Society's earlier commitment to the need for training to be linked to practical experience, and its suspicion of academic courses, his appointment was a notable one, amounting to a change of emphasis, if not a reversal of previous policy. The Parker-Marshall partnership was to continue at Manchester for twenty-one years and, following Parker's retirement in 1898, Marshall succeeded him, serving as president until he died in office twenty-five years later in 1923. 1877, then, was the start of a remarkably long period of stable leadership at the college.

Under Parker, the college's academic standards rose. Relations with Owens College remained close, with Owens' students regularly being offered accommodation at Brighton Grove, and Manchester's students in turn attending classes there. During the late 1870s, Owens was supported in its campaign for university status. In 1883 the college became affiliated to the *Senaticus Academicus*, and soon afterwards the course was also lengthened from three to four years. In 1889 new and more rigorous entrance qualifications were imposed. From then on, all candidates would be examined in reading and delivery, English grammar and composition, "a portion of some one of our English classics", one of the epistles, Scripture history and elementary knowledge of English history, geography, arithmetic and Greek grammar[50]. By then Owens had been incorporated into the new northern Federal Victoria University, and the college had the status of being closely associated with this important development in higher education. The number of students remained at about twenty, similar to Rawdon.

A number of factors were gradually making Manchester's distinctive character less significant. The curriculum, influenced by the requirements of the *Senaticus Academicus* and the teaching at Owens College, was becoming broadly the same as that in the other colleges. The heat had been taken out of the theological controversies of the 1850s and 1860s and, although a strict communion policy was still in place, it seemed to make little difference in practice to which students were accepted for training or the support the college received from the churches. The Downgrade controversy of the late 1880s, and Spurgeon's consequent resignation from the Union, which ten or fifteen years earlier would surely have caused a stir at Manchester, seemed to make virtually no impact at all. One feature of college life that remained important, however, was the involvement of students in mission and preaching in and around the city. In 1878 the committee were told that students had conducted 1,000 services during the course of the past year, and in 1885 they were helping support two mission stations, at Longsight and Hollinwood[51].

Links across the Atlantic, which had always been a particular feature of college life, probably a result of its traditionally conservative theological stance, continued through the 1880s. In 1889 Parker attended the Southern and Northern Baptist Conventions in Memphis and Boston, and visited Baptists in Canada. This was followed by a visit to Manchester of a delegation from the Southern Baptist Convention at the annual meetings in 1890. Overseas links of another kind were made when the first two students were accepted by the Baptist Missionary Society in 1881, to serve as missionaries in India and Africa. Two years later one of them, John Shred, became the first Manchester student to die on the mission field.

During the course of 1891, Marshall was approached by both Rawdon and Nottingham. This caused consternation at Manchester. The House Committee passed a resolution urging him to stay, and offering him an increase of £100 in his annual salary. Such a move, it said, would cause "deep grief", and would not advance Marshall's "comfort or welfare"[52]. The situation at Brighton Grove, though not without inevitable financial worries from time to time, was one with which its supporters were apparently satisfied. They did not want to see it disturbed.

There were good reasons for this satisfaction. The district of Rusholme, a prosperous residential area, had by then been integrated into the city of Manchester, a vibrant and growing modern conurbation at the heart of the British Empire[53]. It had its share of the problems associated with urban life at that time, with areas of desperate poverty, poor housing and short life expectancy. These, however, did not make much of an impact in Brighton Grove. The college's location in a quiet residential road, within easy access of the city centre and its new university, based in modern premises, and led by respected and settled tutors, seemed full of hope.

Ministry and Mission at the End of the Century

Many challenges were common to all three colleges, such as the need to raise money and the huge and varied burden born by their principals for administration, teaching, preaching and fund raising, as well as their own academic work. Other problems differed from place to place. Rawdon faced the disadvantage of its relatively isolated location. Nottingham was seeking to recreate a role for itself in the new post-1891 denominational situation. In Manchester the challenge was perhaps more one of complacency.

The social and economic changes rapidly taking place in England presented all three colleges with new opportunities and dangers, whether they realised it or not. They alarmed many church leaders in all denominations. It was becoming increasingly obvious that the Church as a whole, with the possible exception, in some areas, of the Roman Catholic Church, was failing to reach the vast and growing urban working class. In spite of pouring in resources, it also seemed to have no effective answer to the challenge of urban poverty. The expanding suburban estates presented another kind of challenge: the need to establish new churches to cater for the growing middle-class families who lived there. Mission in an increasingly urban society was also coloured by profound changes in attitudes and behaviour in such spheres as the organisation of labour, popular culture, transport and communication, commercial practice and the status of women.

Many of these changes had so far left the colleges largely untouched. The campaign for women's rights, for example, was still in its infancy, and women had been conspicuous by their invisibility in college life. The occasional matron, female servant or wife had an occasional place in the written accounts of what went on, but the whole field of ministerial education was regarded as almost entirely a male preserve, in its public face, at least. The possibility of women in the ministry was just beginning to be raised. John Clifford had brought it to the attention of General Baptists in an article in the *General Baptist Magazine* in 1880 entitled "Woman as Preacher", arguing in favour of a role for women in the pulpit. He pointed out that in the seventeenth century, some women had exercised a valued public ministry among Baptists[54].

As the century drew towards its close, the challenge of mission in a modern, urban environment, in which the place of women was but one aspect, confronted the whole Christian community. The ministry was central to the answer, and the colleges were in a unique position to address this. Whether the three Baptist colleges in the north and midlands liked it or not, they were involved. Could they play a positive role in contributing towards the answer to the questions being raised, or would they, in the pursuit of academic excellence, retreat into a detached world of academic study? Could they produce a ministry that was able to grapple both with the intellectual challenges of contemporary Biblical and theological scholarship and also relate the Christian Gospel to the practical needs of a changing world?

If they were to attempt an answer to such questions, many believed they needed to work more closely together. The pursuit of co-operation and unity was to dominate the next period of their history.

---

1 *The Baptist*, 3 July 1874.
2 Durham University had been in existence since the 1830s, but was too small to have a significant influence on the development of higher education.
3 University education for women was first provided by Queen's College, London in 1848. Girton College, originally situated in Hitchin, moved to Cambridge in 1872. The federal Victoria University opened its doors to men and women without distinction from its creation in the early 1880s.
4 C.H. Spurgeon, whose Pastors' College was opened in London in 1856, was unique among college presidents in deliberately spurning this way of thinking. Spurgeon, who received no formal training himself, regarded academic qualifications as irrelevant for the ministry.
5 Between 1871 and 1881 rural population fell for the first time in Britain since Census records began. Urban population increased by 25%.

6 R.C.K. Ensor, *England 1870-1914* (Oxford University Press: Oxford, 1936) p.136.
7 John O. Barrett, *Rawdon College (Northern Baptist Education Society) 1804-1954: A Short History* (Carey Kingsgate Press, London, 1954) p.27.
8 Lily Watson, *The Vicar of Langthwaite (new edition)* (James Clarke and Co.: London, 1897) pp.1-93.
9 Skae appears in *The Vicar of Langthwaite* as an abrupt and rather severe Scottish tutor called Alan Keith.
10 William Medley, *Rawdon Baptist College Centenary Memorial* (Kingsgate Press: London, 1904) p.35.
11 Rawdon College Minute Book, 31 March 1869.
12 *Ibid.*, 2 July 1868.
13 Medley, *Centenary Memorial*, p.36.
14 *Ibid.*, 26 February 1869.
15 *Baptist Handbook* 1909, p.479.
16 Rawdon College Minute Book, 1 July 1869. There was long and "anxious deliberation" on the subject before the application was turned down.
17 *Ibid.*, 22 December 1869.
18 Nottingham Baptist College Minute Book, 7 May 1872.
19 Rawdon College Minute Book, 28 September 1876.
20 Medley, *Centenary Memorial*, pp.37-8.
21 *Ibid.*, p.38.
22 It has generally been accepted that Rawdon men were the ones primarily in Spurgeon's sights during the Downgrade controversy of 1887-8.
23 Rawdon College Minute Book, 17 April – 2 October 1878; Minute Book of the Finance and House Committee of Rawdon College, 10 April 1878.
24 Rawdon College Minute Book, 9 January- 25 June 1884,
25 Brian Stanley, *The History of the Baptist Missionary Society 1792-1992* (T and T Clark: Edinburgh, 1992) p.181.
26 As early as 1873 a Rawdon student was undertaking some study at Cambridge (see Rawdon College Minute Book, 25 June 1873).
27 In 1886 Fairbairn left Airedale to establish Mansfield College in Oxford.
28 As well as attending courses at the Leeds School of Medicine, some students from Rawdon had attended courses at the Leeds College of Science from at least as early as 1875 (Rawdon College Finance and House Minute Book, 1 October 1875).
29 Rawdon College Minute Book, 19 December 1883.
30 *Ibid.*, 28 January 1891. Negotiations between the Baptist Union and the General Baptists about amalgamation had been going on for some time, and were to be successfully completed later in 1891. The future status of the college at Nottingham was therefore uncertain.
31 Marshall had been a lay student at Rawdon in the 1860s.

Raising Standards: the 1870s and 1880s

32 The two Congregational Colleges in Yorkshire (Airedale and Rotherham) amalgamated to form the Yorkshire United Independent College in 1888.
33 The story of the Goadby family and its connection with the General Baptist movement is given in Bertha and Lilian Goadby, *Not saints but men: or the story of the Goadby ministers* (Kingsgate Press: London, n.d. (?1908)).
34 General Baptist Year Book 1889, p.66. Carter, *Midland Baptist College*, p.28.
35 Carter, *Midland Baptist College*, p.29.
36 Goadby, *Not saints but men*, pp.242-3.
37 *Ibid.*, p.253. See also the 1890 Baptist Handbook, pp.120-2, where he was described as "a man of good manners and playful humour".
38 *General Baptist Magazine*, April 1880, p.186. There were fourteen students at the College at that time.
39 General Baptist Year Book, 1882, pp.8-10.
40 Nottingham College Minute Book, May 1879. The College had held soirées before, but not on the occasion of the main annual meeting.
41 Annual Report for 1887-8, in the General Baptist Yearbook 1888, p.7.
42 Carter, *Midland Baptist College*, p.25.
43 Nottingham Baptist College Minute Book, 24 June 1889.
44 Carter, *Midland Baptist College*, p.26.
45 All references to General Baptists are to the New Connexion. Those original General Baptists who did not join the connexion had all but disappeared by this time.
46 As part of the amalgamation arrangements, the old Midlands Association was renamed the West Midlands Association.
47 T.W. Davies, "Midland Baptist College" in the *East Midlands Baptist Magazine* vol. 6 (February 1897) pp.21-2.
48 Between 1870 and 1901, the proportion of English Baptist ministers trained in denominational colleges rose from less than half to over 60%. If everyone leaving the ministry was replaced by a college-trained person, and these were distributed evenly among the colleges (neither of which could realistically be expected to happen) there would be a need for about 17 new ministers per college each year. The situation was especially complicated by the fact that Spurgeon's College had far more students than any of the other colleges (see J.H.Y. Briggs, *The English Baptists of the Nineteenth Century* (Baptist Historical Society: Didcot, 1994) p.84).
49 Manchester Baptist College Minute Book, 1874-1899. Report of public meeting held on 2 September 1874, pp.5-11.
50 Manchester College Minute Book, 18 December 1889.
51 Manchester College Minute Book, 3 July 1878. Minute Book of the Manchester College House Committee, 16 December 1885.
52 Minute Book of Manchester College House Committee, 15 April 1891.

53 The 35-mile long Manchester Ship Canal was built between 1887 and 1894. As deep as the Suez Canal, it made Manchester one of the leading ports in the country.
54 John Clifford, "Woman as Preacher" , *General Baptist Magazine* (November 1880), pp.452-4.

Chapter Seven
The Unsuccessful Search for Unity: 1891-1904

The Baptist Union

The drive towards greater co-ordination in ministerial training was partly the result of the growing importance of the Union. A sense of denominational identity had been gradually developing throughout the century, and by the 1890s, the Union, strengthened by its absorption of the General Baptist New Connexion, had become an important centre of influence. Its secretary, Samuel Harris Booth, was an able and respected figure. A new constitution, adopted in 1883, had made its structures more representative of Baptists nationally and given it greater powers and resources. Booth, and other leading Baptists like Richard Glover of Bristol, advocated an even greater denominational cohesion under the banner of the Union. The bitter Downgrade controversy of the late 1880s, as a result of which Spurgeon withdrew from the Union, did not seem to weaken its position. In some respects, the split probably enabled the Union to achieve a more dominant position in the denomination than would have been possible if Spurgeon had remained active within it. An expression of the Union's greater strength was the creation of the Baptist Union Corporation in 1890, paving the way for it to assume greater financial and trust responsibilities.

The colleges were inevitably affected by the rise of the Union, particularly when questions relating to the ministry were raised. As early as 1871 the possibility of a co-ordinated scheme of college training was being investigated, at the initiative of Samuel Green. In 1873 college tutors were made *ex officio* members of the Union. By 1891 the feeling that the ministry was a matter of national rather than merely local concern was widespread. Many were saying that if it was to be effective, decisions about selection and training could not be left entirely in the hands of local bodies, whether they were churches, associations or colleges.

Most of the colleges themselves were aware of the deficiencies of small institutions in providing an adequate preparation for ministry. They aimed to deliver a university standard of theological education as well as give training in the skills ministers needed[1]. Nationally, higher education was rapidly expanding, with universities being opened in several of the larger cities. The colleges found it impossible on their own to keep up with the standards set by these secular institutions. Principals and tutors had an immense range of responsibilities and, even when a college could afford the rare luxury of three full-time academic staff, the burdens and frustrations involved were arduous. Funds had to be raised through voluntary gifts and, while the financial situation was not quite as precarious as it had been earlier in the century, anxieties over money were rarely absent.

At the end of 1890, both Rawdon and Midland were without a principal. Interregnums were always times of uncertainty and opportunity, and the committees of both colleges spent time seriously considering future policy. Midland also went through the throes of constitutional reorganisation following the disappearance of the General Baptist Association in 1891. Soon afterwards Thomas Vincent Tymms and Thomas Witton Davies embarked on their responsibilities at Rawdon and Midland respectively. A new principal meant new priorities and a fresh vision, so there was during 1891-2 an unusual period of openness to change, east of the Pennines at least.

The first attempt at unity: 1891-2

In 1891 the Rawdon committee had hoped to secure the services of J.T. Marshall, tutor at Manchester, alongside that of their new principal, Tymms. Its approach to Marshall was unsuccessful, but the perceived benefit of bringing together the abilities of the tutorial staff at both places may have led to the suggestion of amalgamating. In June of the same year the committee resolved unanimously that such a merger would be desirable and wise[2]. A telegram was despatched to Manchester, and it was mutually agreed to explore the possibility[3]. A conference of representatives of the two colleges took place during the Baptist Union autumn meetings that year, at which it was decided to recommend amalgamation to the college authorities. It was felt that Manchester's position on communion need not be an obstacle, and that it could be preserved in a united college. At the same Union meetings the question of the colleges in general was also discussed more broadly. James Culross, the principal of Bristol College, addressed the Assembly on the subject of "Our Colleges", and the president of the Union, Colonel James Griffin, suggested setting up a Baptist university[4].

In December the committees at both Rawdon and Manchester affirmed their commitment to the principle of amalgamation. The main debating point was how Manchester's views on communion could be safeguarded. Manchester thought this should be done by the "proportionate representation on the tutorial staff and committees" of the two views on communion[5], while Rawdon preferred a less rigid approach, according to which Manchester's stance would be "fully represented" on the committee and the tutorial staff[6]. Diverging interpretations of what this meant in practice led quite quickly to the breakdown of the negotiations. The sticking point was Manchester's demand that the theological professor be a strict communionist, something which Rawdon was not prepared to accept[7]. The theological professor usually took the position of principal too, and perhaps this was the real issue behind the collapse of the talks. Rawdon may have assumed that the recently appointed Tymms would naturally be preferred over the ageing Parker. If Manchester was indeed laying down as a condition of union that the principal be a strict communionist, this was understandably objectionable to Rawdon. The argument over communion had long since ceased to be a matter of vital importance among Baptists, even for the supporters of Manchester College, so it is strange that no way of resolving the issue could be found. Perhaps when it came to it, Parker, given his passionate public advocacy of strict communion twenty-five years before, just could not face any compromise. In any event, it was clear to both sides by June 1892 that the division over communion was not going to be resolved, and the negotiations were brought to an end.

It was not as clear to others, however. At the same time that Rawdon and Manchester were coming to the conclusion that the search for unity was over, John Clifford was expressing his confidence that it was inevitable. Addressing the inaugural meeting of the Midland Baptist College, he spoke with confidence:

> For the next half century, at least, our churches will need four institutions for the effective equipment of their ministry; one in the North, say, at Manchester, and in connection with the Victoria University – Rawdon and Brighton Grove coming together according to the divine decree; one in the West at Bristol, and in association with Bristol University; a third, for the South, in London – Regent's Park and Pastor's College 'now twain, being made one flesh', and gaining their Arts and Science course at University College . . .; and ours in Mid-England, and in vital touch with the Nottingham University[8].

Perhaps Clifford's ambitions for his *Alma Mater* clouded his judgement. It took over seventy years before Clifford's prediction of four colleges came about, and even then it was not in the way he predicted. His remarks do demonstrate, however, that schemes for rationalising college training were very much in the air.

All the colleges received a message from Booth following the Union's spring meetings in 1892, asking their representatives to meet with him to discuss future ministerial training policy. Delegates at the Assembly had expressed a desire to raise standards, broaden syllabuses and see more effective co-operation, and a committee had been set up to see what could be done. At first, Rawdon was reluctant to participate, no doubt smarting after the rebuff from Manchester, but eventually agreed to participate. In 1893, following a conference with college representatives, Booth sent out a set of agreed proposals. In essence, these were that the denomination should establish one college in the neighbourhood of a University College to provide an initial education in Arts for ministerial candidates, and that all other Baptist colleges should become "purely Theological Halls". At the colleges' conference, this had been proposed by J.H. Shakespeare and seconded by Tymms. When the suggestions were discussed by the college committees, however, the response was far from positive. Manchester felt unable to pronounce an opinion because of widely differing reports of the resolutions agreed at the conference. The discussion had been wide-ranging, with references to a common standard of entrance, a common examining board, the exchange of tutors, etc., and the committee did not know quite what to make of it all. Midland approved the general principle of the proposals but deferred any decision on the details. Rawdon supported the idea of a college for preliminary training but was unable to go any further[9]. Faced with such a lack of enthusiasm, Booth dropped the proposals soon afterwards.

From 1895 the Union's attention turned increasingly to the question of ministerial recognition. A scheme for officially recognising ministers whose sense of vocation, ability and training had been approved by the Union was put in place between 1895 and 1898[10]. It did not command much support, partly because it made little practical difference whether ministers were recognised by the Union or not, and being mainly concerned with ministers who had not received a college training, it had little impact on the colleges. The scheme assumed that ministers who had satisfied the colleges as to their fitness were worthy of recognition. It did, however, lead to a list of colleges recognised by the Union for training purposes being drawn up. This comprised all the existing Baptist colleges.

In the years following the unsuccessful talks between Rawdon and Manchester in 1892, Parker's health became increasingly fragile. In 1896, extra tutorial help was arranged at Manchester to cover his absences, and in 1897 he tendered his resignation on health grounds. He died in the following year, after nearly twenty-one years as principal.

At Rawdon, Tymms was assisted by two other tutors, William Medley, and, from 1893, the Scot, David Glass. Glass was responsible for Biblical languages, and had the reputation of being a painstaking teacher. Raising money was an ever-present task, and in 1895 Glass was asked to be the college's financial secretary as well as tutor. As an incentive, he was offered a 5% commission on any extra money he was able to raise[11]. Various other ways of raising money were considered and rejected, including the imposition of student fees and holding a college bazaar.

It was felt that demands on the staff were reaching an unacceptable level, in spite of there being three tutors, generally for about twenty students. The 1894 annual report claimed that the task of training for the ministry had become so arduous that, in their own interests, churches should make as few demands on the tutors for service outside the college as possible. The ministry was more challenging than ever before, owing to "the quickened intellectual activity of the people, the increase of scientific knowledge, the attention given to questions relating to the literary structure of the Bible, [and] the widespread social unrest"[12]. Preparation for such a calling demanded not only the undivided energies of the tutors, but also candidates of the highest quality. Churches were also urged only to recommend candidates in whose "personal piety and intellectual fitness" they had complete confidence. "No College", said the report, "would entertain the idea of training men for the Ministry who were regarded as incapable of gaining a competent knowledge" of Greek and Hebrew[13]. Times had certainly changed since the opening of the academy in Horton ninety years before. But were the demands of ministry really so very much greater?

Sixty years later, H.W. Burdett reminisced about his student days at Rawdon in the *Rawdonian*, the magazine for friends of the college. Burdett started training in 1897. College life as he recalled it was a round of classes, football, debates, rags and talk in the study until midnight. Most students were keen sermon tasters, and when free loved to walk to Leeds or Bradford, "defying rain, hail or snow" to hear some famous preacher[14]. The annual meetings gave the chance for old students to meet, and for past and present students to challenge each other at cricket.

Midland College was smaller than Rawdon, though not by much, and Davies struggled on as the only tutor. Extending the support of the college beyond its old General Baptist constituency, especially into the West Midlands Association area, proved difficult. Student numbers slowly increased through the nineties, from twelve at the beginning of 1892 to fifteen in 1898. Money was short, and in at least one year no new students could be admitted on account of the lack of funds[15]. Frequent use was made of courses run by the University College, and co-operation with the Congregational Institute continued to develop, the two principals sharing teaching with several part-time lecturers. Classes for lay preachers in the area were also run from 1893.

Academic standards at Nottingham were high. In 1895 the Council decided that most students should spend at least two years "wholly devoted to linguistic and scientific studies, as a preparation for the Theological course"[16]. A new five-year curriculum was put in place, with a strong emphasis on languages (Greek, Hebrew and either German or Latin being studied for the first three years) and a wide range of other subjects, including mathematics, political economy and philosophy[17]. Lectures, to which invitations were extended outside the college, were given by visiting speakers in Hinduism and Mohammedanism.[18]

Two of the most able ministers of their generation were studying at Nottingham at this time, Newton Herbert Marshall, who entered the college in 1892, and James Henry Rushbrooke, who arrived in 1894. Marshall looked set for denominational leadership and high scholarly achievement until his premature death in 1914. Rushbrooke went on to become one of the outstanding international Baptist figures of the twentieth century. Both men were protégés of John Clifford. During the 1896-7 session Marshall edited a student magazine called *The Collegian*. This publication described itself as "the organ of the Baptist Students Fraternal Union", a body set up at a conference of ministerial students in Nottingham in 1896. It seems that it only survived for one year. All the Baptist colleges in England and Wales were involved in the Union apart from Spurgeon's College, and membership, which was also open to non-ministerial students at Baptist colleges, stood at 170 in July 1897.

The Collegian offers a remarkable picture of student life and opinion at that time. The first number included an article by "Londiniensis" entitled "Our Denominational Chaos", complaining bitterly about the lack of cohesion among Baptists. An official denominational newspaper, a scheme for accrediting ministers and a federation of colleges to co-ordinate training were all desperately needed. "Let not a superstitious veneration for the Congregationalist principle ... blind us to the higher worth of united co-operation", pleaded the writer. In the second number, these views were endorsed by "Studiosus", who called for "a graduated income tax on all Baptist Churches for the support of the Colleges" and proposed their amalgamation into one powerful institution at Oxford or

Cambridge. It was, perhaps, not surprising that Spurgeon's College viewed the magazine with "disfavour". Correspondence on the application of "collectivist principles" among Baptists continued throughout the year.

Perhaps the most interesting aspect of the magazine, however, is information about college life from the students' perspective. There was a widespread interest in overseas mission, with a fortnightly "missionary band" at Manchester, meeting to study the geography, history and peoples of various mission fields, and a monthly missionary prayer meeting at Nottingham. Examination successes with the *Senaticus Academicus* and London University were reported, and various kinds of social activities described. Rawdon and Manchester students met in February 1897, the "chief event" being the football match, which Rawdon lost 2:1. This was no doubt compensation for Manchester, who suffered defeat at the hands of Didsbury Wesleyan College. In May the matron at Nottingham, Miss McCorkendale, organised an informal entertainment for students and friends, involving items by the choral society, recitations and piano playing. During the summer, Rawdon and Airedale challenged each other at tennis, and the 1897 conference at Regent's Park featured two concerts and a cricket match between the delegates and Regent's Park students. At the conference, "an unlimited supply of cigarettes made the hearts of all the lovers of Lady Nicotine throb with joy"[19].

Davies had made it clear from the start that his interests were "literary and scholastic". He did not want to be responsible for management, and was keen to see someone else appointed as president. He offered to co-operate in any way he could with the College Council in order to see this achieved, including, if necessary, to step down[20]. The Council was sympathetic to Davies' position. It believed that unless "ampler theological teaching" could be provided at the college, its continued existence could not be justified[21]. Davies, like Tymms and many others, including, apparently, the students, was keen to see more effective links between the colleges. The most likely way for these objectives to be achieved was by means of the amalgamation, or at least the closer co-operation, of two or more of the Baptist colleges in the north and midlands. It was not surprising, then, that the issue was raised again in 1898.

The second attempt: 1898 – 1899

Rawdon was responsible for resurrecting the question of amalgamation. The stimulus was a combination of frustration over finances and news of Parker's retirement. A lengthy debate on the wisdom and effectiveness of holding a college bazaar in October 1897 led to a discussion on whether the time was right to approach Manchester and Midland. The committee were encouraged to hear that both the other colleges were ready in principle to consider such an overture sympathetically if it came at the right time[22]. Two months later news came from Manchester that a window of opportunity may have opened. Parker had announced his intention of resigning at the end of the academic year. W. Dale Shaw, the college secretary at Manchester, indicated that "the friends of Manchester College were anxious for amalgamation with Rawdon". He suggested the formation of a joint committee to explore the legal difficulties over Manchester's Trust Deeds on the issue of strict communion[23].

Unfortunately, the delicate process of re-opening negotiations was interrupted by the death of Parker in February 1898. Talking continued for a few months, but by May it had become clear they were getting nowhere. The Manchester committee accused Rawdon of refusing to concede anything. They claimed that what was being proposed was absorption by Rawdon, rather than a genuine amalgamation. Rawdon, on the other hand, accused Manchester of insisting that any united college could only be constituted under the existing Manchester Trust Deed, which it regarded as an insuperable obstacle[24]. The outcome, then, was much the same as it had been six years before.

While the fruitless discussions with Manchester were going on, Tymms heard from Davies at Nottingham. Midland College, he said, were "disposed to favourably consider the question of union with Rawdon". In March 1898 the Rawdon committee decided that pursuing amalgamation with Nottingham should take priority over the negotiations with Manchester, and authority was given for talks to begin[25].

Shortly after the breakdown of the talks with Rawdon, John Turner Marshall was officially appointed Parker's successor at Manchester. Parker's ill health had meant he had already been principal in all but name for some time. With no pastoral experience, his interests were primarily academic, his specialist field being Palestinian-Syriac studies. Five years later the *Baptist Times* described him as being "over-fond of his study, where he becomes a sort of island amid a sea of open books bearing upon his favourite theme, and so situated he beams with happiness"[26]. Whether Marshall was personally involved in the failure of the negotiations with Rawdon is impossible to judge, but he was undoubtedly in a position to enable them to continue had he wanted to. Marshall was joined by Herbert Ellis, who became classical tutor. Ellis had been a student at Manchester under Parker, and at the time of his appointment, was also minister of Parker's old church at Farsley. The feeling that tutorial appointments at the college were something of a closed shop is reinforced by the fact that Farsley was where Marshall himself was born.

The conferences between Midland and Rawdon made good progress. The Midland Council quickly agreed that an amalgamation would "further the interests of Ministerial Education"[27], and two months later the committee at Rawdon reaffirmed its support[28]. When Davies announced that he would be leaving Nottingham to become the Professor of Hebrew and Old Testament Literature at Bangor Baptist College at the end of the year, the need to bring the negotiations to a positive conclusion became more urgent. At the annual meetings in Nottingham in the summer of 1898, Davies expressed his optimism about the prospects of all three colleges coming together. Such an amalgamation, he said, "appears within measurable distance of realisation", and he gave his support to the scheme then being worked out with Rawdon[29].

By the autumn, arrangements for the joint working of Rawdon and Midland had been agreed. These came into effect at the start of the 1899-1900 session. The teaching of all students was undertaken jointly, with the initial arts course being undertaken at Nottingham and the theology course for senior students being taught at Rawdon. Although students were interviewed and accepted by each college separately, they normally lived in Nottingham for the first two years and at Rawdon after that.

Tymms was regarded as principal in both places, assisted by a resident tutor, or "governor", at Nottingham. Existing arrangements for the management of the two colleges remained in place, with an additional joint committee created to oversee the united work and to bring forward recommendations for moving towards a more comprehensive unity.

"Drastic and far-reaching" as these measures were, it was made clear that they were only temporary. They were intended to be in place for just three years, at the end of which they would be reviewed. The ultimate objective was a union that incorporated Manchester too, and at most of the meetings held to draw up the 1899 scheme, reference was made to this. Tymms saw it as a step towards "one united College for the North"[30], and this was the widely, if not unanimously held view in both colleges. Refusing to be daunted by the clear indications of an unwillingness to co-operate from Brighton Grove a year earlier, Tymms went to Manchester in the summer of 1899 to confer with the authorities there about developing joint tutorial work. He was accompanied by George Hill, the leading figure from Nottingham on the joint committee. The precise terms of this approach are not entirely clear, but it seems that the possibility of Midland and Rawdon amalgamating and moving to Manchester was being considered[31]. It may have been a disappointment to Tymms and Hill, but it can hardly have come as a surprise when they returned from Brighton Grove reporting that "the suggestion of united action in Manchester had not been favourably received"[32].

The temporary nature of the arrangements with Rawdon posed a particular problem for Midland. Constitutionally it was still an independent college, but it was deprived of a principal and had become, in effect, little more than a branch of Rawdon. It was unlikely that the future location of any united college would be in Nottingham, so the prospect of closure was a real one. After a delay while the possibility of a move to Manchester was explored, Sidney William Bowser was appointed resident tutor. He had been trained at Regent's Park, and came to Nottingham from the pastorate in Birkenhead.

Initially, the joint arrangements with Rawdon worked well. In 1900 nine Midland students were at Rawdon and five at Nottingham. In addition, Marshall and Rushbrooke, still officially attached to the college, were studying in Berlin, both supported by scholarships available to Midland from its Pegg Trust Fund. Once the prospect of going to Manchester had apparently disappeared, the most likely route towards union with Rawdon, if that were to happen, seemed to be on the basis of a college based on both sites[33].

At Rawdon, however, Tymms continued to entertain union with Manchester, and this sabotaged any possibility of making progress with Midland alone. The lack of movement towards union of any kind was frustrating for everyone concerned. When Midland suggested looking at alternative ways forward, Tymms asserted that "any action which will shut out the prospect of ultimate union with Brighton Grove College would be strongly condemned by the Northern Churches"[34]. Life for the senior students at Rawdon went on much as before, unaffected by talk of union. In the summer of 1899 H.W. Burdett was being entertained by William Medley with roast pheasant and rhubarb wine in celebration of his passing the London BA[35].

The whole Rawdon community was shaken by news of the Boxer rising in China in the summer and autumn of 1900. A large number of missionaries and Chinese Christians were killed, including two missionaries, George B. Farthing and W.A. McCurrach, who had been trained at Rawdon, together with their families. This raised awareness of the dangers of missionary work generally, and at the annual meeting in 1901 a plaque was unveiled commemorating the lives of nine college men who had died on the mission field, including Farthing and McCurrach. Both Tymms and his wife, who had responsibility for the domestic running of the house, suffered from poor health during much of this year, and it was announced in June that they would be taking an extended furlough during much of the 1901-2 session.

At Manchester, the progress of the college under Marshall was not unduly hindered by debates about amalgamation. In 1899 a students' settlement was formed at Longsight, supported by Baptists in the city. Activities at Longsight included a lad's club, gymnastics, a Sunday school, Sunday services and various educational and evangelistic activities. In 1900 the Annual Report included for the first time an account of the work of a college evangelist, A.E. Dearden, whose pioneering work included special missions at Blackpool and services in factories. Links with Victoria University continued to develop, the first-year course at the college being closely co-ordinated with lectures offered there[36]. Overall, the mood was relaxed and confident. The minutes of a committee meeting in June 1901 stated that "in consequence of the pressure of time and the repeated calls of the dinner gong two or three minor matters were taken as considered, in like manner the secretary's report was taken as read"[37].

The third attempt: 1901-1903

Ironically, in view of his enthusiasm for union, it was while Tymms was on furlough in the south of France that the next initiative towards union was taken. It arose as a result of the conviction among the members of the joint Rawdon-Midland committee that the joint working arrangements should not be extended beyond the three years originally agreed. These arrangements gave rise to tensions and administrative difficulties between the two colleges that were unacceptable in the long term. Something more permanent was needed after the summer of 1902. In November of the previous year the committee recommended that another approach be made to Manchester to ask for a conference on possible co-operation there[38]. George Hill, warden for 1902-3, spelt out the logic of the situation at the college's annual meeting a few months later. Efficiency demanded amalgamation, he said. The closure of Midland before finding a permanent site for a united college at a university city was unacceptable to Midland. The closure of Rawdon and a move to Nottingham was unrealistic. Manchester had the best site and the city was already a centre for theological and university education. If unity could not be secured at Manchester, he believed, it could not be achieved anywhere[39].

In December 1901 Manchester agreed to send representatives to a meeting. The committee understood that the matter to be considered was "the proposal of a second Baptist College in Manchester to be worked co-operatively with our own", and it was careful to insist that the meeting would be "consultative only"[40]. It seemed that more than this was achieved, however, for after a series of meetings in early 1902, a draft scheme of amalgamation was drawn up. This entailed continuing with the Manchester Trust Deed for the existing Brighton Grove premises and investments, and setting up a new joint Trust Deed for Rawdon and Midland. The sale of property at Rawdon and Nottingham would finance the erection of new buildings on the Brighton Grove site. The combined college would have four professors, two each appointed by the two sets of trustees, and a governor. It was expected that there would be accommodation for about forty students.

During the spring of 1902, the authorities of all three institutions considered and approved this scheme. At its meeting in March, however, the Rawdon committee received a letter from Tymms, still abroad on furlough, in which he expressed reservations because the scheme did not go far enough. It had "some value as an effort to obviate the legal and other difficulties of the situation, but it does not commend itself as a bold and aspiring attempt to raise the standard of Ministerial Education", he wrote[41]. This did not stop the committee giving it their support. Hoping that the scheme might come into effect at the start of the 1902-3 session, both Rawdon and Midland agreed not to receive any new students in 1902. They were disappointed to discover that Manchester was not going to do the same.

Twelve months notice was required before a formal resolution on the amalgamation and consequent sale of premises could be passed at the colleges' annual meetings, and this was given in all three places in the summer of 1902. It was the first time that many of the subscribers and supporters of the three colleges had been officially told about the proposals. There was some opposition at Rawdon, but overall, support for them was substantial in all three places. At Rawdon, the meeting was told that their existing buildings were "inconvenient and improper" for the purposes of ministerial training. Since sending the letter expressing his reservations, Tymms had returned to the college. Earlier, he had told the committee that he had not expected the scheme to have been approved in his absence. He said that he could not live in Manchester for health reasons, and was also critical of the dual trust idea, believing that it would give rise to "strife and division". For these reasons, he would not be able to be a professor in the new college. At his own request, his views were neither discussed by the committee nor communicated to the annual meeting[42].

It is astonishing that the support of Tymms, the leading proponent of amalgamation, was not secured before the agreed scheme was presented to the wider college constituency. It is also surprising that his objections, which amounted to a threat of resignation if the scheme went ahead, were not publicised, or at least discussed. In spite of his health problems, Tymms, at sixty, would not have been expected to retire for some years.

At Manchester, the amalgamation scheme was not the main topic at the 1902 annual meeting. This was dominated by a celebration of Marshall's twenty-five years at the college, chaired by Alexander Maclaren. When notice was given of the resolution on union, it was emphasised that no compromise would be needed on Manchester's distinctive doctrinal stance. The college deserved congratulation on the foresight of its founders, the annual report claimed[43].

In July, controversy broke out in the *Baptist Times*. The Manchester Trust Deed was criticised as the primary obstacle to college union. This allegation was rebutted by W. Dale Shaw, the secretary of the Manchester committee. Robert Brown claimed that there was "a deep and unanimous desire to retain the college" among ex-students at Rawdon. The scheme was described as "flawed" and hastily put together by another Rawdon supporter, and subsequently defended by George Macalpine, a leading member of the college committee[44]. The controversy also found its way into the pages of the *Baptist Magazine*. Expressing support for the principle of amalgamation, and confidence that it would be achieved, the monthly publication admitted, "We do not like the proposed dual trust for the amalgamated college, and think it would have been far better if the Manchester trustees could have seen their way to sell their buildings to a body representing the three institutions"[45].

The second half of 1902 was a period of frustrating delay. Rawdon blamed this on Manchester's failure to appoint representatives on the provisional committee of the united college, expressing its "strongest disapproval" at this lack of urgency[46]. Manchester blamed the lack of progress on the difficulties Rawdon was having in finding a buyer for its premises[47]. The Midland Council were informed that the delay was because "the preparatory legal work had not yet been completed"[48], and recorded the strong conviction that "every effort possible should be made to begin united work in Manchester in September"[49].

When the provisional committee did eventually meet, problems rapidly, and predictably, emerged. The Rawdon committee urged it to reconsider the possibility of "the temporary occupation of Rawdon College"[50]. It is not clear whether this was because of the difficulty of finding a buyer, or the result of more substantial objections to abandoning the building. Arguments developed over the appointment of tutorial staff. Manchester felt that their right to appoint two of the four professors was being questioned. Rawdon believed that Marshall wanted to hold the chairs of both theology and Old Testament, and were unhappy about this. They were keen to bring in Newton H. Marshall as tutor, but the only way this could be done was if Manchester agreed to appoint him, which they were unwilling to do. Sidney Bowser at Midland complained about not being offered one of the posts. A further and critical difficulty was over the residence of the governor. George Hill had been appointed to this post by general agreement, but Manchester was unwilling to let him take over the principal's accommodation in the main building. Differences also emerged over the new buildings that would need to be built at Brighton Grove[51].

J.H. Shakespeare, by then secretary of the Baptist Union and, since the raising of the Twentieth Century Fund and the building of the new Union headquarters in Southampton Row, a powerful figure in the denomination, was keen to do anything he could to bring the talks to a successful conclusion. Through the pages of the *Baptist Times*, of which he was editor, he condemned the "many rumours" and "unauthorised reports" in the press. Among other things, these had included announcements about appointments for the new united college[52]. By the end of May, it was apparent that rumours about the impending collapse of the talks were correct. No agreement could be reached in time for the united college to start work in September 1903. The negotiations had, in fact, broken down. "It is a lamentable thing", wrote Shakespeare, "and one that makes us almost despair of accomplishing anything in the interests of the Denomination, that the best scheme which Baptists have had before them for many years should have been wrecked in what can only be described as a detail"[53].

Each college broke the news of the failure to supporters at its 1903 annual meeting. At Rawdon, William Medley, who, in Tymms' absence had valiantly held the fort as acting-principal throughout much of the negotiations, summed up the feeling of many who had been involved. "The ever deepening shadow of what bore the name of Amalgamation, but to ourselves meant above all the extinction of Rawdon", he said, "has tended to depress our vitality, and in a measure to injure the effectiveness of our work"[54]. He also criticised the arrangements with Nottingham. It seemed clear that the latest breakdown, accompanied as it was by mutual recrimination and distrust, had brought to an end any possibility of amalgamation in the foreseeable future. The college embarked on an evaluation of its work as an independent institution. The formal link with Nottingham was broken, although a letter offering "such kindly service as we may be able to render them in the present circumstances" was sent[55]. The tutors were asked to continue, at least until the summer of 1904, while a review of staffing was undertaken. Tymms made it clear that he would not be continuing beyond then, and a search for a successor as principal was begun.

1904 was an important year for Rawdon as it marked the completion of 100 years since the creation of the Northern Education Society. Appointing a new principal was the first thing that had to be done if a second century could be embarked upon with any degree of confidence. In January it was decided to approach William Ernest Blomfield of Coventry, and two months later he accepted the invitation. Mrs Blomfield was put in charge of the domestic affairs of the college, and they took up residence at the beginning of the 1904-5 session. Blomfield, a native of Essex, was a graduate of London University, having been trained at Regent's Park College. Before coming to Queen's Road, Coventry in 1895 he had held pastorates in London and Ipswich. He was forty-two. Medley and Glass were asked to continue as tutors alongside the new principal.

Midland, with its smaller student numbers and as the subsidiary partner in the teaching arrangements with Rawdon, faced greater difficulties. The most important decision confronting it was whether to continue at all. The Council resolved that "the work of the College be continued at Nottingham"[56]. Bowser was asked to continue as residential tutor, and contact was made with Richard Glover of Bristol to see if he would consider being appointed principal. When he refused, the option of closing the college was again considered, but in the end it was decided to soldier on under Bowser, making as full use as possible of University College and the Congregational Institute. However, with just seven resident students, a shortage of money and without the stature of a man like Davies at the helm, the task was not easy, as the Council admitted at the 1904 annual meetings[57].

At Manchester, the report of the representatives on the provisional committee was received at a meeting described as "harmonious and hearty"[58]. As at the other two colleges, "considerable excitement and agitation" had attended the proposed amalgamation, and now a fresh start had to be made[59]. A "Forward Movement" was launched to raise money for a third tutor and to develop the already close relations with the university.

Co-operation with the university was about to enter a new phase. Manchester and Liverpool were granted their own university charters in 1903, the 1880 federal arrangements having been abandoned. As a result, opportunities existed for higher education to develop in the city independently. The importance of this became clear later in 1903 when the decision was taken to create a faculty of theology. Existing theological colleges in the city were given the right to affiliate to the university, and their teachers to become lecturers for the new BD course. By the summer of 1904 the college was officially recognised by the university, and Marshall had been given a seat on the board of the new faculty[60]. This meant that from the start the college helped shape theological education at the university. It was from the start entirely non-sectarian and open to all. Five of the six colleges involved in this partnership with the university were Nonconformist bodies.

These changes helped to soften any disappointment over the failure to unite with Rawdon and Midland. For those, like Marshall himself, who could look back over the history of the institution, the progress it had made must have seemed remarkable. In about half a century it had progressed from being a small splinter group on the conservative wing of the Baptist denomination to having a proud place at the heart of Manchester Victoria University's Faculty of Theology.

Reasons for failure

The rather tortuous story of the search for unity between 1891 and 1903 must be seen against the background of moves towards denominational unity during those years. Tymms, the prime mover in the negotiations between the colleges, was closely associated with the Baptist Union, serving as its president in 1896. He worked with Samuel Harris Booth, secretary of the Union until 1898, and then with his successor Shakespeare, and shared their ambitions for a strong and effective national Baptist body. Shakespeare in particular pressed for greater co-ordination and efficiency in the training of ministers, and was profoundly disappointed at the failure of 1903. It proved to be costly, ending any prospect of unity between Rawdon and Manchester for over half a century, and sealing Midland College's fate as a viable institution in the long term.

Earlier attempts at amalgamation had failed, at least ostensibly, because of difficulties arising from Manchester's trust deed. These had apparently been met by the pragmatic, if rather cumbersome, solution of a dual trust deed[61]. One disadvantage of this was that it left the advocates of the scheme open to the charge of ambiguity over what their intentions really were. Was the goal a united northern college, as the *Baptist Times* announced, or was it merely the co-operative working of two institutions on one site? This lack of clarity underlay the arguments over details that took place in 1903. Whether or not Tymms was wise in the way he conducted his part in the whole business, he was right in his judgement that the scheme, as an attempt to achieve unity, was fatally flawed.

Strict communion was still important to some people, but was not really a critical issue, either in the denomination or at Manchester. Principal and tutors were required to adhere to it, but students were accepted, and support from churches welcomed, without any such expectation. If strict and open communionists could be incorporated into other denominational institutions without conflict or compromise, they could have been in a united college.

The real reason why union failed was because, when it came to the moment of commitment, supporters on both sides were unwilling to accept the disappearance of their colleges as independent institutions. For some at Rawdon, the building itself was a critical issue. On more than one occasion in the latter stages of the negotiation, pleas were made for its continuing use. The sense of relief, especially by ex-students, when the scheme fell through was readily apparent. At Manchester, the lack of enthusiasm was even clearer. At first the price they would have to pay for union seemed low, mainly because of the compromises made over the trust deed, and the fact that the united college would be at Brighton Grove. In the end, however, losing the freedom to determine questions of staffing and accommodation proved too much.

Manchester was the most reluctant of the parties, but had signalled this several times before 1903. The difficulties that arose during the last series of talks should not have come as any great surprise to any dispassionate observer of events since 1891. The problem was that those who were committed to amalgamation, like Tymms, were far from dispassionate. Their commitment to achieve their goal meant that they could not, or would not, acknowledge the size of the obstacles.

An underlying tension that the whole episode reveals is one that is a frequent feature of Baptist history, that between local independence and the wider church. Those who argue for unity claim that insisting on independence is selfish and small-minded. Those who defend local freedom argue that to surrender it for the sake of efficiency is a betrayal of principle. Both sides claim pragmatic as well as theological reasons for the stand they take. At the start of the twentieth century, when the Baptist Union was emerging rapidly as a powerful denominational institution, this ecclesiological dispute was raging particularly fiercely. The ultimately unsuccessful search for unity by Rawdon and Manchester can be seen as an example of this tension. The desire to protect the autonomy of each institution proved stronger than any need for greater unity in the denomination as a whole. Retaining independence, however, was won at the expense of the third party in the negotiations, Midland College.

---

1 The exception was Spurgeon's College, which rejected purely academic qualifications as irrelevant for the pastorate.

Unsuccessful Search for Unity: 1891-1904 149

2   Rawdon College Minute Book, 24 June 1891. Although Tymms had not officially taken up his post as principal, and was not at this meeting, it is impossible to imagine that such a decision could have been taken without his knowledge and approval.
3   Manchester Baptist College Minute Book, 24 June 1891. The speedy response of Manchester is notable. It seems that it had been arranged for the two committees to meet simultaneously. They exchanged decisions by telegram.
4   J.E.B. Munson, "The Education of Baptist Ministers, 1870-1900", *BQ* vol.26 (July 1976) p.323.
5   Manchester Baptist College Minute Book, 15 December 1891.
6   Rawdon College Minute Book, 23 December 1891.
7   *Ibid.*, 3 February 1892 and 22 June 1892.
8   Midland Baptist College Report, 1892, p.10.
9   Minute Book of Manchester Baptist College, 28 June 1893; Midland Baptist College Minute Book, 12 October 1893; Rawdon College Minute Book 20 December 1893.
10 Details are given in Douglas C. Sparkes, *An Accredited Ministry* (Baptist Historical Society: Didcot, 1996) pp.9-13.
11 Rawdon College Minute Book, 18 December 1895.
12 Rawdon College Annual Report 1894, p.9.
13 *Ibid.*
14 *Rawdonian* no. 2 (January 1959) pp.3-5.
15 Nottingham Baptist College Minute Book, 1 May 1895.
16 Midland Baptist College Report 1895, p.19.
17 Nottingham Baptist College Minute Book, 22 January 1896.
18 *East Midlands Baptist Magazine* vol. 6 (February 1897) p.34.
19 *The Collegian*, vol.1 nos.1-6, including a supplement on the 1897 conference (November 1896– July 1897).
20 Nottingham Baptist College Minute Book, 15 June 1897.
21 Midland Baptist College Report 1897, p.17.
22 Rawdon College Finance and House Committee Minute Book, 27 October 1897.
23 *Ibid.*, 22 June 1898. Manchester Baptist College Minute Book, 29 June 1898, 13 January 1898.
24 *Ibid.*, 22 June 1898. Manchester Baptist College Minute Book, 29 June 1898.
25 Rawdon College Minute Books, 30 March 1898.
26 *Baptist Times* 11 July 1902.
27 Nottingham Baptist College Minute Book, 26 April 1898.
28 Rawdon College Minute Book, 22 June 1898.
29 Midland Baptist College Report, 1898, p.17-18.
30 Rawdon College Minute Book, 1 March 1899.
31 Nottingham College Minute Book, 4 May 1899.
32 Rawdon College Minute Book, 28 June 1899.
33 Nottingham Baptist College Minute Book, 10 December 1900.
34 Rawdon College Minute Book, 26 June 1901.
35 *The Rawdonian* no. 4 (January 1961) p.3.

36 Manchester Baptist College Minute Book, 29 June 1898.
37 *Ibid.*, 26 June 1901.
38 Nottingham Baptist College Minute Book, 25 November 1901.
39 Midland College Annual Report for 1902-3, pp.10-21.
40 Manchester Baptist College Minute Book, 18 December 1901.
41 Rawdon College Minute Book, 26 March 1902. Tymms was kept in touch with developments while he was away. The committee heard from him regularly during his travels in the south of France, Egypt and Italy.
42 Rawdon College Minute Book, 19 June 1902.
43 Manchester Baptist College Annual Report 1902, p.22.
44 *Baptist Times*, 11 July –29 August 1902.
45 *Baptist Magazine vol.* 94 (August 1902), p.333.
46 Rawdon College Minute Book, 17 December 1902.
47 Manchester Baptist College Minute Book, 17 December 1902. Rawdon had talks during this period with the Church of England about the possible sale of the premises, without receiving an offer.
48 Nottingham Baptist College Minute Book, 2 October 1902.
49 *Ibid.*, 2 December 1902.
50 Rawdon College Minute Book, 25 March 1903.
51 The minutes of the five meetings of the Provisional Committee between 15 January and 20 May 1903 can be found in the Nottingham Baptist College Minute Book. Two sub-committees looked at staffing and legal matters.
52 *Baptist Times* 24 April 1903.
53 *Ibid.*, 29 May 1903. The "detail" was probably the question of the residence of the Governor, which was the immediate reason why the talks were discontinued.
54 Rawdon College Annual Report 1903, p.25.
55 Rawdon College Minute Book, 27 May 1903.
56 Nottingham Baptist College Minute Book, 8 June 1903.
57 Midland Baptist College Annual Report 1904, p.10.
58 Manchester Baptist College Minute Book, 25 June 1903.
59 Manchester College Annual Report 1903, p.18.
60 *Ibid.* 1904, p.9.
61 It was felt by some, at least, that three trusts would be required – one for Manchester, one for Rawdon and Midland and another for the united college.

Chapter Eight
The Great War and the Disappearance of Midland College: 1905-1920

Nonconformity before the war

During the first two decades of the twentieth century, Nonconformity enjoyed an unprecedented degree of national status and influence. This was partly because of its visibility. Since the 1880s a large number of magnificent church buildings had been erected, and by 1900 most of the main towns and cities in the country could boast of at least one, and often several impressive chapels. Leading Nonconformist preachers, such as the Congregationalist Joseph Parker, the Wesleyan Hugh Price Hughes and the Baptist John Clifford were also widely admired and respected. Some stigma was still attached to church life outside the Church of England, but most discriminatory legislation had been removed. The Free Church movement was an influential interdenominational force, with hundreds of local Councils, a prestigious national Council and a large annual Congress. The new century was greeted with confidence by the leaders of Nonconformity. They looked back over a century of almost uninterrupted numerical growth, and saw no reason for it not to continue. Nationally, attendance at Nonconformist places of worship matched that of the Established Church, and in many areas exceeded it.

Politically, Nonconformity was more or less united in support of the Liberal Party. Its principal rallying cry during those two decades was over education. Opposition to the 1902 Education Act mobilised Nonconformists in political protest and lobbying as never before. Their leaders were prominent in the mass movement that demanded the removal of support for church schools from the rates and was one of the principal reasons for the Liberal Party's landslide victory in the 1906 general election. A campaign of passive resistance, led by John Clifford, advocated the non-payment of rates until the Act was amended. Several leading Free Churchmen, including Clifford himself, were imprisoned for their part in the revolt.

Although the campaign over education was ultimately unsuccessful, the excitement and activity it provoked raised the profile of Nonconformity as a force to be reckoned with. In Wales, the call for disestablishment, an issue that had lost much of its steam in England, was also passionate. From 1914, the Great War, for all the challenges it presented to religious belief, provided a platform for Nonconformist social and political advance. Free Church leaders were among the foremost in calling for young men to enlist in the armed services. The army, in which the Church of England held a virtual monopoly of interest, opened its doors to Nonconformist recruits. For the first time, English Free Church chaplains were commissioned as officers.

One of the reasons for this advance into national life was the Welsh Baptist, Lloyd George. A leading figure in the Liberal administration, he rose to become Chancellor of the Exchequer and eventually, in 1916, Prime Minister. Later, he proved to be a mixed blessing, but until 1918, the close relationship between Lloyd George and the Free Churches was of benefit to both parties.

Under the leadership of the tireless J.H. Shakespeare, the Baptists made rapid strides during this period to catch up with the Wesleyans and Congregationalists, both of which were historically wealthier and better organised. Between 1900 and 1905, a quarter of a million pounds had been raised for denominational purposes, a prestigious headquarters had been erected in central London, an official Baptist newspaper had been formed and a world alliance of Baptists had been created. These initiatives resulted in Baptists achieving a greater degree of institutional unity and strength than ever before. For the first time, the Baptist Union became a powerful national body. Subsequently, Shakespeare established the Federal Council of the Evangelical Free Churches, in which all the main Nonconformist denominations shared, with a view to bringing the same unity to the Free Churches as he had to his own denomination.

The colleges were important Baptist institutions, and as such benefited from the advance of their denomination. Their association with the new universities also helped their reputation. Their principals were

The Great War and disappearance of Midland College

widely admired as figures of culture and scholarship. They represented for many Baptists the progress that had been made during the nineteenth century. In the seven years between 1907 and 1913 no less than four of them were elected president of the Baptist Union[1]. Shakespeare was eager to include the colleges in his ambitions for the denomination and the Union. In particular, he needed to gain their co-operation in his schemes for reforming the ministry, which he saw as the key to further progress.

For Manchester and Rawdon, the years between 1905 and the outbreak of the war were a period of consolidation following the unsuccessful attempts to unite over the previous fifteen years. For Midland it was a time of struggle and uncertainty. The war itself was to be a decisive event for all three colleges.

Manchester

At the beginning of 1904 the tutorial team at Manchester was strengthened by the appointment of two part-time tutors to join Marshall and Ellis, Samuel Bull of Huddersfield and John Thomas of Liverpool. Bull, whose responsibilities were for mathematics and philosophy, was accepted as a lecturer at the university. As the college's relationship with the university through the Faculty of Theology grew closer, adjustments were made to fit in with its curriculum. Divinity degrees had been available to Nonconformists in England for the first time in 1898 from London University, and now that the university in Manchester was offering them too, the *Senaticus Academicus* had become largely redundant. Manchester, like the other colleges, discontinued its affiliation.

In 1908 a Board of Studies was formed to administer the college course, dealing with such questions as admission, curriculum and examinations[2]. The demands of the course were strenuous and admission standards high. A new set of regulations emphasised the over-riding importance of preaching, for which a thorough mastery of theology and Biblical studies was regarded as essential. The normal BD course was three years for those who already possessed an arts degree, and six years for those who did not. Students who showed "lack of diligence" became subject to new disciplinary procedures. They were expected to complete their course, and any who might be tempted to accept a call from a church and leave prematurely were warned that they would neither be recognised by the college nor recommended for recognition by the Baptist Union[3].

In his history of the Faculty of Theology, Ronald Preston described the university's theology course as "the most comprehensive initial theological degree in the country"[4]. The faculty established professorial chairs in Biblical criticism and exegesis, comparative religion, Semitic languages and literature and Hellenistic Greek. There seemed no question in the minds of the tutors and committee that it provided a good training for the Baptist ministry, and that it was appropriate for the college to be an integral part of the university. In line with improving the academic standing of the college, Marshall was keen to enlarge the college's library. He donated most of his personal collection of books to the college in 1905, and a few years later Alexander Maclaren, minister at Manchester's Union Chapel from 1858–1903, did the same.

The college's academic advance took place against the backdrop of the city of Manchester itself. For many years a major industrial centre, made even more so by the opening of the Ship Canal in 1894, it was also vigorous culturally and commercially, with a proud tradition of radicalism and progress in its civic life. In 1900 the city's tram system was electrified. The *Manchester Guardian*, edited by the Unitarian, C.P. Scott, and the Halle Orchestra, along with the University, became lasting monuments to the city's cultural achievements. In 1903 Emmeline Pankhurst, with her two daughters Christabel and Sylvia, founded the Women's Social and Political Union in the city[5]. Alan Kidd, in his history of the city, described it as "the first of the industrially based cities of the nineteenth century to create a cultural identity distinct from that of the traditional London-Oxbridge axis"[6]. It was an interesting and stimulating place to be a student.

Manchester College staff and students in 1913.
The principal, J.T. Marshall, is seated fourth from the right.

The ministry and the Baptist Union

Marshall was elected vice-president of the Baptist Union in 1908. His election coincided with a powerful speech by Shakespeare on the "arrested progress of the Church". Shakespeare, like many in the denomination, had been dismayed by the news that there were fewer members of Baptist churches in England and Wales in 1907 than there had been the previous year. This was the first drop in membership in living memory. Membership figures on their own were not a reliable measure of influence, and as a proportion of the total population they had been falling since the 1880s, but it was still a shock for many to see the decline reported in the *Baptist Times* in January 1908. Aware that it was a long-term problem, Shakespeare blamed it on "our defective Denominational system, which fails to use to the best advantage such resources as we do possess" and "changing conditions of social and national life". His proposed remedy centred on the ministry, which was, for him, "the root and secret of the whole matter". "What the Church needs more than anything else today", he said, "is leadership in its ministry"[7].

For some years Shakespeare had been planning a radical overhaul of the ministry. His dream was for a co-ordinated national approach to selecting, training, deploying and supporting ministers. In 1909 a scheme was presented to the spring Assembly. After a year of consultation and debate, a revised version was commended to the churches in 1910. Shakespeare hoped to get the colleges on board, but resistance from most of them, and outright opposition from Spurgeon's, made this impossible. The 1910 scheme was therefore mainly concerned with the settlement of ministers in churches and their financial support, and the selection and training of ministerial candidates in the colleges was not included. Realising that no comprehensive scheme could ignore them, however, Shakespeare wrote asking for their support in setting up an association of colleges and an inter-collegiate board. He suggested that the board should be given authority to enquire into admission policies, and have at least some say in recommending which candidates should be accepted. The Manchester committee supported the creation of these structures, but only as long as it retained ultimate control over admission and over referrals to the board[8].

During 1911 representatives from all the colleges, except Spurgeon's, agreed the constitution and functions of the inter-collegiate board. It included representatives from the Baptist Union, and its task was to confer on a wide range of matters relating to ministerial selection and training, including the supply of candidates, financial support for students, college curricula, settlement and post-collegiate study. Its powers were consultative and advisory only[9].

The board first met in September 1912, and survived for three and a half years. One of its first tasks was to investigate the number of candidates admitted for ministerial training. During the five years 1909-13, Manchester accepted 20 of the 62 applications it received, Rawdon 18 from 45 and Midland 11 from 24[10]. At face value, these figures suggest that Manchester was the most popular, and the choosiest, of the three. Many of the rejected applicants were nevertheless invited by churches to become ministers, sometimes, the board heard, with "disastrous results". They identified this as a major weakness in Baptist ministerial recruitment. Neither the Union nor the colleges could prevent a church from inviting an untrained person to be its minister. One way of addressing the problem might have been for the colleges involved in the board to follow Spurgeon's example and run less academically demanding courses. The tendency, however, was in the opposite direction. Manchester, proud of its partnership with the university, was typical in not being prepared to lower its standards. The board suggested the setting up of a "preparatory school or college" for preliminary training before admission to a theological college. This idea was not new, and, as one of its consequences may well have been to lengthen training courses still further, was not likely to prove popular. In any event, nothing came of it, partly due to the start of the war.

The board made little practical impact on life at Manchester. By the autumn of 1914 the college treasurer, W. Dale Shaw, was complaining that the other colleges were not taking attendance at its meetings seriously, and cast doubt on its value[11]. The war no doubt made meetings difficult, if not impossible, but its failure was fundamentally due to the unwillingness of the colleges to sacrifice their independence for the sake of any central denominational policy.

In 1914, Marshall was elected Dean of the Faculty of Theology at the university. This, like his year as president of the Baptist Union four years before, was a considerable honour for the college. The committee was eagerly anticipating the forthcoming jubilee celebration of 1916. Marshall suggested possible building projects and new lectureships in such contemporary subjects as comparative religion, youth work and sociology[12]. The college was proud of its past achievements and keen to build on them. A dispute with the Baptist historian W.T. Whitley over references to the college in his history of the Lancashire and Cheshire Association showed that it was also protective of its reputation. Whitley was closely associated with Rawdon, which may not have helped his relationship with Manchester. Summoned to meet the college's house committee in 1913, he was told that his account of the college's origin and work was "not fair", "meagre" and "insufficient". He expressed regret and promised to make corrections in subsequent editions of his book[13].

War

In 1914, Britain found herself at war with Germany. All thought of jubilee celebrations was soon abandoned, although the Manchester College secretary, Charles Rignal, produced a substantial history. In his review of the previous fifty years he defended the college's stand with feeling, asserting that it would agree to nothing that might prevent "the faithful discharge of its obligations to truth and principle" [14]. He also included a list of past students and a summary of their ministerial careers. Of the 206 men he included, nearly 80% had completed a course of between three and five years. No fewer than thirty-four had gone abroad, either immediately after their training or later in their ministry, ten of them as missionaries, mostly with the Baptist Missionary Society. Sixteen past students had left the denomination, twelve to join the Church of England[15].

As the war progressed, its impact on the work of the college grew. Young men, whether already students or contemplating training for the ministry, came under increasing pressure to enlist, or engage in some kind of war service. Initially, the committee limited itself to a promise of sympathetic treatment for any students who decided their duty lay in the armed services[16]. In the spring of 1915, it was decided to ask all applicants whether they had offered themselves for war service, and if not, why not[17]. Conscription was introduced in 1916, and although existing ministerial students were usually allowed to complete their course, numbers at the college rapidly dropped. In the summer of 1916 it was agreed, in conjunction with Rawdon, not to accept any new students for the duration of the war, unless they had been definitely rejected by the military authorities. All existing students were expected to do some form of Christian work among soldiers during the summer and Christmas vacations[18].

During the course of 1917 it seemed increasingly likely that the remaining students would be called up, and it was decided to close the college that summer and offer the use of the building to the Red Cross. Marshall and Ellis continued to be paid as tutors, but were encouraged to seek outside preaching engagements to help alleviate the cost. Marshall continued to reside at Brighton Grove, accommodating the two students still at the college in his own house[19]. At first, the Red Cross declined the use of the premises, but in July 1918 began using them as a convalescent home for wounded soldiers. Students whose courses had been interrupted by the war undertook service in a variety of capacities, both in the army and in civilian occupations. Two were conscientious objectors and one served as a chaplain.

The comprehensive disruption caused by the war gave the college authorities an opportunity to review their work and draw up new regulations for its resumption once it was over. Particular attention was given to student discipline. Conversation with college servants was forbidden, studies were to be kept in order and properly ventilated and monitors and prefects were to ensure that the premises were kept tidy and safe. Committee members were, perhaps, mindful of earlier problems, such as when one student suddenly left the college in 1915 after a "moral lapse" with his fiancée[20]. The curriculum was also reviewed and, after consultation with ex-students, redrawn. Homiletics was to receive more attention, and several new subjects were introduced, such as sociology and the Christian ministry, under the general heading of "the Kingdom of God in the modern world". The linguistic demands of the course were relaxed somewhat, with only New Testament Greek being demanded as compulsory. The general tendency seems to have been to emphasise practical skills rather more and academic ability rather less. The war confronted students and staff with the stark realities of human need, and no doubt played its part in contributing to this change. The "great aim" of post-war training would be "especially to enable men to preach the gospel more effectively"[21].

Henry Townsend

Once the war was over, it soon became clear that changes would have to be made in staffing as well as in the regulations and curriculum. Marshall told the committee that he was not well enough to take a full part in the post-war reconstruction of the college. He would still be able to teach, and did not want to resign as principal, but was keen to avoid any responsibility for the discipline of the students, which he found especially stressful. He also wanted to remain in residence at Brighton

Grove, in order to avoid the anxiety of looking for alternative accommodation, and suggested that a resident tutor be appointed, to live alongside him in the college and be responsible for discipline and the administration of the house. He went further, recommending Henry Townsend of Huddersfield for the post[22].

Townsend had been a student at Manchester under Marshall and a member of the Board of Studies since 1909. He was one of the first to be made a Doctor of Divinity by London University, following his thesis entitled "The Doctrine of Grace in the Synoptic Gospels". He had pastoral experience in Leeds and Huddersfield. In Marshall's eyes, he was also qualified for the position because, although married, he had no children, and so could be accommodated at Brighton Grove without unduly disturbing the household.

The situation was a sensitive and complex one, raising a number of questions for the committee to consider. In the light of Marshall's long years of service and desire to continue as principal, it was difficult for them to reject his proposals. Marshall himself thought that any possible problems between him and Townsend could be overcome with good will on both sides. The potential for conflict was, however, considerable. For one thing, the division of responsibilities between Townsend and Marshall was not straightforward. In effect, Marshall was asking to be principal in name only. This put Townsend in a very difficult position. On a domestic level, the relationship between the two men, and more importantly their wives, would inevitably be an uneasy one. The principal's wife was traditionally responsible for domestic matters. In the case of the Marshalls, their unmarried daughter was also living with them, and shared in the work of the house, which added to the complications. The question of domestic servants and the accommodation of guests would also need to be sorted out. The position was made even more difficult by the presence of a lay student, John Reddihough, who had been living with the Marshalls for the latter part of the war.

The prospects of a happy outcome seemed remote, but the committee felt they had no option but to go along with Marshall's proposals. Townsend was invited to become vice-president, house governor and tutor in the philosophy of religion. Ellis continued in his position as the third tutor. Mrs and Miss Marshall were asked to continue responsibility for catering, with Miss Marshall and Mrs Townsend acting jointly as "hostesses"[23]. Predictably, these elaborate arrangements soon came to grief once the college reopened in 1919. Within a few months it became clear that the Marshalls would have to move out. Accommodation was found for them in a house in the vicinity, Townsend was appointed principal and his wife put in charge of domestic affairs.

Several students whose courses had been interrupted by the war returned in 1919, joined by others who were starting their training. A pamphlet addressed to officers and men in the armed services had been produced by the colleges, appealing for candidates for the Baptist ministry, and several of those responding had been accepted by Manchester. At the annual meetings in 1920, eleven probationary students were accepted as full students, having by then completed their first year of training[24].

The war had led to a new curriculum, a new set of regulations and a new principal. It meant, in many respects, a new start for the college. Another sign of changing times was the permission to practise open communion granted to the Longsight Mission, whose management committee was appointed by the college, and where many students gained practical experience in ministry[25]. The three tutors, however, all had long association with the college before the war. How significant the changes would prove to be only time would tell.

Rawdon's centenary celebrations

Unlike Marshall at Manchester, Blomfield was more a pastor and preacher than a scholar. He came to Rawdon in 1904, following the retirement of Tymms, after twenty years of ministry, during which he had gained the reputation of being "an earnest, devoted and hard-working pastor"[26]. He arrived at the time of the centenary celebrations. This provided a good opportunity for re-launching the college's work following the collapse of the amalgamation discussions with Manchester and Midland the previous year. In a letter to the committee before moving, Blomfield said he attached "very great importance" to the raising of new capital for the college, and urged a generous response to the centennial appeal for £5,000 already launched. He also emphasised that Mrs Blomfield should be given "a free hand in the control of the household"[27].

The centenary celebrations in June 1904 included an address by Medley, tutor since 1869, in which he outlined the history of the college since its formation. He emphasised the contrast between the cramped, dingy premises at Little Horton and the "fine gabled frontage" of Rawdon. The history of the college, he said, was "a desperate, and at times almost a hopeless struggle for an educated ministry, against a great mass of prejudice almost everywhere prevalent in our denomination"[28]. This effort to improve the education of ministers continued with the decision to seek affiliation to the new university in Leeds later in 1904. Some students were also encouraged to take the degrees in divinity now available at London.

In 1905 Medley announced his retirement. This gave the new principal the opportunity to secure the services of one of the rising academic stars of the denomination, Henry Wheeler Robinson. Blomfield's ministry in Coventry had briefly overlapped with that of Robinson, who was minister in one of the other churches in the city. Robinson had, like Blomfield, been trained at Regent's Park College. He had also studied at Oxford and Edinburgh Universities, and on the continent, before two short pastorates, the first at Pitlochry in Scotland. His particular field of study was the Old Testament, but as this was also Blomfield's main interest, he was appointed as tutor for Church history and philosophy.

Robinson had wide-ranging academic interests and an enormous capacity for hard work, and he brought a daunting spirit of academic rigour to the college. Prior to his appointment in 1906 he had been the college's external examiner in Hebrew. In that capacity Blomfield had urged him not to spare the students in his reports but to "search them with fire". He rose at 5 a.m. and often remaining up working until 2 a.m. During his first seven years at Rawdon he produced four major published works. Blomfield described him as "perhaps the most outstanding scholar we have in our Church"[29]. While he was at Rawdon, several Baptist ministers who went on to have notable academic careers received their training, including Arthur Dakin and Laurance Henry Marshall, later principals of the colleges at Bristol and Rawdon respectively[30].

Blomfield's two main objectives were academic excellence and financial security. The college entrance examination was demanding. It included tests in Greek, Latin, English, Scripture knowledge and mathematics[31]. Establishing a link with Leeds University did not prove as straightforward as it was in Manchester, and it was not until 1914 that Blomfield and Robinson were recognised as lecturers, and not until 1915 that a formal scheme of affiliation was agreed. In the meantime, the emphasis was on gaining a London BD. The isolated location of Rawdon, and its small size and limited resources, made this a particular challenge.

Financial security was less of a problem because of the wealthy Yorkshire businessmen who supported the college. In 1905, J.C. Horsfall was appointed treasurer. He insisted on personally meeting any deficit on the college annual accounts until his death in 1920, and also financed the renovation of the premises during the war[32]. Substantial legacies and gifts were received at various times from the Macalpine and Bilbrough families. The committee regularly met at the Liberal Club in Bradford or Leeds, where lunch was provided by one or other of its more prominent members[33]. One of the main advantages of being relatively secure financially was that the tutorial staff could be expanded. In 1905 Harold Charles Rowse, an ex-student without pastoral experience, was appointed as a fourth tutor, with responsibility for arts subjects[34].

A few Rawdon students were successful in receiving Baptist Union scholarships. These were available from the Twentieth Century Fund, which had been raised by Shakespeare between 1899 and 1902, and were usually used for study abroad. In 1910 Arthur Dakin received a doctorate of theology from Heidelberg University. Student achievements, however, were not always so encouraging. In 1907 five students failed the London University matriculation examination, a disappointment over which the committee expressed its "serious view"[35]. At about the same time, a student resigned because he had got married, and shortly after that another was asked to leave because "he had not given sufficient proof of repentance for dishonesty committed earlier in the term, and that his failure to pass the Inter BD examination was morally unsatisfactory"[36].

Other students were dismissed in 1911, 1913 and 1914 because of "dishonesty in the examinations" or "moral delinquency"[37]. In an institution of only about twenty students, these resignations, dismissals and suspensions must have had a significant effect on the spirit of the house. The pressure to succeed was considerable. Blomfield and Robinson were single-mindedly committed to discipline and hard work, neither man having much time for outside interests. Perhaps as a consequence of this, Robinson collapsed in the spring of 1913, and for some weeks was seriously ill.

The Union's schemes for ministerial training and support were discussed at Rawdon, and in general supported. Representatives were appointed to the inter-collegiate board in 1911. It did not provoke much interest, however, and contributed little, if anything, to the work of the college.

The impact of the war was, as at Manchester, profound and far-reaching. Students were encouraged to enlist, and by the summer of 1916, only five were still in training. Difficulties in securing domestic servants meant that these five were boarded out at the beginning of 1917, and the college was closed for the remainder of the war. Unlike Manchester, where the premises were offered for use by the Red Cross, the committee at Rawdon used the opportunity to renovate and modernise the interior of the building. Blomfield also continued his efforts to secure greater financial security. The Horsfall family funded an exhibition for a student to study for a degree at Leeds University in memory of their son Cedric. Three other similar gifts were received, in addition to a medical missionary exhibition and other student prizes. As a result the college reopened in the autumn of 1919 in a significantly improved state, both financially and in its premises.

One of the students whose course was interrupted was John Middlebrook. He was one of many who faced a "terrible dilemma" in deciding on the right course of action[38]. He joined up in the early part of the war, was wounded in 1916 and had an arm amputated. Later in the year one of his fellow students, Harry Robson, was killed in action[39]. In the autumn of 1917 Middlebrook returned to Rawdon to continue his studies. The college was by then closed, and he was given individual tuition by Robinson, at that stage acting temporarily as minister at South

Parade Baptist Church in Leeds. Seventeen of the twenty-one men who joined him at Rawdon in 1919 were new to the college. Most came as "battle scarred 'veterans'"[40]. Some of those whose studies had been interrupted, like Middlebrook's, decided not to return[41]. The experiences of the students naturally made a difference to college life after the war. When students went out to take services, Blomfield told the churches what they had been through, sometimes in lurid detail[42].

Manchester's example was followed when a board of studies was created to oversee the curriculum. Early in 1920 it recommended that there should be two classes of student, one group working for a certificate of religious knowledge at London University and the other the Leeds BA. The usual course would be for three years, but students not studying for a degree should normally expect to remain for a fourth year of study. The board also recommended training in child psychology and the conduct of Sunday schools, and suggested a year's post-college placement to gain practical experience[43]. The war seemed to have resulted in a relaxation of the college's strict academic regime, and a greater emphasis on the practice of ministry.

The spirit of change brought about by the war was reinforced by the departure of Robinson. In January 1920 he resigned his position, having accepted an invitation to succeed G.P. Gould as principal of Regent's Park College. Two months later the committee wrote to invite Alfred Clair Underwood to take his place. Like Robinson, Underwood was a scholar. He had been trained at Midland College and studied at Oxford, and since 1911 had been professor of Church History at Serampore College in India. He had taken up his place at Rawdon by June 1920, when no fewer than sixteen probationers were accepted as full students of the institution after completing their first year's training. Altogether, twenty-one students had been in residence during the first full session after the college re-opened in 1919[44]. In the autumn of 1920 those who were continuing were joined by five new men.

The end of Midland College

Sidney Bowser was resident tutor at Midland from 1905 to 1910. He was often referred to as the principal, and in 1910, by which time the prospect of appointing someone else had been abandoned, he was officially given the title. He was respected by students and by the churches of the east midlands, being elected as president of the association in 1909. Until then John Douglas provided additional tutorial help. The number of students varied between about ten and sixteen. The college's finances were a constant anxiety, and cast a cloud over all attempts to resolve the difficult question of its long-term future. In 1906 a special emergency committee was set up to consider this, and in October of that year a public meeting was held in the Derby Road Church in Nottingham. Prominent supporters of the college, including John Clifford and Charles Aked of Liverpool, appealed for more generous giving so that the work could continue[45]. This was not forthcoming, and less than two years later Joseph Bright, the warden, announced that a doubling of the college's income was required in order to remove doubts about its future prospects[46].

At the 1907 annual meeting, the emergency committee was asked to write to Shakespeare about the possible establishment of a Baptist college at Cambridge[47]. The advantages of this possibility had been raised, by Shakespeare and others, at various times since the two ancient universities had opened their doors to Nonconformists in 1870. Shakespeare's reply to the committee indicated that he would be willing to discuss the matter if the college council definitely approved the principle of moving to Cambridge. In spite of encouragement from Rushbrooke to take up this offer, the council decided not to pursue it any further[48].

In 1912 the number of students had declined to ten. Co-operation with the Congregational Institute and University College continued to be a life-line for the college. A second special committee was appointed to enquire and report "as to the desirability of the continuance of the College, as to the present regime and the possibility of making income and expenditure meet"[49]. Soon after this, Bowser resigned, apparently to enable a complete reorganisation of the college to take place, and there is no record of the committee delivering its report. The college's 1913 annual report announced that E.J. Roberts of the Melbourne church had been appointed to act as tutor for the 1913-14 session. As the college matron was also leaving, students would reside in private houses. A

Midland Baptist College's premises in Nottingham

"house governor" would live at the college and deal with correspondence. College debts remained stubbornly around £1,000[50].

The onset of the war meant that the supply of students soon dried up completely. In November 1915 activities were suspended. During the latter stages of the war the premises were used as a hostel for soldiers. In 1918 the re-opening of the college was debated by the college authorities. An endowment fund called the "Clifford Diamond Jubilee Fund" was launched, but the response was meagre. The West Midland Baptist Association, which had always been lukewarm in its support, questioned the wisdom of it re-opening at all. The prospect of a "University scheme for the East Midlands" raised hopes a little at the 1919 annual meeting, but the reality was that the war had put the final nail in Midland's coffin[51]. In July 1919 the Council recommended to the trustees that the premises be sold. They were bought by the YMCA. The proceeds from the sale, and the college's other assets, such as they were once debts had been met, were devoted to the support of students training for the Baptist ministry elsewhere, and to help create the "John Clifford Chair" for General Baptist Biblical and theological teaching at Rawdon. Appropriately, the first beneficiary of this was A.C. Underwood, a student under Bowser, upon his appointment as tutor at Rawdon the following year. Most of the library was donated to the new Baptist Women's Training College at Havelock Hall in Hampstead[52].

The closure of Midland College was not marked by any celebration of its achievements over the 123 years of its life. A series of articles in the *Baptist Quarterly* by W.J. Avery, the house governor through the war and a past student, went some way to paying tribute to its work, but in reality its passing was mourned by only a few[53]. Its most prominent advocate, John Clifford, was well into his eighties by 1920. The New Connexion of General Baptists, which had created and sponsored the college for most of its existence, had disappeared thirty years before, and was little more than a distant memory for most people. The attempt to give the college a new identity by forging a vital connection between it and the Midlands churches had not been successful. The failure of the amalgamation discussions with Rawdon and Manchester in 1903 was a fatal blow, and since then its eventual demise had seemed probable.

There might have been a more positive, and fitting, conclusion had the council had the courage and realism to close the institution before the war, perhaps by means of an arrangement with Rawdon or another college. By 1920, activity in Nottingham had already been more or less at a standstill for four or five years. The fact that the college continued to play a positive part in the training of ministers for so long after 1891 was largely due to the influence of Davies, whose scholarship and leadership until his resignation in 1898 kept hope for the longer-term future alive. In spite of its small size and financial problems, the college continued to play a positive role in training ministers right up to the war, and even in 1914 most of its accommodation was still being used by students in training.

Altogether, about 300 Baptist ministers were trained under the auspices of Midland College, in its various guises. These included some of the best known ministers and missionaries in the denomination, including in its later years John Clifford, J.H. Rushbrooke and A.C. Underwood. As long as it survived, it was a reminder to Baptists of the General Baptist element of their inheritance, which goes back to the very first Baptist church on British soil in 1612. Like the New Connexion and the General Baptist Missionary Society before it, it had now disappeared altogether, absorbed into the mainstream of Baptist life.

In a small way, the colleges at Manchester and Rawdon were beneficiaries of Midlands' demise. With no other college now situated between them and London and Bristol, they could freely promote themselves in the midlands without the risk of being accused of an unseemly rivalry. At Manchester, the committee was eager to welcome new subscribers from Midland's constituency and to stake a claim on the proceeds of the sale of property[54]. Rawdon benefited most, however, mainly because of the money received for the John Clifford Chair[55].

The historical links between Midland and Rawdon are one reason for regarding the history of the former as part of the story of Northern Baptist College. These links were especially strong during the four years of shared teaching between 1899 and 1903. During that period, and for some time before, Midland had shown the greatest enthusiasm over co-operating or uniting with its two northern neighbours. The decision to make money available for a professorial post at Rawdon in 1921 reflected a particular sense of kinship. Theologically, Manchester's strict-communion policy and more conservative doctrinal stance was more alien to Midland's character than Rawdon's more open and liberal tradition. Older historical ties also drew Midland and Rawdon together. Dan Taylor and John Fawcett, the eighteenth-century founding fathers of the two colleges, were friends and neighbours in West Yorkshire, and frequently met to discuss the training of ministers. They would, no doubt, have found the panelled rooms, terrace and towers of Rawdon, as well as much of the curriculum taught in its lecture room, hard to comprehend, but there was something fitting about their legacy being reunited in the Yorkshire Dales.

Educating for ministry

The pursuit of high academic standards was a major goal of college life during the pre-war years. Preaching was regarded as the key to ministerial effectiveness, and a thorough theological education as the key to good preaching in the twentieth-century world. Marshall, Medley and Robinson were all primarily academics. Marshall and Medley, whose long service provided the mainstay of teaching at Manchester and Rawdon, had no significant pastoral experience in the local church.

An important catalyst for this emphasis on education was the creation of universities at Manchester, where divinity degrees were available, and Leeds. The standard of ministerial competence became the possession of degrees in both arts and divinity. The ideal was to have studied at Oxford or Cambridge, or in Germany as well. There were other qualities regarded as necessary in a good minister, but without high intellectual ability and accomplishment, these were regarded as insufficient. Many men were discouraged from applying to college, and others failed the entrance examination, because they could not make the grade academically.

The historical context goes some way to explaining this attitude. Opportunities for advanced theological study in England before the start of the twentieth century were so few that once they became available, they were eagerly grasped. Degrees in theology were valued as evidence of a long coveted equality of ability and status with ministers in the Established Church.

Baptist scholarship flowered especially in the field of Old Testament studies. Marshall, Robinson and Davies all gained a national, if not international reputation for their work. The Scriptures have always been at the heart of Baptist life, so this is, perhaps, not surprising. Possibly it was also because the mastery of Hebrew and other Semitic languages was an impressive sign of intellectual stature.

Expertise in Old Testament studies was valuable, but whether it had much to do with ministry and mission in early twentieth-century England was less certain. The unrelenting pursuit of a highly educated ministry seems strangely divorced from the most urgent needs of the churches. Many contemporary observers recognised that the churches' biggest challenge came from the urban working class, which was, to a very great degree, alienated from them. Six years studying for a divinity degree was not the obvious qualification for meeting that challenge. Even the better educated and growing suburban middle class, many of whom showed a preference for the many new opportunities for leisure activities over attendance at church, had needs of other kinds.

The challenge of effective evangelism and of finding answers to the many troubling questions raised by contemporary society was, as it always has been, urgent and demanding. Ministers needed to help their congregations to relate their Christian faith to issues such as war, urban poverty, Britain's role in the world as an imperial power and the changing patterns of work, leisure and family life, yet their training for ministry did little to prepare them to do so.

The tragedy of war brought a stark note of reality to the colleges. It was impossible to reject men who sensed God's call to ministry while undergoing war service because they did not know any Latin or their grammar was not up to scratch. This perhaps helps to explain the unusually high number entering Manchester and Rawdon in 1919. Once they embarked on their training, both students and teachers traumatised by war inevitably viewed ministry differently. Mastering irregular Hebrew verbs and classical Greek took on a different perspective in the light of the millions slaughtered on the Western Front. The practice of ministry became more important, and the pre-war calls for attention to be given to psychology, sociology and economics became more urgent.

The 1918 Representation of the People Act acknowledged for the first time that voting was not the exclusive right of men with property. All men over the age of twenty-one and all women over thirty were enfranchised. In the general election of that year Labour became the official Opposition in the House of Commons for the first time. The experience of the war demanded changes of attitude and behaviour throughout the country. In their own way, Rawdon and Manchester faced similar demands.

1. W. Henderson (Bristol), J.T. Marshall (Manchester), W. Edwards (Cardiff) and G.P. Gould (Regent's Park). Apart from Spurgeon's College, whose relationship with the Union was tenuous, and Midland, the only English college not to have its principal serve as president during the first two decades of the century was Rawdon. However, T. Vincent Tymms did so in 1896, and W.E. Blomfield in 1923.
2. Manchester Baptist College Minute Book, 15 July 1908.
3. *Ibid.*, 19 December 1907.
4. Ronald Preston, "The Faculty of Theology in the University of Manchester: The first seventy-five years", in *University of Manchester Faculty of Theology seventy-fifth anniversary papers 1979* (University of Manchester: 1980) p.8.
5. Radical ideas regarding the role of women affected Baptists too. In 1894, the church at Moss Side took the unprecedented step of appointing a female delegate to the national autumn Assembly. After discussing the matter, the Council of the Union decided that women were eligible (see E.A. Payne, *The Baptist Union: a short history* (Carey Kingsgate Press: London, 1959) p.150.
6. Alan Kidd, *Manchester* (Ryburn Publishing: Manchester, 1993) p.159.
7. J.H. Shakespeare, *The Arrested Progress of the Church* (Baptist Union: London, 1908). See especially pp.21-4.
8. Manchester Baptist College Minute Book, 21 December 1910.
9. *Ibid.*, 20 December 1911.
10. Inter-Collegiate Board Minute Book, 20 May 1914.
11. Manchester College House Committee Minute Book, 28 October 1914. A month earlier Dale Shaw and Marshall had written to G.P. Gould, the chairman, to say that unless attendance from the other colleges improved, they would themselves stop attending (letter dated 30 September 1914 in the Minute Book of the Inter-Collegiate Board).
12. Manchester Baptist College Minute Book, 15 July 1914.
13. Manchester College House Committee Minute Book, 22 October 1913.
14. Charles Rignal, *Manchester Baptist College 1866-1916: Jubilee Memorial Volume* (William Byles and Sons Ltd.: Bradford, 1916), p.235.
15. *Ibid.*, pp.247-266. Rignal's statistics need to be treated with care. Names could be removed from the list of past students by the committee if it saw fit.
16. Manchester College House Committee Minute Book, 9 September 1914.
17. *Ibid.*, 5 May 1915.
18. *Ibid.*, 29 June and 1 November 1916. Manchester College Minute Book, 11 July and 13 December 1916. The students were threatened with expulsion if they failed to contribute to the war effort in some way.
19. Manchester College Minute Book, 11 July 1917. By the end of 1917, only one student was left.
20. Manchester College House Committee Minute Book, 16 June 1915.
21. *Ibid.*, 10 April 1918 and 9 April 1919.
22. *Ibid.*, 9 April 1919.
23. Manchester College Minute Book, 9 July 1919.

24 *Ibid.*, 14 July 1920.
25 *Ibid.*, 15 December 1920.
26 W.N. Town, "W.E. Blomfield" *BQ* vol.7 (October 1934) p.163.
27 Rawdon College Minute Book, 22 June 1904.
28 William Medley, *Rawdon Baptist College Centenary Memorial* (Kingsgate Press: London, 1904), pp.6, 7 and 13.
29 See Ernest A. Payne, *Henry Wheeler Robinson: Scholar, Teacher, Principal. A Memoir* (Nisbet and Co. Ltd.: London, 1946), pp.50-53, 69.
30 It is of interest to note that both these men were, like Blomfield, ministers at Queen's Road Baptist Church in Coventry before their college appointments.
31 Rawdon College Annual Report for 1906, p.10.
32 Rawdon College Minute Book, 16 March 1921.
33 *Ibid.*, 16 December 1908, 31 March 1909, etc.
34 A 1910 brochure advertising the college actually lists five tutors, Blomfield, Glass, Rowse and Robinson being joined by A.S. Lowry, who gave instruction in elocution.
35 *Ibid.*, 11 September 1907.
36 *Ibid.*, 21 September 1910.
37 *Ibid.*, 20 November 1911, 17 December 1913, 16 December 1914.
38 J.B. Middlesbrook, "Rawdon: 1914-1921 – Years of Transition" in *The Rawdonian* vol.6 (January 1963) p.3.
39 Rawdon College Minute Book, 20 December 1916.
40 Middlebrook, p.5. See also the Rawdon College Minute Book, 25 September 1919.
41 Rawdon College Minute Book, 18 June 1919. Three of those who had enlisted and failed to return to the college are mentioned. One wanted to work with the YMCA, one to work in Africa combatting malaria and a third to continue in the army.
42 Middlebrook, p.5.
43 Rawdon College Minute Book, 10 March 1920.
44 *Baptist Times*, 2 July 1920.
45 *Baptist Times*, 18 October 1906.
46 *Baptist Times*, 10 July 1908.
47 Midland College Minute Book, 4 July 1907.
48 *Ibid.*, 25 July 1907.
49 *Ibid.*, 28 June 1912.
50 Midland College Annual Report, 1913, pp.10-11.
51 *Baptist Times*, 6 June 1919.
52 W.J. Avery, "The Late Midland College", *BQ* vol.1 (1922-23) pp.334-6. Havelock Hall was opened in 1920 for the training of Baptist deaconesses, or sisters, as they were known for a short time. The Baptist Union had taken over responsibility for the selection, training and deployment of deaconesses in 1919.
53 *Ibid.*, pp.218-222, 263-269 and 327-336.
54 Manchester College Minute Book, 17 December 1919 and 21 April 1920.
55 Rawdon College Minute Book, 16 March 1921. It amounted to £275 per annum, a significant sum, although not enough to fund the post on its own.

Chapter Nine
The Inter-war Years

Changes in society and church

The collapse of Liberalism, both as a coherent political force and a social and economic principle, provided the background to the fortunes of Nonconformity between the wars. Even before the war, the Liberal Government, urged on in particular by Lloyd George, had departed from its traditional emphasis on individual freedom by creating labour exchanges, bringing in a national scheme of health insurance and providing for centrally-funded old age pensions. The demands of the war had driven the Government to intervene in other areas of the nation's social and economic life. After the war, confronted by the failure of the economy to rebuild itself following a brief period of recovery in the immediate post-war period, it found itself unable to escape responsibility for national economic management. Taxation increased and import tariffs were introduced. Attempts to recover pre-war conditions, such as the decision to re-establish the value of sterling in terms of the price of gold and the return of mines and railways to private control, led to immense economic and political strains.

The Liberal Party itself, formerly the main vehicle of Nonconformist political hopes, did not survive the war as a national force. Labour, representing the newly enfranchised working classes, became the main party of opposition, forming minority Governments in 1924 and 1929. The most damaging feature of the economic difficulties was mass unemployment, rising to three million in the 1930s. Particularly hard hit were the older industrial centres in South Wales, Scotland and the north of England. Newer industries provided some employment opportunities, but these were mainly in the south of the country. There was considerable migration into the London area.

While poverty and deprivation was the experience of many, especially in the north, large numbers, particularly from 1930 onwards, began to enjoy the benefits of industrial and economic progress. These included the increased availability of motor vehicles. Between the wars, the number of private cars on the roads increased nine-fold. Buses replaced trams in the city and, in the country, provided public transport in areas inaccessible by rail. Increased opportunities for travel were accompanied by the development of a huge and varied industry devoted to popular entertainment which included the radio, the press and the cinema.

Church life was naturally affected by these changes. The predominant overall feature of the period was a slow but unrelenting decline in membership and attendance. This was most marked within Nonconformity. Its enthusiastic attachment to Victorian and Edwardian Liberalism was now an irrelevance, and made responding to the new circumstances of post-war Britain difficult. There was no large-scale flight from Baptist and other Nonconformist churches, the decline in Baptist membership between 1925 and 1939 amounting to about 7%, but it was nonetheless a serious and seemingly insoluble problem.

At the end of the conflict, hopes were high for a greater degree of co-operation between the churches. Many felt that the need for church unity was one of the primary lessons to emerge from the war. The formation of the Free Churches' Federal Council in 1919, and discussions between Church of England and the Free Churches about unity seemed to offer ways of achieving it. However, these failed to materialise into anything substantial, and ecumenism was probably in a less healthy state in 1939 than it had been in 1914.

The grand hopes with which the century had opened for the advance of the Free Church idea as the dominating principle in English church life had disappeared for ever by the mid-1920s. The denominations that had stood together on social and political issues and had happily co-operated in mission were divided, both among themselves and internally, politically and theologically. Differences between theological conservatives and liberals, in part fuelled by disillusionment with German scholarship, emerged as a significant feature of church life. Among Baptists, criticisms of what was seen as modernism on the part of denominational leaders like A.C. Underwood, Wheeler Robinson and T.R. Glover became increasingly forthright.

For English Baptists, the departure of the two most prominent pre-war figures, Clifford, who died in 1923, and Shakespeare, who resigned as secretary of the Baptist Union in 1924, marked the end of an era. Melbourn Evans Aubrey, who took Shakespeare's place, consolidated the position of the Union at the centre of denominational life through the creation of a superannuation scheme for ministers and the further development of the Union's departmental structure. The leading figure among English Baptists during the inter-war years, however, was not Aubrey but J.H. Rushbrooke. Rushbrooke's sphere of service was European and global, rather than national. Among his many wide-ranging activities as first European Commissioner, then European Secretary, and finally General Secretary of the Baptist World Alliance, he drew the colleges at Rawdon and Manchester into his schemes for providing training for Eastern European ministers.

Among Baptists the possibility of women ministers slowly gained acceptance. Among several notable pioneers was Margaret Hardy, who was invited to preach at Regent's Park Church in London in 1920. Conscious that it was a rare opportunity, she chose the topic "The Place of Woman in the Church". She asked whether the Christian church was to be the only institution refusing to profit by women's gifts. "Will it be deaf to a message because it is delivered by a woman's lips?"[1] In 1926 the Council of the Union affirmed that there was no reason in principle why women should not become accredited ministers. In that year the official list of ministers included the names of three women. Edith Gates was at Little Tew and Cleveley in Oxfordshire and Maria Living-Taylor worked alongside her husband, who was also a minister, in the Sion church in Bradford. Neither of them had received college training. Violet Hedger was the first to pass through a denominational college. Trained at Regent's Park, she was ordained in Derby in 1926 and served as minister of the Littleover church there for three years. A few years later she became the first woman to be appointed to sole pastoral charge in the county of Yorkshire when she was inducted to the pastorate of North Street Baptist Church in Halifax[2].

Continuity at Manchester

Following his appointment in 1920, Henry Townsend remained principal at Manchester throughout the inter-war period. He had a close relationship with his predecessor Marshall, who continued to teach at the college until his death in 1923. Townsend had entered Manchester for training shortly after Marshall's own appointment as principal in 1898 and had maintained close links with the college throughout his ministry. Between them, the two men led the college for over fifty years. Manchester was used to continuity in its leadership. All of its principals were Manchester men who were already well known and had a close relationship with their predecessors.

The historian Kenneth Brown has suggested that one of the reasons for Nonconformist decay in the late nineteenth and early twentieth centuries was the inadequate training its ministers received, and that this was largely due to the college principals. In particular, he cites their long periods in office and lack of experience of secular life as handicaps in enabling them to provide training that was relevant to contemporary needs[3]. He concludes that the Baptists generally emerge better than the other denominations. The other Baptist colleges were not as inward-looking as Manchester, and his allegation that many principals were out of touch with changing times seems to be justified in the case of Marshall. Townsend's experience of church life had been within a fairly limited sphere, but, unlike Marshall, he had the advantage of several years in the pastorate, in Leeds and Huddersfield. During that time he had served on the Free Church Council and with local Sunday Schools. He had also worked for his London University DD on the doctrine of grace in the synoptic Gospels, a thesis that was published in 1919. He was one of the first to receive the degree from the university.

Townsend was a prominent figure in academic, denominational and Free Church affairs. Like his predecessor, he was elected dean of the Faculty of Theology in 1926 and became president of the Baptist Union in 1936. Always a keen advocate of the cause of Nonconformity, he urged the amalgamation of the two national Free Church bodies, and saw this achieved during the second World War with the formation of the new Free Church Federal Council, of which he was Moderator in 1944[4].

Theologically conservative, he was an outspoken opponent of all forms of Catholicism and resisted attempts to achieve organic church unity, whether within Nonconformity or between it and the Church of England. He believed that, for Baptists, differences over baptism were a decisive obstacle.

Townsend was associated with the college as a student, a committee member, principal and principal emeritus for fifty-six years. It was said that "to get at the facts was the object of his own academic study", to which end "he slogged at his studies"[5]. He was remembered by his students as "a little man with glasses and a brilliant red gown"[6]. He stood firmly within Manchester College's tradition of doctrinal and ecclesiological conservatism.

Few substantial changes took place at Manchester between 1920 and 1939. The committee spent its time on accepting new students, deciding on their order of seniority, and receiving reports from the tutors on academic progress and from the treasurer on college investments. The death of Marshall in 1923 and the illness of the other tutor Ellis led to the appointment of William Solva Davies of Carlisle as tutor in Biblical languages and exegesis in 1925. The college treasurer since 1885, W. Dale Shaw, whose father William Shaw had been instrumental in founding the college in 1866, died in office in 1929, bringing to an end another remarkable example of continuity in that key position. Later in 1929 a new library was opened.

Correspondence with the Baptist Union occasionally provoked discussion at the college. At the end of 1929 a dispute with the Union arose over the future of an Estonian student who had been recommended to the college for training by Rushbrooke, and was about to complete his course. The Union was eager to see him return to Estonia for ministry, as had been the original intention, but the Manchester committee was quite prepared to recommend him to the churches for ministry in England. The student's personal circumstances and the state of the churches in Estonia were given as the reasons for this. The committee refused to accede to the Union's wishes, even after a special appeal from Aubrey. After his settlement as minister at Rawtonstall, the Union's ministerial recognition committee refused to allow him onto its list of probationary ministers. It seems that he did soon afterwards return to his own country[7]. It is impossible to draw any firm conclusions from this incident, but it suggests an independence of spirit and a narrowness of vision on the part of the college.

The committee was similarly unimpressed with the Union's attempts to exercise greater control over admission to the ministry through the colleges in the early 1930s. It protested that "the time was not ripe for denominational control of the Colleges". Townsend was authorised, however, to try and secure a greater degree of co-operation at the revived united college board. Four years later little progress had been made. The committee decided to let the suggestion of establishing common entrance and leaving examinations for students "lie on the table for the time being"[8].

The number of students in training varied from year to year, but there is no evidence of any significant overall decline during the inter-war years. 1937 and 1938 were poor years, with only three students starting their courses in each of those years[9], but other years in the decade had higher intakes. Twenty years later, in 1955, there were still thirty-three ministers and missionaries in active service who had been trained at Manchester in the 1930s[10]. Townsend continued to look for academic and preaching ability in the candidates who were accepted for training. "Before admittance to college", he wrote, "the utmost significance is attached to strength of character, to capacity for study, to the quality of previous Christian work, and especially the gift of preaching"[11]. Financially the college also remained on an even keel. Townsend was remembered as a principal who was able to increase the financial resources of the college, enlarging its capital funds and establishing a medical missionary scholarship[12].

Overall, it was a time of stability and little change, in which the college remained relatively unaffected by outside factors, supported faithfully by those churches that appreciated the solid, traditional training it provided. Possibly, after the shock of the war and the economic and political turmoil of the following two decades, they found security in an institution that represented earlier values. The challenges of changing political and economic circumstances, which greatly affected many of the people of Manchester and the north, and nationwide social and cultural developments made little impact at Brighton Grove. The

The Inter-War Years 181

college's lack of interest in initiatives from the Baptist Union was a sign of this conservatism. Manchester, of course, was not alone in this. The challenge of the emerging twentieth century was one that the whole of Nonconformity was struggling to meet[13].

Townsend's personal preoccupation with upholding Free Church principles, resisting moves towards union, and speaking out against Catholicism seem somewhat anachronistic and irrelevant in the light of events in England and abroad since 1914. It would be wrong, however, to blame Townsend alone for the apparent lack of any serious attempt to address the main issues confronting the churches in their mission. This was beyond the capacity of most of his contemporaries. One's judgement of a small institution with slender resources, led by hard-pressed men sincerely trying to stay true to their principles and serve the churches as well as they could, should not be too harsh.

Floreat Rawdona!

The 400 people who attended the annual meeting at Rawdon in 1920 were encouraged by news of a healthy financial situation and more applications for training than the college could accommodate. They also welcomed Underwood as the new tutor, who had filled the vacancy left by Robinson's departure for Regent's Park. Underwood had gone to Serampore from Midland. Apart from his knowledge of Indian Christianity, about which he had published a number of books, his main area of expertise was church history. His appointment meant that the number of tutors remained at four, Blomfield and Underwood sharing the work with Glass and Rowse, who had between them over forty years experience of teaching at the college.

The encouraging start to Rawdon's post-war work was given a further boost when the news came from the trustees of the now closed Midland College that they were offering Rawdon the income from the Joseph Davis Charity. This offer was gratefully accepted, and a John Clifford

Rawdon College

Chair was created. Underwood was the natural choice for the position and was appointed as its first holder in May 1921. John Clifford's death two and a half years later led to additional donations towards this cause, and eventually enabled the college to establish a second medical missionary scholarship in 1925.

Less encouraging was the response to the board of studies' recommendations about the need for a greater emphasis on practical training, with opportunities for post-collegiate placements in churches or other institutions. This bore little fruit, and it was to be another six years before any steps were taken to do anything about this.

Financial security was one of Blomfield's constant goals. Together with John Horsfall, the college treasurer until his death in 1921, and

Blomfield's wife Ellen, who kept the college accounts, he managed to avoid the problem of debt that had sometimes dogged the college in the past. Blomfield appreciated his wife's "most watchful solicitude of the College finances"[14], and the committee later paid tribute to her "unusual capacity for all business matters"[15].

Academically the college's reputation grew, with doctorates of divinity being bestowed on the principal in 1922 and on Underwood in 1924, from St Andrew's and London Universities respectively. Blomfield was formally presented with his academic robes at a meeting of the committee. Members of the committee expressed delight at the "gorgeous apparel" and his account of the capping ceremony at St. Andrew's[16].

1922 was also the year in which Blomfield was elected vice-president of the Baptist Union. His presidential address at the Assembly the following year was entitled "The Baptist Churches and the Ministry of Tomorrow"[17]. In it he pleaded for "a higher conception of the ministry" and greater co-operation within the denomination for its recruitment and training. "In our revolt from sacerdotalism", he said, "we have swung to an extreme, and our sense of the sacredness of the minister's vocation has been obscured". Concerted action was needed, he believed, not only for initial training, but also for in-service training, to prevent ministers losing their "vitality and freshness". Arguing the need for college training for all ministers, he resurrected the proposal for a two-tier scheme of training. The colleges, he suggested, could provide a university standard theological education, and the Union take on responsibility for pre-collegiate training in special schools, or under the supervision of experienced ministers. He defended colleges like his own from accusations of theological liberalism, asserting that Biblical criticism strengthened, rather than weakened, belief in Jesus Christ as Lord. He appealed for consideration and decency in controversy, and a concentration on the things that mattered most of all, rather than "our particular theological label". He believed that students should be allowed to form their own theological opinions, and that the role of the colleges was to give them the ability to do this:

> I do not reckon it to be a teacher's mission to look upon students as so many empty vessels into which he is to pour his own or anybody else's ideas. ... Students are Christian men with minds of their own, and they should be encouraged to grapple with the problems of faith and form their own theology.[18]

The 1923 assembly at which Blomfield gave his address was an important one for Baptists as far as the ministry was concerned in other respects too. It adopted a statement in which the terms ministry and ordination were defined. The ministry was defined as "an office within the Church of Christ conferred through the call of the Holy Spirit and attested by a particular or local Church", and ordination as "the act of the Church by which it delegates to a person functions which no man can properly take upon himself". These definitions became important reference points for the denomination, and were printed annually in subsequent *Baptist Handbooks*. The statement formally sanctioned the use of the terms, about which there has often been considerable controversy among Baptists, but it did not advocate or encourage the more centralised concept of the ministry which both Shakespeare and Blomfield were keen on. It was also at this Assembly that the decision to revive a united collegiate board was made.

In the early 1920s significant changes in theological atmosphere were taking place, among Baptists and others. The division between theological conservatives and liberals took on a new importance, becoming a significant and public feature in denominational life for the first time since the controversies centred on Spurgeon in the 1880s. The formation of Christian Unions at universities, as a direct response to the Student Christian Movement's perceived modernism, and the creation of the Fellowship of Independent Evangelical Churches were signs of this in the wider church. Rawdon was accused of promoting liberal views of the Bible, as some of Blomfield's remarks in his presidential address suggest. These accusations were often centred on Underwood, but this did not prevent him from taking over the principalship when Blomfield retired in 1926.

The tendency towards a polarisation of theological opinion further distanced Rawdon and Manchester from each other. Contact between them had been minimal since the beginning of the century, and the differences in both theology and background between Townsend and Underwood made the prospect of any joint approach to ministerial training remote.

Although not as close as in Manchester, and at times frustrating, Rawdon's relationship with Leeds University was important in several ways. It brought about a closer co-operation with the other theological colleges in the area as they made use of its courses. This was especially true of the Congregationalists' Yorkshire United College, which had taken over the use of Airedale's building. From 1921 the tutors of the two colleges and the Wesleyan college in Leeds, together with others, met from time to time as part of a Leeds and Bradford theological circle[19]. The relationship with the Congregationalist college deepened in 1926 when J.B. Allan was appointed jointly as tutor for Hebrew and Old Testament studies. An ecumenical project of this kind was an unusual, if not a unique, event. Allan, whose time was divided equally between the two colleges, assumed Blomfield's teaching responsibilities at Rawdon following his retirement. In 1932, the arrangement with the Congregationalists having come to an end, Underwood turned to an old Serampore colleague who had retired and returned to England a few years earlier, George Howells, to take over Old Testament teaching.

In 1927, links with the university were put on a more formal footing when procedures for the recognition of tutors at the college as university lecturers were put in place. Theology degrees were not offered at Leeds until the 1930s. Existing theological colleges were not as closely involved with the creation of the Faculty of Theology as those in Manchester, and Underwood was disappointed with the choice of theological professor[20]. Three years later, when the university decided in favour of a BA degree in theology instead of a BD, this was felt to fall short of what Rawdon needed, especially in the teaching of Hebrew[21]. Ironically, the university then went on to poach Rawdon's tutor in Hebrew and Old Testament studies. Just two years after John Noel Schofield had come as tutor to Rawdon in 1935, on the recommendation of Robinson at Regent's Park, he was approached by the university and appointed a lecturer there.

Like Manchester, Rawdon found itself caught up with Rushbrooke's activities at the Baptist World Alliance. Students from Poland, Estonia, Holland and Latvia undertook training at the college from 1922 onwards. An increase in the level of practical ministerial experience and training was eventually achieved in 1926, although it did not amount to a significant shift in the balance of the curriculum. An extra week was added to the beginning of the academic year devoted to such things as Sunday School teaching, pastoral work, sermon-making and psychology[22]. In 1930, two students were given the opportunity for three weeks of intensive training in Sunday School work at Westhill Training College in Birmingham[23].

The Rawdonian appeared in 1929. Launched as an annual publication with production largely in the hands of the students, it appeared six times before being discontinued during the war years, and was then revived in 1950. The first issue included a list of things one student learnt while at Rawdon that were not on the college curriculum. These included:

> How to light my own fire, sweep my own study, and make my own bed.
> How to pour tea at the breakfast tables.
> How to blow the college organ.
> How to get up at 6.45 am on a Sunday morning.
> How to sprint uphill in order to catch the Leeds tram.[24]

The students were also mainly responsible for laying the new tennis courts that year.

When the supporters of the college met for its annual meetings in 1930 they saw that work had started on an extension to accommodate six or seven more students. They watched David Glass lay the foundation stone. They also enjoyed hearing the college song, *Floreat Rawdona!* sung for the first time. With words and music by Carey Bonner, the leading Baptist musician and composer of the time, who had studied at Rawdon, it was dedicated to the "past and present members of the brotherhood" and set to a rousing tune.

> On northern height, 'mid woodlands fair, bedecked in leafage green,
> A stately Hall of Learning stands, o'er Vale of Aire the Queen;
> Her grey stone walls, with turrets crown'd, both storm and time defy;

And for that College Beautiful, our love shall never die.

Chorus: Alma mater, Alma Mater, Ever in our thoughts so near,
Ever to thy sons so dear – loyal hearts we bring to thee,
Proudly now we sing of thee – Floreat Rawdona!
Floreat Rawdona! Gratia Christi floreat!

Within her walls we toiled and thought, and dreamed the dreams of youth;
We caught the vision of the Christ – the Life, the Way, the Truth.
With trusty comrades mingling there, we learned to play our parts,
And found that priceless gift of God – the fellowship of hearts.

Right worthy names are on her scroll – the noble men who taught;
The valiant soldiers of the Cross, who for the faith have fought;
The hero-souls, in lands afar, who gain'd the martyr's crown,
And by their witness bravely borne, won deathless, high renown.

Up, Rawdon men! And aye, maintain the spirit of the past;
Think truth, keep pure, act out your creed, and for your Lord stand fast!
Live Christ; and let the humblest task your utmost pow'rs engage;
Here, pledge your troth, to keep unspoiled, your glorious heritage.[25]

A significant milestone occurred in 1936 with the retirement of David Glass at the age of seventy-four. He had served the college as tutor for forty-four years and also as financial secretary for twenty-nine. He was appointed professor emeritus, and Laurance Henry Marshall became tutor in his place. Marshall had been trained at Rawdon between 1905 and 1911, during which time he had also studied in Berlin and Marburg as a Baptist Union scholar. He was minister of Victoria Road Baptist Church in Leicester, and already a member of the college committee. A gifted and enthusiastic student of the New Testament, he had spent five years as professor of practical theology at McMaster University in Toronto, where he had been forced to defend himself against persistent criticism for holding modernist views. Describing his teaching style, students later recalled that "as he opened the pages of the New Testament he was like a master jeweller sorting precious stones", and that in a private tutorial he "waxed so enthusiastic over a passage . . . that he thumped the chair in which he was sitting as if he had been addressing a large congregation", then apologised[26].

The arrival and departure of tutors, modifications to the curriculum, improvements to the premises and the introduction of electric power during the inter-war years at Rawdon could not hide the fact that, like Manchester, continuity rather than innovation was the order of the day. Those associated with the college were keen to retain its traditional ethos and values, as *Floreat Rawdona!* poetically demonstrated. The transition from Blomfield to Underwood did not involve any change in policy, and in spite of demands in some quarters for a new look at the training of Baptist ministers, no substantial initiatives were taken. Changing location or co-operating with other Baptist colleges did not feature in committee debates. The shared appointment of a tutor with the Congregationalists was an interesting development, but was motivated by pragmatic needs at the time and proved a short-lived experiment. Relations with the university did not develop significantly. A few concessions were made when new academic disciplines and practical training were introduced, but only at the margins of the training provided.

After the large intake in 1919, student numbers remained about the same, usually with about seven or eight being admitted each year. One noticeable change was the introduction of men from continental Europe. No women were admitted, and there were no women on the committee, in spite of the fact that women were beginning to appear among the ministers of Yorkshire Baptist churches[27]. Rawdon was less conservative than Manchester, but it was still reluctant to make changes in the way it approached the business of training ministers.

It must have been an enormous relief at both colleges to see a return to normality after the war, a process helped by a good number of students applying for training in the immediate post-war years. Student numbers remained more or less stable and financial security was maintained. Both institutions were able to improve their premises, Manchester adding a library and Rawdon more student accommodation. Both seemed broadly happy with the pattern of training they had inherited and gave little evidence of wanting to make reforms.

The northern colleges' response to these changing times, then, was basically one of retrenchment. The effect of ministerial training on church life is long term, and the consequences of the colleges' activity was only felt much later. With hindsight, it could be said that they should have taken a lead in developing new patterns of ministry and ministerial training. Brown uses a statistical analysis of Baptist ministers and quotations from the Nonconformist press after the war in arguing that, to a large extent, responsibility for the denomination's loss of vitality in the twentieth century lies with the kind and number of ministers its colleges were producing during this period[28] There were other factors at work too, but the lack of imagination, energy and confidence required for change is evident. The fact was that Townsend, Blomfield and Underwood, together with their colleagues, belonged to an age ill-equipped to cope with the realities of a modern world torn apart by war. Sadly, the country was thrown into another global conflict before any new generation of teachers could begin to shape the ministry in ways more appropriate for the new society. The colleges would find their work disrupted once again.

---

1   *Baptist Times*, 28 May 1920.
2   Douglas Sparkes, *An Accredited Ministry* (Baptist Historical Society: Didcot, 1996) p.32. Ian Sellers (ed.), *Our Heritage: the Baptists of Yorkshire, Lancashire and Cheshire 1647-1987* (Yorkshire Baptist Association and Lancashire and Cheshire Baptist Association: Leeds, 1987) p.95).
3   Kenneth D. Brown, "College Principals – a cause of Nonconformist decay?" in *Journal of Ecclesiastical History* vol 38 (1987) pp.236-253.
4   The history of the various Free Church Councils can be confusing. The National Council of Evangelical Free Churches was formed in the 1890s and the Federal Council of Evangelical Free Churches in 1919. They amalgamated in 1940 to form the Free Church Federal Council.
5   Manchester Baptist College 1955 Annual Report, pp.9-10.
6   So described by the Rev. Edmund Pilling, a student at Rawdon College between 1946 and 1953, in a personal conversation with the author.
7   Manchester College Minute Book 18 December 1929, 17 December 1930 and 16 December 1931
8   *Ibid.*, 17 December 1930 and 12 December 1934.
9   *Ibid.*, 18 May 1938.
10 Manchester College Annual Report, 1955, pp.20-22.

11 Henry Townsend, *The Claims of the Free Churches* (Hodder and Stoughton: London, 1949) p.37.
12 Manchester College Annual Report, 1956, p.18.
13 Kenneth D. Brown, *A Social History of the Nonconformist Ministry in England and Wales 1800-1930* (Clarendon Press: Oxford, 1988) especially pp.223-30. Brown's analysis is not entirely convincing, but he helpfully highlights the problems of adjustment faced by the Nonconformist ministry in the early twentieth century.
14 *Ibid.*, 20 March 1929.
15 *Ibid.*, 4 October 1939.
16 *Ibid.*, 30 December 1922.
17 W.E. Blomfield, *The Baptist Churches and the Ministry of Tomorrow* (Kingsway Press: London, 1923).
18 *Ibid.*, p.21.
19 Elaine Kaye, *For the Work of the Ministry: a History of Northern College and its Predecessors* (T and T Clarke: Edinburgh, 1999) p.196. Church of England priests were among those involved in the circle.
20 Rawdon College Minute Book, 13 December 1933.
21 *Ibid.*, 21 October 1936.
22 Rawdon College Minute Book, 30 September 1926.
23 *The Rawdonian*, no.2 (June 1930).
24 *The Rawdonian*, no.2 (June 1930). *The Rawdonian*, no.1 (June 1929).
25 Carey Bonner, *Floreat Rawdona! College Song, arranged for Baritone Solo, and Unison Chorus* (first sung at the College conference, 23-25 June 1930). Not long before this performance Bonner had been elected vice-president of the Baptist Union. For Bonner, see *The Baptist Hymn Book Companion* (London: Psalms and Hymns Trust, 1962), p.257. The music for three hymns in the current Baptist hymn book, *Baptist Praise and Worship* (Oxford University Press, 1991), was composed by Bonner: these are Sommerlied (377), Adsum (522), and Tilak (601).
26 Henry Bonser, *A Memoir of the Author*, in L. H. Marshall, *Rivals of the Christian Faith* (Carey Kingsgate Press: London, 1954) p.8.
27 Maria Living-Taylor in Bradford and Violet Hedger in Halifax.
28 Kenneth Brown, "Patterns of Baptist Ministry in the Twentieth Century" in *BQ* vol.33 no.2 (April 1989) pp.81-93.

Chapter Ten
The Second World War and its Aftermath: 1939-1964

The Second World War

Like the Great War, the Second World War was a turning point in national life. Although similar in the disruption and suffering it caused, its impact was more immediate and extensive. The Government's direction of labour soon affected most people of working age, not just the men and women in the armed services and those involved in the production and supply of military equipment. Many women and retired people were added to the work force because of the demands of the war. Its massive cost cast a shadow over the nation's economy for many years. International trade was disrupted and rationing was not discontinued until 1954.

In spite of profound changes in international relations after the first war, Britain still had the status of a world power, but after 1945 the country's weakness was all too apparent. Outside help was needed, not just for the rebuilding of industry but for basic needs. America and Russia, the latter strengthened by the emergence of the Soviet Union, became globally dominant, politically and militarily. Responsibility for economic and social restructuring lay with the new Labour Government, elected with a clear mandate for change in 1945. Eager to implement the 1942 Beveridge Report, which recommended the universal provision of social insurance by the State, and with Labour's long-standing commitment to nationalisation, this government embarked on a radical programme of reformation. Coal, railways, gas, electricity and steel were all brought into public ownership, and the National Health Service was created, within which medical diagnosis and treatment were provided free of charge for all.

Internationally, the start of the Cold War, symbolised by the blockade of Berlin in 1948 and the suppression of the Hungarian uprising eight years later, was an ominous sign for the future shape of world politics. It became clear that nuclear power, first harnessed to terrifying effect by America, was to be a decisive factor in the new world order. Britain's first nuclear bomb was detonated in 1951, and the first nuclear power station started producing electricity five years later.

India's independence in 1947 demonstrated once for all that the idea of Empire was no longer relevant, and the Suez crisis of 1956 made clear that Britain's ambitions as a world military power were over. The country's relations with its former colonies took on a different form. Withdrawal from overseas responsibilities was accompanied by the arrival of Commonwealth citizens, all eager to make the most of the employment opportunities they had been told existed in post-war Britain. The first to arrive, in the mid-1950s, were immigrants from Jamaica.

In 1953 the coronation of the young Queen Elizabeth reinforced the feeling that the war years could be consigned to history and a new start in the nation's history could be made. By the mid to late 1950s a sense of economic prosperity grew, with full employment and an increasing range of consumer goods becoming available.

In church life, among the more dramatic events were the evangelistic meetings of the outspoken American evangelist, Billy Graham, in 1954 and 1955. The final rally of his 1954 tour, when 180,000 people gathered at Wembley to hear him preach, seemed to be evidence of a thirst for spiritual experience during those years. Some hoped for religious revival. In general, however, churches were struggling to maintain their numbers, with membership and attendance dropping significantly in most of the mainstream denominations. Baptist churches lost about 14% of their membership between 1941 and 1957, as rapid a decline as they had ever experienced[1].

As had happened between 1914 and 1918, the war had brought the churches closer together, and one of the main features of the immediate post-war period was the development of closer ecumenical co-operation. The amalgamation of the two national Free Church councils into the Free Church Federal Council was evidence of this, but not as important as the birth of the British Council of Churches. Both councils were products of the war years, the latter bringing together representatives of the main non-Roman Catholic churches under the Presidency of William Temple, Archbishop of Canterbury[2]. After the war conversations on Church unity took place over the course of several years at the initiative of Temple's successor, Geoffrey Fisher.

The leading Baptist figure in the ecumenical discussions after the war was Ernest Payne. He was appointed general secretary of the Baptist Union in 1951, after serving for eleven years as a tutor at Regent's Park College. A keen advocate of the importance of the Union and of church unity, his influence over Baptist affairs was considerable. His book *The Fellowship of Believers*, first published in 1944, was a powerful defence of the importance of Baptists working together, and helped shape the Union's statement of 1948 on *The Baptist Doctrine of the Church*. Naturally interested in ministerial training, he played an important part in the development of the colleges at Rawdon and Manchester.

A report on Baptist church polity, commissioned before the war and published in 1942, helped determine the pattern of ministry in the post-war years. It encouraged the development of the role of the denomination's General Superintendents, urging them to provide spiritual leadership. It also recommended that the United Collegiate Board should co-ordinate the theological education provided by the denominational colleges.

Kenneth Dykes and changes in the student body at Manchester

The impact of the war on the colleges was more immediate than it had been in 1914. Conscription was immediately introduced, and although theological students already accepted for training were at first exempted, it was soon clear that college life would be disrupted in a major way. No new students were admitted after 1939. At the end of 1941 most of Manchester's premises were requisitioned as a training centre for the RAF, and by the summer of 1944 the college was closed altogether. Townsend, who resided in the college, became the only tutor once Davies was asked to "look for other work" because of the uncertainty about the future[3]. Townsend was heavily involved in Free Church matters, and was elected president of the new Free Church Federal Council in 1943.

By the end of 1944 plans had been drawn up for the re-opening of the college after the war. George Farr, a member of the committee and a student at the college during the first part of the war, was appointed tutor in Biblical languages, literature and exegesis, following a short pastorate in Birmingham. Thirteen candidates were accepted for training, with a view to them starting once they had been released from military service and the premises had been re-occupied. The need for the training to be undertaken within the scope of the university syllabuses was re-affirmed. The college planned to supplement this theological study with practical courses and experience in such areas as youth leadership and pastoral theology. It also hoped to take advantage of non-theological courses on offer at the university such as sociology, psychology and economics[4].

The college's 1945 annual meeting took place in the immediate aftermath of the declaration of victory in Europe. Townsend was congratulated on the twenty-fifth anniversary of his appointment as principal, an achievement none of his predecessors had matched. He was busy trying to arrange for the building to be handed back from Government control, including the removal of a Spitfire machine from the lecture hall[5].

The 1945-6 session began with four men in training. By the end of it, the number had increased to eleven, of whom four were married. Some of the married men lived in lodgings, others at home. Given their wartime experience, it was not surprising that they found some of the pre-war disciplinary practices irksome. Gradually numbers increased, so that by the end of 1947, twenty-four students had been admitted. Some were degree candidates, but most studied for a certificate in theology. With ex-servicemen particularly in mind, the university introduced a BA course in theology, enabling ministerial students to gain a degree in theology without having to spend six years studying for both BA and BD degrees. In 1947 the Ministry of Works finally left the building, enabling the college to re-occupy the whole site once more. It became clear that the cost of repairing the premises from damage done during the war would be substantial. Routine maintenance, neglected for several years, would also be expensive. The demands of the building were to be a big drain on the college's financial resources for some years.

Manchester College staff and students in the late 1950s. The principal, K.C. Dykes, is seated fourth from left. M.H. Taylor, later to become principal of Northern Baptist College, is standing fourth from the right in the first row.

In June 1948 Townsend told the committee he would be retiring a year later. Kenneth Dykes was appointed in his place[6]. Dykes was a son of the manse, having been brought up among the Strict and Particular Baptists of Suffolk. Originally intending to become an actuary, he had entered Manchester College for training in 1932, graduating in arts and divinity. Since 1938 he had been the minister of the Myrtle Street and Wavertree churches in Liverpool, during which time he undertook research for an MA into the doctrine of original sin. He was a pacifist. One of his students later recalled the impression he made:

> It is impossible to imagine him physically thin, or without his pipe, or failing to punctuate any occasion at which he was present with

appreciative grunts, sitting restless and hunched in his chair with hands that were rarely still[7].

Following his election, Dykes spent several months studying in Zurich with Emil Brunner, before taking up his appointment in the autumn of 1949. He was thirty-nine, and brought with him a young family. From his student days Dykes was dogged periodically by bouts of depression, and from time to time this affected his work as principal. His wife Beryl became matron, assuming responsibility for the college's domestic arrangements, and Townsend was given the title of Principal Emeritus.

Dykes' financial and organisational abilities were soon put to the test in endeavouring to restore the premises to an adequate state of repair. Throughout his principalship worries about the cost of maintaining the premises were almost constant. In 1950 an appeal for £5,000 was launched. Slowly the money came in, although not quickly enough to meet the needed expenditure. The discovery of dry rot in 1951 made the need even more urgent. The college had significant capital assets, upon which it relied for annual income, but its financial viability was an ever-present cause for concern. In 1958 it was reported that its resources were "not only slender but are also poised on a knife edge of uncertainty"[8]. Dykes was keen to take advantage of Local Education Authority grants, a new source of income made available by Government reform of higher education funding. These became an important source of funding for all colleges after the war. Hopes were expressed of giving Dykes and Farr some badly needed secretarial assistance, but this never materialised. The question of the adequacy of their salaries exercised the minds of the committee during 1951, and small increases were agreed the following year[9].

Domestically, the principal and his wife tried to create a family atmosphere at Brighton Grove, eating with the students each evening. For Dykes, a close relationship with the students was an important dimension of training. Any student wanting to get engaged to be married was expected to talk his plans over with him before making an announcement.

The link with the university was one of the greatest assets of the college. Professors such as H.H. Rowley and T.W. Manson made

Manchester a leading international centre for the study of theology, and Biblical studies in particular. Dykes and Farr were both recognised lecturers in the Faculty of Theology[10]. The annual reports, and information given to prospective candidates, emphasised this close relationship. In 1960 it was stated that 80% of the tuition provided for students was given by the university[11] A medical missionary scholarship tenable at the university was also available.

It seems that the college was no more successful in implementing wartime plans for a stronger emphasis on practical training than it had been after the Great War. In 1953 the Superintendents complained that training in homiletics and other practical aspects of ministry was seriously defective[12]. An entrance examination required high standards so that full advantage could be taken of what the university offered. There was a preference for "men with a grammar school education"[13]. Academic ability was not, however, the only condition for admission. "The utmost significance", a brochure given to potential applicants said, "is attached to strength of character, the capacity to labour, the quality of previous Christian work, and especially the gift of preaching".

In 1953 the college enjoyed the novel experience of a female student. Dorothy Evans, a BMS missionary in East Pakistan, applied to study theology while on furlough. Dykes agreed to overcome the problem of her accommodation by offering to put her up in his own house. He told the board of studies that "the students had no objection to her taking certain meals with them and using the common room at certain times"[14]. When the time came for the official list of college students to be printed in the 1954 annual report, it agreed that her name could be included[15]. She was described as "a student in a special class"[16]. When Evans left in 1956 to resume her work in East Pakistan, she was referred to as "the first woman student to be accepted for training at this college, and it is with pride that we now formally invest her with the status of old student"[17].

Although Evans was not a ministerial student, and not the first woman to be trained at a Baptist college in England, her presence marked a notable new development in the history of Manchester College. Apart from domestic staff and the female members of principals' families, she was the first woman to play any official role in the life of any of the colleges that form part of its story. Until her arrival, students, academic staff and committee members had all been exclusively male.

In 1958, controversy over doctrinal orthodoxy broke out within the student body. Dykes told the board of studies that a group of three students, which he called "the I.V.F. Group", owing to their strong support for the conservative theological stance of the Inter-Varsity Fellowship, were exercising a subversive influence and working against "the tradition and thought" of the college[18]. A similar problem arose five years later when the student body was told that criticism of the college's teaching in the churches could not be tolerated. At least two probationary students were refused permission to continue their studies over the issue. Perhaps it was in response to this unsettled spirit that A.S. Clement, the college secretary, described the college as Conservative, Evangelical and Liberal in the annual report in 1962, acknowledging as he did so that defining those terms was not easy[19]. It seems that, in the eyes of some of the students at least, the college's traditional reputation for conservatism was no longer deserved.

Amongst the 1960 intake were three unusual students. In different ways, they were signs that fundamental changes were taking place in the kind of students coming to Manchester. The first was a second female student, another BMS missionary, Miss M.H. Tissington, following in the footsteps of Dorothy Evans. The second was G. Bidston who was accepted as a "student pastor", and the third was H.S. Myrie, a Jamaican from the Derby Road church in Nottingham.

Bidston asked to continue as pastor of the Bethel Baptist Church in Bootle while he trained. Although this was regarded as an "unusual" and "impractical" request by the board of studies, he was allowed to do so, on the understanding that his duties at Bethel would be limited to vacations[20].

The college authorities greeted Myrie's arrival with uncertainty. He was encouraged to apply to Calabar College in Jamaica after his probationary year at Manchester, presumably with a view to pursuing his ministry there. This he did, but found it impossible to settle back in his own country and soon resigned. According to David Jelleyman, a missionary on the staff of Calabar College, he was treated badly by the

The Second World War and its aftermath: 1939-1964 199

student body there. Myrie re-applied to Manchester, with the enthusiastic support of his association, and returned to continue his studies in 1962.

The Myrie case raised the question of the acceptance of West Indian candidates for ministerial training. Some years earlier, a Jamaican had been trained at Rawdon, supported by the Jamaican Baptist Union, for ministry in Jamaica, but Myrie was the first in either college to be trained for ministry in Britain[21]. The principals and tutors of the colleges discussed the issue of admitting Jamaicans resident in this country for ministerial training at their annual conference in 1962. Two or three applications had been received and there was considerable uncertainty about whether the men concerned could find openings for ministry at the end of their training. They concluded that "until the situation is clarified colleges would be running a great risk in admitting Jamaicans"[22]. The question was raised again in 1965. The minute book restricts its record of the debate on that occasion to a reference to the "interesting discussion" that followed[23].

The mixed character of the student body, both ethnically and in terms of gender, was reinforced with the arrival of a post-graduate student from India, C. Lal IIminga, in 1961. Two years later Tissington indicated that she would not be continuing her service with the BMS in India following her training and wanted to be considered a regular ministerial student, so becoming the first female minister trained at Manchester. Rawdon College had accepted their first female ministerial student, Cynthia Allegro, the year before. Like the issue of Jamaican candidates for ministry, the question of women ministers was discussed at the annual conference for principals and tutors. In 1963 they agreed that "there was no theological objection to any office in the church being open to any suitable person, male or female", and that although the training offered to women might be different in some respects, they should be treated equally with men[24]. The official acceptance of women ministers within the denomination had been agreed by the Baptist Union nearly forty years earlier, when the names of women first appeared on the accredited list of ministers. Numbers since then had been small. The main problem was securing an invitation to be a minister from a church. The Superintendents acknowledged in 1964 that they had failed to find openings for any of the three college-trained women seeking settlement, and in 1965 Leonard Champion, principal of Bristol College, admitted that he could not see much future for women ministers[25].

Tissington, Myrie and Bidston were all, in their different ways, signs of things to come. Manchester was not resistant, it seems, to accepting new kinds of students for training. By 1960 it was also prepared to accept married men with families, unlike most of the other colleges[26]. If these developments continued they would inevitably change the ethos and pattern of training, based as they had been for a century on the notion of single young men living together in community.

A.C. Underwood and L.H. Marshall at Rawdon

The war years brought considerable changes to Rawdon, quite apart from the impact of the war itself. The financial resources of the college were increased by a substantial legacy from the estate of Ellen Blomfield, the widow of the previous principal, who died in July 1939, and by James Mursell's gift of a valuable collection of stamps. Between them, these added over £9,000 to the college's capital. The human resources, on the other hand, were depleted by the deaths of Harold Rowse in 1940 and David Glass in 1942. Until his death, Rowse was tutor in philosophy. He also maintained a valuable link with northern ministers by leading their annual conference. Glass had been teaching at the college for fifty years, the last six of them officially in retirement. He had become, according to the college committee, "a living stone in the structure of Rawdon"[27].

Underwood and Marshall continued their work at the college until dwindling student numbers enforced its wartime closure in 1944. One of the benefits of the lessened demands on the two men during the war was the opportunity it gave them for writing. Underwood's *A History of the English Baptists* and Marshall's *The Challenge of New Testament Ethics* were both completed in 1945, and are among the most notable books published by Baptist scholars in the twentieth century.

At the end of the war the relationship with Leeds University came under scrutiny. Three other theological colleges were linked to the university: the Methodists at Headingley, the Congregationalists in Bradford and the Anglicans at Mirfield. Degree students took the BA in theological studies. Most theology undergraduates, however, did not study for a Leeds degree at all, opting instead for a London BD. All the affiliated theological colleges had serious objections to the BA course, and before the war Rawdon was the only one to support it. In 1945 it was decided to continue allowing some students to take it, while pressing for improvements in the course, because of the benefits of association with the university. The possibility of moving the college into Leeds was considered and rejected. The advantages of Rawdon's situation for quiet and concentration, and the importance of maintaining its independence, were crucial considerations in coming to this decision[28]. In 1945, a preliminary approach from a woman led to a rather anxious debate about the possibility of admitting female students. However, when the approach failed to materialise into a formal application the matter was pursued no further[29].

Rawdon was able to resume a full programme of training at the end of the war more quickly than Manchester. It did not face the same problems of derequisitioning and costly repairs. Eric Rust, a minister in Huddersfield, was appointed as tutor to take Rowse's place. By the summer of 1946, eighteen men were in residence and receiving training. Five more were admitted later that year, and a further eleven twelve months later. Some were engaged to be married, and the committee received three requests for permission to marry between 1946 and 1948. It refused them all[30].

Underwood's lecturing style was formal, and he was remembered for his aloof, strict style of leadership. Marshall, on the other hand, was energetic and enthusiastic, preaching as much as lecturing his Greek classes. Mrs Underwood supervised the domestic staff. Compared with Manchester, the accommodation was comfortable and spacious, each student having a bedroom and a study, as well as the use of extensive grounds and sports facilities. Student life was lively, with a strong emphasis on sport, especially football, fives and tennis. Although the atmosphere was in some respects monastic because of the isolated location, the common room was frequently the venue for an impromptu student choir, and water fights between students in the two wings of the building were a popular amusement:

At times in true conformity with past Rawdonian behaviour battles between East and West raged as furiously as any battle of the Roses – water flowed freely, sometimes mingled with blood, through the corridors and into the studies[31].

Morning prayers were led by Underwood, and were accompanied by a formal shaking of hands by tutors and students. This was followed by breakfast, and lectures either at the college or in Leeds, at the university or the Methodist College. The journey to Leeds was usually done either by bus or cycle. The small café near the bus stop in the village of Rawdon offered free coffee in return for help with the washing up. Afternoons were free for recreation, and the evenings reserved for private study. The day closed with evening prayers led by one of the students. On Saturday morning the weekly sermon class was held, and on Sunday morning most students walked the short distance to Apperley Bridge train station as the first stage of their journey to a preaching appointment.

In April 1948 Underwood died suddenly, still in his early sixties, shortly after hearing news of the death of his son Donald who worked with the Colonial Service in Nigeria. He had devoted the whole of his working life to training ministers, first at Serampore College in India and then at Rawdon. Marshall was immediately asked to take his place, in spite of the fact that he was three years older than Underwood, and he took up the principalship in the summer.

Unlike Underwood, Marshall had considerable pastoral experience. He was also a lively and popular teacher. The responsibilities of being principal were wide and varied, however, and one of the most difficult challenges was over domestic arrangements in the house. Marshall's daughter Ruth was initially given responsibility for this, but gave up after a couple of years, weary of the isolation[32]. Now with only two tutors, adjustments had to be made to the teaching programme. Church history courses were taken at the university and Hebrew at the Methodist College in Headingley under Norman Snaith. In 1950 a thorough investigation of future staffing was held, including the possibility of co-operating with other colleges. Although both Manchester and Rawdon now had new principals, there was still some resistance to working together. However, in 1951 it was agreed to conduct a joint financial appeal to churches in the north of England[33].

A revival of the college magazine was one of the initiatives taken by Marshall. Before the war this had been published for a few years as a student publication, but it had not appeared for ten years. From 1950 it was an important annual link between the college and the churches. In the first issue Marshall described his priorities as principal. "Evangelism steadied by education" was his aim, as it had been, he claimed, for his predecessor William Steadman. The ability to read the Bible in the original languages was vital. "Sound theology is indispensable to vigorous Christian life and work", he wrote. "The soothing syrup of sentimental appeals" was not enough[34]. In 1951 he wrote in favour of social and recreational activities in church life, commending uniformed youth organisations, sports clubs and even whist drives and dancing[35].

Marshall also arranged for the conversion of one of the classrooms into a memorial chapel, funded largely by the money received from the sale of Mursell's stamp collection. This included the creation of a large stained-glass window in Mursell's memory[36].

As Marshall approached seventy, anxiety grew over his successor. The committee had no enthusiasm for Rust taking over, in spite of his eagerness to have the position. Ernest Payne, who had just been appointed secretary of the Baptist Union, suggested John Barrett, Superintendent for the northeast of England, but the committee was unhappy about any interference from the Union, and Payne's initiative probably hindered any chance Barrett might have had[37]. When Rust was given leave of absence to be a visiting lecturer at Crozier Seminary in the USA for the whole of the 1952-3 session, the staffing position became critical. William Hough, a schoolteacher from Leeds who had been trained at Rawdon and served as a minister earlier in his career, was asked to cover his classes for the year.

The combined anxiety over staffing, both teaching and domestic, and the future of the college, seems to have become too much for Marshall. In the autumn of 1952 he suffered a health breakdown and was ordered to have three months complete rest. It seemed likely that his work at Rawdon was over. Hough was made acting-principal, and started making temporary arrangements for the students' classes. New Testament lectures were held at the Methodist College. Visiting lecturers, including Howard Williams from Leeds and John Barrett, were called in to help, and the senior student, Edmund Pilling, gave lectures in New Testament Greek to the junior men. Within a few months, Rust sent a letter of resignation to the committee, having been offered a permanent position in America, and, after a few months as an invalid, Marshall died. Consequently, as the college approached its 150th anniversary in 1954, Hough was left holding the fort on his own. Rawdon was left without any permanent tutorial staff, and the committee faced the urgent challenge of finding a principal who could rescue the institution from a predicament that threatened its whole future.

D.S. Russell

In March 1953 David Syme Russell was appointed principal, with responsibility for teaching Hebrew and Old Testament studies, homiletics and pastoral studies. Russell, a Scot, had been educated at the Baptist College of Scotland, Glasgow University and Regent's Park College. Later, he was to receive the degree of DLitt for his published work on Jewish apocalyptic undertaken at Rawdon. Aged thirty-six, he brought to the post youth, energy and scholarship, with a special interest in intertestamental apocalyptic literature. He came to Rawdon from an eight-year ministry in Acton. Although not due to take up the appointment until the summer, Russell moved into temporary accommodation at the college straight away. His first major step was to secure the services of G.H.C. Angus, recently retired from the principalship of Serampore College and living in London. Angus agreed to take responsibility for New Testament teaching in return for a nominal salary and lodgings during term time. Hough was made a permanent member of staff, with responsibility for teaching philosophy of religion and Christian ethics. In October 1953 the three men were formally inducted at a ceremony conducted by Ernest Payne. They were joined by a new college secretary, J.G. Hobbs, minister at Westgate, Bradford. A financial appeal was made to the churches for help.

Coming to Rawdon at such a time was a major challenge, especially for someone with no previous connections with Yorkshire, but Russell rapidly won over local people with his "vigorous advocacy of the college" and "his warm personality and ready wit"[38]. The 1954 annual meetings, when the 150th anniversary was celebrated, provided a good opportunity to mark this new start in the life of the college. About 1,000 people were present in a large marquee erected in the college grounds. Subsequent annual Open Days drew large numbers from throughout Yorkshire, and together with the "Rawdon lectures", given by members of staff at weekends or in the evening, were important in strengthening ties with local churches and widening the scope of the college's work. In 1957 a "Friends of Rawdon" scheme was created, aimed at mobilising support for the college more effectively.

The eleven years of Russell's principalship were marked by almost constant difficulties over securing adequate domestic help. Staff turnover was rapid, and much of the work had to be done by the principal and his wife Marion themselves. On occasion the principal could be found stoking the boiler and his wife cooking the students' breakfast. The elaborate and now ageing buildings required frequent attention, and students and tutors were regularly involved in such tasks as gardening and laying tarmac. Central heating replaced coal fires in the library and studies, and deteriorating roofs were replaced.

Academically, the college was strengthened in 1956 with the appointment of a third permanent tutor, Ernest Moore, who took over some of Angus's work and responsibility for teaching church history. Continuing dissatisfaction with the theological teaching available at Leeds University still meant that most degrees were taken externally through London University, a situation that was not ideal in various respects[39]. There was a constant question mark over the value of the college's affiliation to Leeds. Access to the city was not easy, and the syllabuses of the two universities were quite different. Russell, although recognised as a lecturer at Leeds, soon realised the disadvantages of Rawdon's isolation, and became increasingly keen to do something about it. As early as 1955 he had informal discussions with Dykes about co-operation with Manchester, but nothing practical came of these. In 1958 the Congregationalists decided to close their college in Bradford and to unite with their college in Manchester. When the Methodist college in

Headingley also closed, the opportunities for Nonconformists to share teaching in West Yorkshire disappeared altogether.

In 1955 the first woman, Mrs Barritt, was appointed to the college committee, following a debate in the previous year which had concluded that "nominations may be made for people of either sex"[40]. Russell maintained strict student discipline in the house. The day began at 7.30 a.m. with prayers, and men were expected to exercise in the afternoons and be in their studies without fail in the evenings. Student numbers remained at a satisfactory level, reaching thirty in 1955. Visiting students from Europe occasionally spent the summer term at Rawdon, including two from Italy in 1957, one from Germany in 1961 and one from Spain in 1962. The occasional non-white face was to be seen among the students, but none bound for the home ministry. Azariah Mackenzie, a Jamaican supported by the Jamaican Baptist Union, whose general secretary he later became, received training between 1951 and 1953, before returning to Jamaica in 1953, and a Southern Rhodesian, G.C. Magaramombe, was at Rawdon between 1960 and 1961.

Cynthia Allegro was the first female student. She arrived in 1962, and was joined in the following year by another, Marjorie Forster[41]. Allegro, who was initially accepted for a one-year course, subsequently extended to three, was the first woman to be accepted as a ministerial candidate at either Manchester or Rawdon. At the time of her admission to the college she was working as a Baptist deaconess at Wolston Baptist Church near Coventry, and returned there as minister at the end of her course. She had been a professional ballet dancer before her deaconess training. In spite of the difficulties facing women ministers in finding churches prepared to have them, she was determined to become an ordained minister, and had the support of her church. She believed that the distinction between deaconesses and women ministers was no longer valid, as most of the former were in full charge of a church. Before finishing her course, she explained her convictions in the college magazine, urging churches to "search deeply in their hearts" over their reluctance to call women ministers[42].

The needs of married students, and the desire of others to marry, continued to raise problems from time to time. The general rule was that married students should live apart from their wives during term time, and that single students, once they had been accepted, should not marry until they had completed their training. This was a sensitive and sometimes perplexing issue. One student, who was due to start his course in 1956 after military service, was given permission to marry when it was realised he would be thirty-two by the time he finished[43]. Another was allowed to live out of college with his wife and young child during the 1958-9 session[44]. Another was asked to withdraw for at least one session, after which he could apply for re-admission if he wished, because he had got married without seeking the principal's consent[45]. Another was given permission to marry because of the illness of his fiancée[46].

Various attempts were made to improve the practical element of training. Apart from lectures in homiletics by the principal, evangelistic campaigns were conducted in nearby towns, and summer pastorates undertaken. Some students attended short residential courses at the William Temple College and the Luton Industrial Mission. The isolated location of the college did not make work in the community easy, but visits were made to a nearby home for elderly men run by Bradford City Council. In 1962 a scheme of minister's assistants was instigated, to enable senior students to spend time alongside experienced ministers in local churches[47]. The emphasis, however, remained on the academic side of training. A combination of the desire to see high academic standards maintained and the persistent difficulty of getting domestic staff led to a determined drive to unite with Manchester at Brighton Grove.

The creation of Northern Baptist College

The initiative that eventually led to a united college came from Rawdon. At a committee meeting in March 1961 the academic and practical problems facing the principal and staff were spelt out in uncompromising detail. During the previous autumn an investigation into the "present position and future policy" of the college had been launched, and its report urged an immediate approach to Manchester about amalgamating. The most urgent need, the committee was told, was for adequate domestic help. The college's remoteness and the lack of good staff accommodation had resulted in a series of unsuitable applicants. Many of those who were appointed stayed only briefly, sometimes just a few days.

On the academic front, Rawdon loyalties had been divided between the universities in Leeds and London, and this led to inevitable inefficiency. This was made worse by the fact that neither university offered the kind of theological teaching Russell and the tutors felt was needed. The report stated that the weakness of the college's location was already leading to a decline in the quality of applicants, and that it would become increasingly hard to attract the best qualified tutors. Russell and the committee were well aware that the other Baptist colleges were situated in university cities.

Added to these difficulties were the financial problems. Economically, the report claimed, the college as it stood was not viable because of its size. Each student cost the college £400 each year to train which, in spite of Russell's strenuous and usually successful efforts to find funding, was unrealistically high.

In the light of these threats to the college's future, the report outlined three possible courses of action. The first was to remain at Rawdon and try to cope with the difficulties. Russell said that this would be unacceptable to him personally because the strain on his wife and family had become intolerable. The second was to move elsewhere as an independent college. This would not solve the problems of economic viability and would not be acceptable "from the denominational point of view"[48]. The third course of action, and the one favoured by Russell, was to move to Manchester, creating a new college in a new building in union with the college there. Such a step would make domestic arrangements easier, and would provide students and staff with the academic stimulus of a nearby university with a good Faculty of Theology, closely integrated with several other theological colleges. Russell said that this option would have the backing of the Baptist Union, which might make available some funds from its planned Ter-Jubilee Fund to help finance the move, and that Manchester was willing to consider it[49].

It has been said that there are none more tenacious in their loyalty than the alumni and supporters of a theological college[50], and Russell had to use all his tact and skill to persuade those at Rawdon that this was the way to go. He had prepared the ground through personal contacts with

Payne at Baptist Church House and Dykes at Manchester[51]. He had also won considerable affection and goodwill in Yorkshire by the way he had helped rescue Rawdon from its critical state when he was appointed and his commitment to its cause over the subsequent eight years. It was, nonetheless, a significant victory for him when the committee agreed to make an informal approach to Manchester about the proposal. The following month a meeting duly took place. Russell spelt out the logic of union. "Rawdon has a good building but a poor site", he said, "whereas Manchester has a good site and not so good a building". He insisted on two conditions to a merger in Manchester. One was that the united college should have a new name, and the second that it should have new buildings, either at Brighton Grove or on a new site[52].

Over the next few months momentum for union rapidly built up. The Manchester committee gave its support to pursuing the matter and what had started out as an informal opportunity to confer became a formal joint committee. It soon became clear that the Brighton Grove site was the best location for the new college. The Rawdon Brotherhood, comprising ex-students, gave Russell a vote of confidence at their annual conference in the summer. It was decided to invite Payne to be a member of the committee. Naturally enough, several obstacles had to be overcome in the early stages. Dykes' health was a matter of concern. He had fallen victim to one of his bouts of illness when the joint committee first met in April 1961 and was also absent for its second meeting in July. He was back in August, however, and chaired the meeting in October. The Rawdon men were also worried in case they lost the substantial sum left to the college in James Mursell's will, but were reassured this would not happen.

The nature and design of the new premises in Manchester, the amount of money that would have to be raised, the saleability of Rawdon, the staffing of the new college and the legal implications of merger were all debated anxiously between the summer of 1961 and the spring of 1962. It was agreed to plan for accommodation for sixty students and four tutors, and for the building work to be done in stages, gradually replacing the existing property. A dispute between the architects of the two colleges briefly threatened the scheme, until one withdrew from the committee.

The total cost was estimated at £150,000. This included the purchase of two houses adjacent to the Brighton Grove site. Valuers were appointed to estimate the likely selling price of the Rawdon building. They "could indicate no saleable use" for it, suggesting that the site might raise £10,000. Payne suggested that £20,000 might be available from the Union's Ter-Jubilee Fund. In spite of objections from Dykes that the scheme was "quite out of touch with reality", it was agreed to launch a general financial appeal to meet the shortfall in funds[53]. J.B. Middlebrook, Home Secretary of the Baptist Missionary Society, who was about to retire, agreed to be the Commissioner of the appeal.

Discussions between Russell and Dykes about staffing were not easy. The respective responsibilities of the two principals had to be resolved, as did the teaching duties of Russell and Farr, both of whom were Old Testament specialists. Hough and Angus indicated that they would retire when the merger took place. Whether Moore would have a position in the new college was not at first certain.

None of these obstacles was allowed to prevent progress being made, and it was soon decided that the new college should be opened in the summer of 1964. If this was to be realised, the two annual meetings in 1962 were vitally important. In Manchester, approval was gained fairly easily. The only stipulation was that the existing library-chapel should be retained in the new building. In 1961 that part of the building had been improved by the addition of an apse, with a view to making it more suitable for use as a chapel, and Dykes was eager not to see it disappear. No problems were encountered over the requirements of the trust deed, an insuperable obstacle in previous merger negotiations[54].

At Rawdon, progress was not so easy. Various objections were raised to the closure of the college, and questions raised about its necessity. Could not the united college be at Rawdon? Was proximity to a university really so important? How could severe damage in the college's relationship with the Yorkshire churches be avoided? The general committee itself was divided on the question. Russell, however, was determined to press ahead. The make-or-break occasion was a special meeting for college subscribers called for 27 October 1962. Well over a hundred met to hear Russell and Hobbs, the college secretary, present the case for union. It was ultimately approved by 98 votes to 17. In the light

The Second World War and its aftermath: 1939-1964

of this result, the general committee gave it their backing. Fortified by this support, the Rawdon members of the joint committee returned to the detailed negotiations over the design of the new building. Dykes' objections to various elements of the architect's plans were overcome and planning permission was secured[55].

The cover of the final edition of Rawdon College Magazine (1964), depicting the principal, D.S. Russell, supervising the students' departure for Manchester

During the course of 1963 the Baptist Union Corporation was appointed trustee of the building[56]. This was a condition attached to the £20,000 grant from the Ter-Jubilee Fund. It was also agreed that the name of the college should be Northern Baptist College. A constitution was drawn up, providing for the appointment of a board of governors in place of the general committee. The president of the Baptist Union, H.L. Watson, laid the foundation stone for the first phase of the new building on 9 October, ninety-one years to the day that the original Manchester College foundation stone had been laid. A residential block for thirty-six students, a dining hall, kitchen block and two tutors' houses were erected alongside the old building, with a view to both being used until the second phase was started.

Russell and Dykes became joint principals, with Farr and Moore the two other tutors. A matron and bursar were also appointed. The student body had traditionally been understood as a kind of extended family centred on the principal and his wife. This had already been modified by the earlier appointment of matrons and other domestic staff, but the creation of Northern Baptist College meant an effective abandonment of this model. Personal adjustments had to be made, especially by Marion Russell and Beryl Dykes, but more importantly it marked a change in the character of college life. All four tutors also had to adjust to new relationships and responsibilities. One of Russell's and Moore's particular duties was to see the Rawdon students doing London BD and diploma courses through to completion.

In the penultimate issue of the Rawdon College magazine Russell gave a brief outline of the historical relationship between the two colleges. "We cannot afford to be parochial in this matter", he wrote. The new college provided many new and significant opportunities. Its greater size would make it "a powerful Baptist witness in the North". Its close connection with the university would prove beneficial for students and staff. The academic staff would be free to develop training in new directions, something which the heavy demands of teaching and administration in the separate colleges had hindered. The development of extra-mural work amongst the churches was one possibility. Russell acknowledged that the move to Manchester would make maintaining links with the churches in Yorkshire more difficult[57]. Middlebrook, in an article promoting the financial appeal, warmly commended the new venture. Writing of the remoteness of Rawdon and the "long and arduous walk" to the nearest station, he said that no committee had any right to continue to subject principals and their wives to the "heartbreaking and dreary business of conjuring up from nowhere cooks and housemaids"[58].

The last annual meeting at Rawdon took place in June 1964. Russell and Hobbs spoke of the "Rawdon tradition". Presentations were made to the tutors. The agent had not made any progress with the sale of the premises and the officers were given authority to sell or lease them at the most advantageous terms available. They were eventually sold in 1966 to the Roman Catholic College of Trinity and All Saints in Horsforth, Leeds, as a hostel[59]. The final *Rawdon College Magazine* included an article by Angus on the benefits of the move to Manchester. It would, he said, help relations with other denominations and with "the world"[60].

The final months of Manchester College were understandably not as emotional for its supporters as at Rawdon. There was to be no move of site, and although building work was going on apace, the old building was still, initially at least, in place, and the two tutors remained in post. The 1963 annual report included a full description of the new premises. The existing college building stood on what would become the quadrangle lawn, its readers were told, and would continue to remain in place until the final stage of building took place[61]. The committee assured supporters that the amalgamation and resulting demolition of the premises had not been the consequence of any decline at Manchester. On the contrary, student intake over the previous decade had been higher than in the pre-war years, and the academic results had been good[62]. The 1964 report was produced under the heading "Northern Baptist College". Thirty-one ministerial students were listed as starting the 1964-5 session. Ten of them had been admitted by a joint interviewing panel and were described as Northern students. They joined eleven from Manchester and ten from Rawdon[63]. This was significantly less than the combined total in the two colleges during most of the post-war years. Numbers at Rawdon in particular had understandably dropped in the years immediately prior to the merger. The unused accommodation was taken up by non-ministerial students at Manchester University.

On 8 October 1964 the *Baptist Times* reported on the amalgamation under the heading "Two Colleges become One". Strictly, the union had to wait somewhat longer while the lawyers sorted out the necessary formalities, and the official opening did not take place until 1965. The work of Northern Baptist College really began at the start of the 1964-5 session, however, even though the demolition of the old building and the erection of the new went on for another three years. A service and act of dedication were conducted at the start of the new session by Leonard Champion, president of the Baptist Union. The two proud institutions at Rawdon and Manchester had effectively disappeared, bringing their separate traditions and resources together into a new venture.

Many things had been gained by the merger, and these were repeatedly emphasised. But some things had also been lost. A remark of Russell's about his Rawdon students summed up both gains and losses. "They miss the trees", he said, "but they are glad to be among the lassies"[64]. The loss of the building and its setting above the Aire in Cragg Wood was a significant one. Yorkshire Baptists felt it particularly keenly, but Rawdon had far wider significance as a symbol of northern Baptist life and an impressive monument to Victorian Nonconformity for over a century. To some extent it still is, although access to what is now an exclusive block of luxury apartments is difficult. For all the practical obstacles to maintaining it, Rawdon was also a unique resource for reflection, study and community life.

The communal, family atmosphere that had characterised both Manchester and Rawdon was disrupted by the merger, and to a large extent was lost for ever. In many ways it was an outdated setting for ministerial training anyway, and had been under threat for some time in both places. The increasing number of applications from married men, some with families, and from women, had already made the traditional model of a residential community of single men unrealistic.

New approaches to theological study were also challenging old preconceptions. The emergence of BA degrees, rather than the traditional BDs, at both Leeds and Manchester, and the development of theology as an academic discipline not linked to the ministry, was broadening the perception of what it meant to study theology. The idea of a seminary for ordinands, in which there was a strong emphasis on Biblical languages, the philosophy of religion and systematic theology, seemed increasingly out of touch with trends in the universities.

These changes were naturally regretted by some and welcomed by others. The long-term impact was not immediately apparent, and would not become so until new principal and tutors were appointed. Even in the autumn of 1964, however, it was clear that they were likely to transform

The Second World War and its aftermath: 1939-1964 215

the nature of ministerial training in the north of England in a more profound way than had ever happened before.

D.S. Russell, K.C. Dykes (joint principals) and E.A. Payne (general secretary of the Baptist Union) at the official opening of Northern Baptist College in 1965, with Professor William Mansfield Cooper, Vice Chancellor of Manchester University

The momentum that led to the successful amalgamation of the two colleges, after several earlier failed attempts, was the result of several unavoidable factors. One was financial. The pressure on small institutions like Rawdon and Manchester was becoming intolerable. Small numbers of students had always made the cost of training and accommodation expensive, but with rapidly rising costs, particularly staff wages, this became impossible to cope with. Ageing buildings made the problem worse. Colleges of all denominations were being driven to merge, as it became impossible for them to function effectively, or even to survive as separate institutions.

Another factor was the personalities of the two principals. They were largely responsible for overcoming previously fatal hostility to merger. In the case of Dykes, this was mainly because of his refusal to allow Manchester's trust deed, which committed the college to reformed doctrine and to strict communion, to become a stumbling block. The issue had long ceased to be a matter of vital concern, but the conservatism of previous principals had meant it had become a convenient excuse for not going forward. Under Dykes, such matters had not been seriously raised as a problem at all. On the other side of the Pennines, Russell's ability to overcome the historic opposition to merger among Rawdon's supporters was vital. County loyalty was not, perhaps, quite as vigorous by the mid-twentieth century as it had been in previous generations, but it still existed, and Russell's personal qualities of persuasion and determination were important in winning the doubters over.

A third factor that contributed to the successful outcome of negotiations in the 1960s was denominational. The part played by the Baptist Union under the leadership of Payne may well have been decisive. Payne himself was a keen advocate of the scheme, and played an active part in it from the start. In practical terms, the grant of £20,000 from the Ter-Jubilee Fund was crucial[65]. Although only a fraction of the total cost, it was offered at an early stage, and played a major part in overcoming the objections of those, like Dykes himself, who doubted whether the money could ever be raised.

There were other powerful arguments in favour of amalgamation, such as the academic advantages of closeness to Manchester University, the benefits of a modern, vibrant city and the possibility of working with other Nonconformist colleges. These, however, had all been in existence for some time, and it seems that financial, personal and denominational factors were the most decisive in making it happen in 1964. The advantages of union had been recognised by many people for more than seventy years, and in many ways it is surprising it took so long to achieve. Efficiency and common sense, however, were not, and never have been, the only factors guiding Baptists in making their decisions.

For those with a sense of history, there was something fitting about a united college for the north being situated in Manchester. It had originally seemed likely that Steadman's academy would have been founded in Manchester in 1805. Only the arrival of Gadsby slightly earlier had prevented this from happening, and had led Steadman to Bradford instead.

---

1   Ernest A. Payne, *The Baptist Union: A Short History* (Carey Kingsgate Press Ltd.: London, 1958) p.268.
2   Both the Free Church Federal Council and the British Council of Churches had their inaugural meetings in Baptist Church House in Southampton Row, London. In spite of some war damage, the Baptist Union kept its headquarters there throughout the war. The formation of the British Council of Churches anticipated that of the World Council of Churches in 1948. The intention had been to launch the latter in 1941, but this was prevented by the war.
3   Manchester College Minute Book, 9 June 1943.
4   *Ibid.*, 13 December 1944.
5   Hundreds of girls were trained as inspectors of aircraft parts at Brighton Grove during the war. One of them went on to marry a college student.
6   Although the recommendation for the appointment came officially through the usual committee channels, it seems that Townsend had Dykes in mind as his successor for some years before his retirement.
7   Michael H Taylor's tribute to Dykes at his funeral, 15 July 1985.
8   Manchester College 1958 Annual Report, p.8.
9   Manchester College Minute Book, 20 June and 12 December 1951 and 25 June 1952. Farr's appointment was officially part-time, with half his salary being paid by the University.
10 Ian Sellers describes Farr's lectures as "carefully inscribed on a variety of sheets of paper, card and what often looked like parchment flown in directly from the Dead Sea" (Ian Sellers (ed.), *Our Heritage: The Baptists of Yorkshire, Lancashire and Cheshire 1647-1987* (Yorkshire Baptist Association: Leeds, 1987) p.107).
11 Manchester College 1960 Annual Report, p.9.
12 Minutes of Superintendents' Conference held at Regent's Park College, 1-3 September 1953.
13 *Manchester Baptist College: Information for Prospective Candidates* (no date, but probably mid- or late-1950s) p.4. Minutes of Principals and Tutors Conferences, 1956.
14 Manchester College Board of Studies Minute Book, 10 June 1953.
15 *Ibid.*, 20 May 1954.
16 Manchester Baptist College 1954 Annual Report, p.7.
17 Manchester Baptist College 1956 Annual Report, p.9.
18 Manchester College Board of Studies Minute Book, 10 December 1958.

19 Manchester Baptist College 1962 Annual Report, p.8.
20 Manchester College Board of Studies Minute Book, 13 September 1960.
21 The debate surrounding Myrie's training is recorded in the board of studies minute book, 13 September 1960 – 4 December 1963.
22 Minutes of Principals and Tutors Conference, March 1962.
23 *Ibid.*, March 1965.
24 *Ibid.*, March 1963.
25 *Ibid.*, March 1964 and March 1965.
26 Among the other colleges, only Bristol was also able to do this.
27 Rawdon College Committee Minute Book, 7 October 1940. In a sense this is still true today. Glass's name is inscribed on the foundation stone laid for the college extension in 1930.
28 Rawdon College Committee Minute Book, 24 October 1945.
29 *Ibid.*, 24 October 1945 and 6 March 1946. The woman concerned decided to undertake training as a deaconess instead.
30 *Ibid.*, 16 October 1946, 5 March 1947 and 23 June 1948.
31 T J. Neal, "Those were the days", in *Rawdon College Magazine* no.5 (1954) p.27. Neal entered Rawdon in 1946.
32 Letter from Barrett to E.A. Payne dated 1 July 1950 (Payne MSS).
33 *Ibid.*, 24 October 1951. A special committee's suggestion that closer co-operation should be sought with Manchester in particular was rejected at a meeting in June 1951. There is some anecdotal evidence that the personal relationship between Underwood and Townsend was poor, which goes some way to explain why there was so little contact between the institutions at this time.
34 *Rawdon College Magazine* no.1 (1950) pp.4-5.
35 *Rawdon College Magazine* no.2 (1951) pp.2-5.
36 The window is now in the chapel of Luther King House at Brighton Grove.
37 Correspondence between Marshall, Barrett and Payne in January 1952 refers to the "feeling" that existed at Rawdon about London controlling appointments in the north. Barrett asked Marshall for his name not to be considered for the principalship because of the difficulties that had arisen over Payne's suggestion (Payne MSS).
38 David Milner, "The Last Days of Rawdon and the Formation of Northern Baptist College" in J.H.Y. Briggs (ed.) *Bible, Church and World* (Baptist Historical Society: London, 1989) p.23.
39 In 1961 a committee also complained about deterioration in the quality of the London BD (Policy Committee Minute Book, 2 February 1961)
40 Rawdon College Committee Minute Book, 27 October 1954 and 27 October 1955. It is, of course, remarkable now that the absence of women on the college committee was tolerated up until this point.
41 Forster resigned within a few months because of her engagement to the senior student.
42 *Rawdon College Magazine* no.15 (1964) pp.20-1 and *Northern Baptist College Magazine* no.1 (1965) pp.15-17). Allegro was ordained in 1965.

43 Rawdon College Committee Minute Book, 18 January 1956.
44 *Ibid.*, 27 June 1958.
45 *Ibid.*, 20 October 1960.
46 *Ibid.*, 8 March 1962.
47 *Ibid.*. An undated leaflet (probably issued in 1963 or early 1964) outlining the "Pastoralia" undertaken at the various colleges also mentioned courses at Westhill College in Birmingham on work with children and young people.
48 Presumably this meant that the Baptist Union would not support such a move.
49 Rawdon College Policy Sub-committee Minute Book, 2 February 1961 and Rawdon College Committee Minute Book, 20 October 1960 and 9 March 1961.
50 Geoffrey Rusling, "David Syme Russell: A Life of Service", in J.H.Y. Briggs (ed.), *Bible, Church and World* (Baptist Historical Society: London, 1989) p.9.
51 In a personal conversation with the author, Russell described his conversation with Dykes on a seat in Salendine Nook Baptist Church graveyard. Dykes was apparently keen to amalgamate.
52 Report of Informal Meeting between the Rawdon College "Small Committee" and the Officers of Manchester College, April 1961.
53 Minutes of Joint Committee, 20 November 1961. Initially, the appeal was to be for £75,000. This was later reduced to £50,000. Both Payne and Dykes were uneasy about making a general appeal for funds. Dykes found the prospect "shocking" (Minutes of Joint Committee, 19 March and 5 July 1962).
54 Manchester Baptist College Annual Report, 1962, pp.18-21.
55 Dykes did not want to be "looking at a brick wall for the next fifteen years", nor did he want the proposed quadrangle layout looking "like a city street" (Joint Committee Minute Book, 13 September and 21 November 1962).
56 Joint Committee Minute Book, 27 February 1962.
57 *Rawdon College Magazine* no.14 (1963) pp.10-12.
58 *Ibid.*, p.14.
59 They were subsequently converted into a block of luxury apartments.
60 *Rawdon College Magazine* no.15 (1964) p.13.
61 Manchester College 1963 Annual Report, p.5. Was there, one cannot help wondering, still some lingering hope that the old building would not have to be demolished?
62 *Ibid.*, p.10.
63 Northern Baptist College 1964 Annual Report, p.2. In one place the number of ministerial students is given as 32.
64 Reported to the author by both Farr and Russell in personal conversation.
65 One of the objects of this fund was to assist ministerial training. It was agreed that in the case of the new college in Manchester, a lump-sum payment should be made, rather than future payments out of accrued interest.

Chapter Eleven
Northern Baptist College
1964-1978

It is impossible to achieve a proper historical perspective and to assess the real significance of the changes that occurred when considering the most recent events in the college's life. There must, therefore, be a sense of provisionality, not only about any evaluations or conclusions that are made, but also about the description of these events. The story is incomplete without these years, however, and an attempt has to be made. Many of the actors in it are still alive, and each one has a different story to tell. The account given here is susceptible to a variety of interpretations.

Society and church

The last four decades of the twentieth century (the period covered by chapters 11 and 12) saw enormous changes in almost every area of human society. The rate and scale of change in such basic things as culture, technology, family life and international relations was unprecedented. Behind much of it was the onward march of Western-style capitalism, creating powerful corporations capable of influencing the lives of billions of people. Companies such as MacDonalds, which opened its first restaurant in Britain in 1974, and Microsoft, which came to dominate the computer software market, represented the global economy that developed during this period. Remarkable technological developments revolutionised manufacturing, entertainment, medicine, communications and warfare.

Many of these changes took place against the backdrop of the Cold War, which was often a driving force behind them. This stand-off between East and West brought with it the threat of nuclear war, a constant anxiety throughout much of the period. When the Cold War came to an end, symbolised by the collapse of the Berlin Wall, anxieties over global instability did not disappear. Attempts to create workable political structures to match the power of global commercial and financial organisations were largely unsuccessful.

In Britain, many traditional industries virtually, or in some cases completely, disappeared. This did not occur without serious unrest, especially during the 1970s, culminating in the miners' strike of 1981. Under Margaret Thatcher's premiership in the 1980s, many of the socialist ideals underpinning the Labour Party's post-war reforms were abandoned. By the time of her resignation in 1990, the vigorous confrontations between the political left and the political right that characterised the previous two decades had largely disappeared.

Other tensions surfaced in several British cities in the 1980s, fuelled by a sense of injustice and discrimination within black communities. The country was becoming a genuinely multiracial and multicultural society. Increasingly, closer links were established with continental Europe. Membership of the European Economic Community was achieved in 1972 and confirmed by a referendum in 1975. Since then the opening of the channel tunnel in 1990 was the most potent symbol of Britain's growing sense of a European identity.

In family life and personal relationships, the equal status of men and women in employment was affirmed by the Equal Pay Act of 1970. The 1969 Divorce Act also had a major impact on marriage and family life. Changes in personal and family life are subtle and difficult to evaluate, but the decline in respect for the institution of marriage over the latter decades of the twentieth century seems to have been as important as any.

Another feature of late twentieth-century Britain was the emergence of youth culture. From the arrival of the miniskirt and the Beatles in the mid-sixties, the fashion and music industries, largely aimed at teenagers and young adults, mushroomed. At the other end of the age-scale, the combination of a lowering birth rate, improving standards of living and better health-care resulted in a significantly older population and larger numbers of active pensioners.

For many Christians, a growing sense of society's secularisation, and the marginalisation of church and theology, at least in their traditionally understood forms, led to calls for greater efforts to relate Christian thinking to contemporary social and political questions. Two other important features of these years for churches were the ecumenical movement and the charismatic movement. Serious attempts were made in the late 1960s and early 1970s to achieve a greater degree of organisational unity among the denominations. In 1972 the United Reformed Church was created when Congregationalists and English Presbyterians came together. At about the same time the union of the Methodist Church and the Church of England just failed to gain the necessary majority among the Anglicans. The World Council of Churches and the British Council of Churches, both formed in the 1940s, provided the main forum for interdenominational co-operation. The momentum towards organisational unity had faltered by the end of the 1970s, however, with the emphasis being placed more on local, informal partnerships than on large organic schemes.

The charismatic movement, with its emphasis on informality in worship and personal experience, had a profound effect on many Baptist churches in particular. Often rejecting traditional denominational forms and structures, it contributed to the breakdown of barriers between denominations. Charismatic churches were often among the most rapidly growing sections of the Church. Some remained within the older denominations, and others grouped themselves into new organisations, in order to develop structures independent of the constraints of history.

Baptists, in common with most church groups, saw their numbers steadily decline. Both the ecumenical and the charismatic movements, in different ways, tended to contribute to a reduced sense of denominational identity. One of the most important institutional events was the sale of Baptist Church House in London and the relocation of denominational headquarters to Didcot in 1989. This released significant funds for denominational use, much of which was used to support the work of the ministry, particularly in training and the provision of pensions.

The governors, principals and staff of Northern Baptist College, now housed in new buildings at Brighton Grove, sought to respond to the challenges of these decades in the training they provided. It proved to be an exciting time of change. The college pioneered new approaches to ministerial and lay training, and often proved itself ready to embrace both the risks and the opportunities presented to it by the late twentieth century.

Getting Started

The first few years at Brighton Grove were a time for completing the premises and adjusting to new circumstances. Attachment to Rawdon and Manchester lessened with each new intake of students and soon disappeared as the physical reminders of the old college were removed. Miss M. Wass and Mrs E.M. Newton became bursar and matron respectively, appointments that constituted a new approach to the domestic side of college life[1].

Northern College Magazine first appeared in 1965. Of the thirty-one students present during the 1964-5 session, there was one woman, Cynthia Allegro, and one black student, Heckford Sharpe. The magazine's theme of unity was understandable, given the amalgamation of the two colleges, but the energetic advocacy of church unity was nonetheless remarkable. Russell looked forward to the time when ministerial training would be done on an ecumenical basis[2]. Dykes applauded moves towards unity and discussed how the issue of baptism could be overcome[3]. Various other writers contributed to the theme and were unanimously positive about the prospects and importance of church unity. Other articles included one by Cynthia Allegro arguing the case for women ministers[4] and one reporting an address by the general secretary of the Student Christian Movement appealing for action by the United Nations to end apartheid in South Africa[5]. In hindsight, one can see how these topics of ecumenism, the ministry of women and social justice set the scene for the future.

The official opening of the first phase of the new premises took place on 16 June 1965. The main speaker was Ernest Payne, whose support for amalgamation had been crucial. The quadrangle was completed and the old building demolished during 1966 and 1967. Two tutors' houses, occupied by the Russells and the Dykes, completed the suite of buildings. In October 1966 the amalgamation scheme was formally approved by the Secretary of State for Education and Science, and the governors officially took over responsibility for the college. By the autumn of 1967, sixty-two study-bedrooms were available for occupation, of which just twenty-three were occupied by theological students and the rest by lay students from the university.

Old and new premises together at Brighton Grove.
The transition from one to the other was spread over about three years.

From the start, the new premises at Brighton Grove were a great asset. Accommodation was similar to the combined space at Rawdon and Manchester, but student numbers had declined, and most of it was never taken up by Baptist ministerial students. It is doubtful whether mixing ministerial and lay students was a deliberate plan in the design of the building, although from early on the benefits were recognised. For a start, renting out rooms to the university generated income, as Manchester College had discovered. In a general way, Russell regarded more frequent contact between ministerial students and others at the university as one of the benefits of the move to Manchester[6].

A novel feature of the new college was its official link with the Baptist Union. In return for help from its Ter-Jubilee Fund, the Union Corporation became the trustee of the college and the Union was given the constitutional right to be represented on the governing body. The Union was entitled to two governors, one of whom was usually the general secretary. In addition, the four Area Superintendents from the north and midlands, themselves employees of the Union, were ex-officio governors[7]. This link was a reminder that the Union, as well as Rawdon and Manchester, had been involved in the birth of Northern. It ensured good channels of communication between Union committees and the college staff, something that was of mutual benefit when questions of ministerial training and accreditation were being discussed.

In the summer of 1966 Russell informed the Governors that he had accepted an invitation to become the General Secretary of the Baptist Union when Payne retired. It was a happy coincidence that this opportunity arose just as the scheme towards which he had worked for over six years was drawing to its successful conclusion. The new college probably owed its existence more to his vision and determination than to any other single factor. The final event in the rather drawn-out process was a service of thanksgiving in November 1967. Appropriately enough, Russell, who had by then taken up his new position, was the preacher. The congregation was given an historical sketch of the origin of the college and a description of the premises, which were called "neo-Georgian" in style. Of the old Manchester College, only the chapel had been retained, although even that had been re-faced with bricks matching the new building.

The two years following Russell's departure were difficult. For much of the time Dykes was unwell. In his absence, Farr was appointed acting-principal. Some governors expressed doubts about Dykes' ability to fulfil the responsibilities of the principalship. They thought there was a need for fresh "vision and vigour" to grasp the many opportunities facing the new institution. A committee was appointed "to consider the Principalship, Staffing and Policy of the College"[8]. Early in 1969 the governing body agreed that "in the light of the history of Mr. Dykes' illness" he be immediately relieved of all responsibilities. Arrangements were made for his early retirement in the following October and steps were taken to find a successor[9]. In February the *Baptist Times* announced that "owing to prolonged illness" Dykes would be on leave of absence until his retirement[10].

Dykes himself did not want to leave. The cyclical nature of his illness, which rendered him incapable of working for lengthy periods every few years, was no doubt a major factor in the governors' decision. Also important, however, was the growing feeling that a whole new approach to ministerial training was required. The field of theological education was coming under the spotlight, partly as a result of an international conference in Canterbury in 1966 sponsored by the World and British Councils of Churches. Experiments were being tried in different parts of the world and in Britain many felt that considerable fresh thinking was needed.

Among Baptists, the ministry was also coming under scrutiny. In 1961 a report on *The Doctrine of the Ministry* had been produced for the Baptist Union, raising many questions about the nature of ministry among Baptists. It was followed in 1967 by the creation of a Commission on the Ministry, which produced the innovative and radical *Ministry Tomorrow* report in 1969, just at the time that Dykes' future was being decided. The commission's chairman was Norman B. Jones, the superintendent of the north-western area of the Baptist Union and an influential figure on the board of governors.

One of the conclusions *Ministry Tomorrow* came to was that the financial impoverishment and frustration of ministers lay at the heart of a crisis in church life. It advocated a smaller number of "professional" ministers, supported by part-time or non-stipendiary "supplementary" ministers. This would lead to a varied pattern of ministry dependent on the size and circumstances of churches. Groups of churches and teams of ministers were envisaged. Colleges would become centres of theological education, providing different types of training for professional and supplementary ministers as well as lay people. The report specified five key areas of training: spiritual discipline, the use and interpretation of the Bible, the use of language, personal relationships and pastoral theology. It emphasised the need for theology to be linked to the practice of ministry, rather than approached as an isolated academic discipline.

Although many of the ideas in *Ministry Tomorrow* were not adopted by the denomination as a whole they are important because many of those relating to theological education were taken up by Northern. Those who were eager to see Northern experiment with new approaches to training doubted whether Dykes was able to provide the required leadership for this.

Once Dykes' retirement had been agreed, the search for a replacement began. Norman Jones was on the nominating sub-committee, and the first choice was one of his colleagues on the Commission on the Ministry, Morris West of St Albans. After initially agreeing to accept nomination, West subsequently withdrew. The sub-committee next turned to one of the gifted younger members of the governing body, Michael Taylor, minister of the Hall Green church in Birmingham. Taylor had been a student at Manchester during the 1950s, and, after studying at Union Theological Seminary in New York, had ministered in North Shields for six years before moving to Birmingham in 1967[11]. Still in his early thirties, it was a bold recommendation. After a lengthy discussion by the governors, his appointment was agreed. Taylor asked for the first term of his appointment to be a period of personal preparation, in which he could "review and assess the situation"[12]. It was spent at Regent's Park College. His teaching responsibilities started in earnest at the start of the 1970-71 session.

Michael Taylor

Ministry Tomorrow had made ministerial training a contentious issue among Baptists. When George Beasley-Murray, principal of Spurgeon's College, was told about the ideas it contained he wrote to Dykes saying that if its ideas were implemented it would spell disaster[13]. Others were eager to see changes made. In January 1969 an ecumenical gathering of theology students at Swanwick, organised by the Student Christian Movement, forcibly expressed its dissatisfaction with the way their colleges were run. The students believed that theological education should be undertaken ecumenically, not in a "closed and sectarian" manner, and that it should be built upon the study of cultures and society, equipping students for the practical demands of ministry[14]. Taylor was sympathetic to their point of view. Disappointed with the Baptist Union's 1967 *Baptists and Unity* report, he was much involved in encouraging Baptists to be positive in their response to ecumenism. His own experience of ministry in North Shields had also convinced him of the uselessness of theological education without the ability to apply it to people's actual experience of life[15].

Michael Taylor

Taylor spelled out his views in a document entitled "The Church in Training", written in December 1969. This provided the starting point for his work. The opening affirmation, "Dissatisfaction with theological education is widespread", set the scene for the proposals it contained[16]. Taylor argued that a constant dialogue between the Church's Biblical and theological heritage and the contemporary secular situation was necessary if Christian truth was to be comprehensible. Theological education, he believed, was for the whole Christian community, rather than a few experts, and should be aimed at enabling Christians to engage in the service in the world to which God had called them. The minister's role was to help the church to minister, often by pioneering new forms of service. Just as the forms of the Church were becoming more varied and flexible in response to a changing society, so forms of ministry should change. A much more diversified approach to ministry was required, in which distinguishing between lay and ordained ministers would no longer be relevant and in which working in teams would become the norm.

Taylor envisaged an initial programme of basic training for lay and ministerial students, which would include three elements: church and mission in the contemporary world, thinking theologically, in which group work and case studies would be important, and personal formation, which would include the development of "a viable form of spirituality realistic for life in ministry"[17]. Ministerial selection and training would follow the completion of this basic course. Ministerial training would be divided into general training, dealing with worship, communication and people, and special training. Academic work, which for ministers would normally be of degree level, would be undertaken at the same time, interspersed with the other elements. Denominational training, such as Baptist principles and history, would normally be done after the main ministerial training had been completed. Colleges would also be responsible for supervising continuing in-service training for ministers, especially in the early years of ministry. The whole approach was based on the radical assumption that the "local, residential congregation" was no longer the norm for church life, and that therefore preparation for ministry could no longer take this for granted.

Taylor went on to say that all theological education should have five qualities. First, it should be open, both to "the outside world" and to other academic disciplines, avoiding isolation. Second, it should be ecumenical. Third, it should be relevant, not just by the inclusion of instruction in practical skills but by relating theological study to the actual experience of mission. Fourth, it should be corporate, with an emphasis on teaching and learning by all in small groups. Fifth, it should be flexible, subject to constant review and conducted by staff members who change regularly.

These ideas constituted a radical departure from the kind of training undertaken at Manchester and Rawdon. Traditional academic disciplines like systematic theology and philosophy were largely ignored, and, while Taylor was eager to incorporate study of the Bible, the place of Biblical languages and textual criticism was downplayed. The model of a group of people preparing themselves for full-time pastoral ministry by living together for three or more years, attending lectures and engaging in private study, with occasional opportunities for practical training and experience, had disappeared. Taylor's manifesto made no reference to Northern's existing practice or its past. It was a brave new vision by a gifted young idealist, shaped during a period buzzing with new ideas. Taylor was passionate about the task before him and unafraid of the future, anxious "not of being too extreme, but of being too blind and unimaginative and too mild"[18].

Taylor circulated his paper at the college's education committee in April 1970. He made some specific suggestions for immediate implementation. These included the formation of an ecumenical fourth year course and the abolition of the courses in homiletics, systematic theology and Baptist history and principles and the sermon class. In his opinion, these subjects would be better covered in project and group work. He was also keen to investigate possible ways in which the college might provide part-time training. The minutes of the meeting record that "the general pattern was approved"[19]. When the governors heard about the proposals a month later they congratulated Taylor and gave their support[20]. He wasted no time in putting them into practice. A fourth-year "training for ministry" course was instituted that autumn in conjunction with other Nonconformist theological colleges in Manchester. Seven Northern students participated in this. The sermon class was replaced by discussions involving tutors, students and congregation after hearing a student preach in a local church. Plans were made for lay training courses. Contact was made with the Anglicans and Methodists to explore Baptist involvement in the joint training college they were discussing, and conversations held with them and others about a proposed Theological Education Council for Manchester[21].

In 1971 the association between Taylor and radical thinking became firmly fixed in the denomination as a whole. Principal Henton Davies of Regent's Park College was elected vice-president of the Baptist Union in 1970. He wanted to introduce a serious theological dimension to the 1971 Assembly, and asked three leading scholars to deliver addresses on key contemporary themes. Alongside presentations by others on God and the

Holy Spirit, Taylor was asked to speak on "The Incarnate Presence: how much of a man was Jesus Christ?"

Taylor's address had an explosive effect on the Baptist community. Delivered with a typical honesty and clarity, it confronted the question of the meaning of the Incarnation in the modern world. Having acknowledged the need to express Christian truth in ways that were relevant, rather than simply using the language of ancient creeds, Taylor confessed, "I think I must stop short of saying categorically, Jesus is God". "I do not say that Jesus is God, but I do say with the New Testament that God was in Christ or that I encounter God in Jesus". The difference between Jesus and other men was one of degree rather than of kind. He was more of a man than other men, fulfilling the potential of humanity more fully, and in him God was reconciling the world to Himself. Taylor acknowledged the problems of any confession of faith that sought to put faith into words. "I am not committed to a confession of faith, I am committed to a Person", he said. He admitted his preference for addressing the issue of the Incarnation by means of the challenge Jesus presented to contemporary society rather than abstract statements of faith [22].

Many Baptists were shocked and disturbed by what Taylor had said. For a college principal to use the Assembly platform to express such unorthodox views, apparently with the support of the president and, if its report of the occasion was anything to go by, with the sympathy of the *Baptist Times*, threatened denominational unity[23]. Leading conservatives led the protests. Douglas McBain of Streatham said the denomination faced "a huge crisis of confidence" if "strong, Bible-based, evangelical convictions" were abandoned or wittered away[24]. In October a large gathering at Bloomsbury Central Baptist Church heard David Pawson of Guildford attack Taylor's views in an address entitled "How Much of a God was Jesus?"[25]

Demands were made of the Baptist Union Council to repudiate what Taylor had said and to reaffirm the Union's declaration of principle, which describes Jesus Christ as "God manifest in the flesh". In November 1971 the Council did reaffirm the declaration, but to the dismay of many conservatives attached an addendum to its resolution urging toleration. Its failure to clearly disassociate itself from Taylor led to Beasley-Murray's resignation as Council chairman. For bodies like the conservative Baptist

Revival Fellowship the issue was "the toleration of heresy within the Body of Christ". Its officers and committee members resigned from the Union's accredited list of ministers in protest and there was talk of "secession"[26]. Major disruption at the 1972 Assembly was avoided, mainly because of a strongly worded resolution reasserting the declaration of principle moved by Cyril Black. The unease provoked by Taylor's address did not quickly abate, and in some quarters was still being felt thirty years later.

Quite why the incident gave rise to such strong and lasting feelings is an intriguing question. Baptists were generally more conservative than other denominations, and views such as those expressed by Taylor were disturbing for many, but they were not by any means unusual or extreme, given the theological climate of the time. Reaction to the growing influence of liberal theology, through the publication of such books as Bishop John Robinson's *Honest to God* in 1963, was probably significant, giving rise to a determination not to see such ideas gain a hold within the Baptist denomination. The clarity and force of Taylor's delivery made it hard for those who disagreed with him to ignore what he said. There were those, including the leading elder statesman of the denomination, Ernest Payne, who doubted the Council's wisdom in allowing a difficult and potentially divisive subject to be dealt with in such a way on such an occasion[27]. Controversy was probably unavoidable, although the depth of feeling it generated was surprising. In theology as in politics, the late 1960s were a time of considerable passion and protest.

The impact of the furore on the college was significant. The college received "a number of letters" expressing "concern and apprehension" because Taylor was "held to have called in question the deity of Christ". As a result, a resolution supporting the principal was passed by the governors:

> From our knowledge of Principal Taylor, from the evidence of his work in the College and from the evidence of his devotion and dedication to Jesus Christ as Lord, we affirm our confidence in him as Principal of the College and give him our full support. We further believe it to be essential to a College that freedom of speech be assured to the College Principal and that his academic integrity be respected[28].

There was one abstention and no dissenters. A few churches subsequently wrote to say they would be withdrawing their support for the college. Probably the most important and worrying consequence of the 1971 controversy, however, was the decline in the number of ministerial students. Numbers were already dropping, with only twenty in training during the 1969-70 session. By the start of the 1972 session this had dropped to thirteen, and continued to be less than twenty throughout the 1970s. Within ten years of the amalgamation of the two colleges, ministerial students numbered only about a third of the total being trained at Rawdon and Manchester in the years immediately before they merged.

It is impossible to say how much of the decline was the direct consequence of the 1971 Assembly. Nationally, the number of Baptist ministerial students dropped by about a fifth between 1968 and 1973. Northern's decline was much more rapid. Other factors may have played a part in this. The disruption caused by the amalgamation, the almost constant building work between 1964 and 1967, the early departure of Russell and the illness and enforced early retirement of Dykes did not make a positive start easy. As a new college under new leadership, Northern was seeking to establish its identity on the basis of a distinctive modern approach to training, emphasising the importance of relevance to contemporary culture and ecumenical co-operation. Taylor's *Baptist Times*' article, *Tuned in to the Seventies*, part of a series on the colleges run by the newspaper in 1971, pulled no punches over the rejection of older training methods. Group work, projects and part-time training were all integral to its work, he said[29]. It was bound to take time for this to be understood and win support, even in the most favourable of circumstances. The controversy connected with Taylor's address added an extra difficulty to an already challenging situation.

The arrival of the Methodists

From 1972 onwards the variety of developments at Northern was dramatic, and for some outside observers at least, somewhat bewildering. No doubt the relatively small number of students and the college's reputation for radical innovation made experimentation easier. Co-operation with other theological colleges in Manchester continued to deepen. Arrangements were made to run the first-year course on an ecumenical basis. In the summer of 1972 the Methodist Conference decided that its training establishment in Manchester, Hartley Victoria College, would have to close because of the cost of maintaining it. The plan was to move its work to Bristol and unite with the college there. This posed a threat to the joint training courses Taylor was developing with them and the Congregational college. With plenty of rooms available at Brighton Grove, Taylor persuaded the governors to offer accommodation to Hartley Victoria as a way of preventing an immediate closure. This offer was accepted, and in October 1973 the Methodists moved in. The senior tutor, Richard Jones, was accompanied by one other tutor and thirty students, the majority of whom lived out of college. Taylor was keen to discuss a long-term partnership with the Methodists, and from the outset his intention was to enable them to remain permanently and to integrate work wherever possible[30].

The retirement of Farr in 1973 raised the question of future staff appointments. Taylor wanted to appoint a second full-time tutor under the age of forty to take Farr's place. Moore's position as a part-time tutor at the college seemed under threat for a while, but a way forward for him to stay was opened up when arrangements were made for the new appointment to be a joint one with the Congregationalists[31]. In May 1973 David Goodbourn was invited to take this up, the Baptist college paying two-thirds of his salary and the Congregational college one-third[32]. Goodbourn was just twenty-five. A graduate in politics and economics at Durham University, he had been responsible for student work at the Baptist Union for two years and then undertaken campaigning and educational work as director of the Baptist World Poverty Education Programme. As a layperson, he had no ministerial experience, and was appointed specifically to help develop lay training and to teach in the fields of social studies and adult education. Taylor saw the appointment as a step towards the development of the college as an ecumenical regional resource centre for lay and ministerial training.

As relations with the Methodist and Congregationalist colleges grew closer, the possibility of a united institute or college was aired. Co-operation was also developing with the Anglicans through their North Western Ordination Course (NWOC), which had been established a few years earlier for part-time ministerial training, mainly in the Church of England. The course used the college premises for its residential training weekends. In 1973 two Baptist students were also being trained under the auspices of NWOC. Taylor reassured the governors that he was involved in lecturing on the course and that there was no difficulty about its acceptance by the Baptist Union for ministerial recognition purposes[33].

Student life was naturally affected by these changes. Baptist ministerial students were by now only a small minority of those resident on the premises. They were out-numbered by Methodists, and there were more lay students using the building as a university hall of residence than both Baptist and Methodist ministerials together. Others, many of them married, lived off-site and came in for training, either on a full-time or part-time basis. The staff was also increasing in number and variety, not only with the arrival of tutors from other denominations, but also by the appointment of a domestic superintendent, who took over the matron's duties as well as becoming responsible for property maintenance and vacation conferences, and a secretary. Mr V.J. Ahern was appointed domestic superintendent in 1970, and held the post until his death in 1987. Mrs Rhoda Smith was secretary for over twenty years.

The growing diversity of people and courses and the increasingly ecumenical nature of training meant that the separate identity of the college became less distinct. This was a natural consequence of Taylor's ambition for an ecumenical, rather than a denominational, centre for theological education. An important expression of the unity he sought to achieve was the weekly communion service in the college chapel. Usually given the name Eucharist, an unfamiliar term for most Baptists, it was organised ecumenically and open to all. It soon came to be seen as the primary means whereby the people who lived and worked at Brighton Grove could find and demonstrate their corporate existence as a Christian community. It was ironic that it was held in a chapel erected specifically for worship by strict Baptists. Most of Taylor's predecessors in Manchester would have objected on principle to anyone other than those baptised as believers by immersion sharing in such a service[34].

Early in 1974 the governors met to consider a national report on the Baptist colleges. This had been produced by an advisory group established in response to *Ministry Tomorrow*. It had come to the conclusion that the future need for ministers did not justify four colleges, and urged closer cooperation between them and the consideration of mergers. Northern, it said, was "weak in ministerial students at present", and should pursue further the development of joint training with other denominations. The governors may have been happy with this endorsement of ecumenical work, but were in general critical of the report's findings. They challenged its assumption that training was best done in residential colleges where students were predominantly ministerial. They also questioned the report's emphasis on ministerial training, rather than the training of the whole church, and regretted that it did not take the ecumenical dimension more seriously. More attention should have been given, they said, to a college as "an ecumenical resource centre for the education and training of the whole church in a region"[35].

Small though the number of its Baptist ministerial students was, and different as was its approach to training from that of the other colleges, Northern had confidence in the direction in which it was moving. It may have embarked on a risky venture, but it sensed that it had an opportunity to achieve something important and new. Trusting in the energy and vision of its principal, it was not afraid to play the role of pioneer.

Developing new courses

Goodbourn and Taylor spearheaded the development of several initiatives in lay training, as part of their vision for the college as a regional resource centre for theological education. Even though they were primarily designed for lay students, little distinction was made in practice between lay and ministerial students; courses and other training events were attended by both. Some were specifically directed at Baptists, but most were deliberately organised across denominational lines.

The most important organisational development was the creation of the Manchester Christian Institute. This formally came into existence in 1977 after four years of discussion and planning involving most of the main denominations. As early as the autumn of 1973, when the Methodists moved into the Brighton Grove premises, the establishment of such a body was raised at a governors' meeting[36]. A working party was set up to explore how it could be done, and in May 1974 it proposed an institute that would incorporate the United Reformed Church and Congregationalists in the form of their Northern College, the Methodists, the Unitarians, NWOC and the William Temple Foundation, as well as Northern Baptist College. The aims of the institute were:

- to encourage the mutual involvement of ministers and laity in the practice of theology.
- to endeavour to respond to and derive much of its emphasis from the actual situations, problems, opportunities and tasks of individuals and groups, whether they find their main centre of interest outside or inside the church.
- to establish recognised links between its member bodies and associates[37].

Taylor saw it as a vehicle for the realisation of his goal of relevant, ecumenical training for the whole Church. He hoped that the institute would offer courses for ministerial candidates, ministers and the laity, and would pioneer "a number of less traditional policies" with regard to theological education[38]. He reassured the governors that the proposal did not amount to the setting up of a united college. In 1976 they agreed to be one of the institute's sponsors and to provide an office for it at Brighton Grove. The other sponsors were Northern College, which provided training for both the United Reformed Church and the Congregationalists, the Methodist Division of Ministries, the United Reformed Church, NWOC and the Anglican Diocese of Manchester. The Unitarian college became an associate member. A representative of the Roman Catholic Training Centre at Upholland was co-opted onto the institute's council at its first meeting in September 1977. Taylor and Goodbourn were the Baptist representatives. It was primarily Taylor's creation, and he was appointed secretary. Goodbourn was given the task of "making it work"[39].

The institute provided an official framework to existing co-operation, and gave fresh impetus to training on an ecumenical basis. It was described by the *Baptist Times* as "an information network and co-ordinating office" for Christian education and training[40]. In many ways its creation belonged more to the general development of church co-operation in Manchester than to the history of the college itself. The college was at the centre of its work, however, both physically, as its premises were used as a base, and also because of the involvement of Taylor and Goodbourn.

By 1977 the college was making its resources available to the wider church through various kinds of open courses, visiting Baptist churches to hold conferences and organising events at Brighton Grove. The latter included Saturday conferences for local people called "talkabouts", which dealt with particular topics of interest, weekly courses for ministers and lay people, including college students, on such subjects as the practice of theology and counselling ("Tuesdays at Brighton Grove"), and occasional "meet the author" events. Accommodation was also made available for ministers on sabbatical study leave. In addition the institute developed its own ecumenical programme of adult education.

In 1975 Taylor and Goodbourn attended an international conference in Windsor on the future of theological education. One of the main themes to emerge from this was that

David Goodbourn

training for ministry and the practice of ministry belonged together. They should therefore not be separated but be undertaken side by side, the work of ministry itself being the basis of training. The experience of theological education in developing countries, and especially in India, lay behind this idea. It met with an enthusiastic response from Taylor and Goodbourn. They decided that such a pattern of training should be introduced at Manchester. At the meetings of the education committee and the governors in the following Spring they received support for this to be investigated. It was given the title "an alternative pattern of training", or APT, and work soon got underway to sort out the details of how it could be implemented[41].

As well as Taylor's and Goodbourn's attraction to the principle behind this method of training, it was also relevant for the continuing anxiety over low student numbers. In the mid-1970s there were consistently only around twelve altogether training for the Baptist ministry, a few of whom were part-time students taking the North West Ordination Course. Efforts were made from 1976 onwards to publicise the college more effectively in the churches in an attempt to reverse the downward trend. Apart from the college's unpopularity in many churches because of Taylor's reputation for holding liberal theological views, it was also becoming evident that a residential style of training was not appropriate for all those who desired training for ministry, especially older students with family responsibilities. Church-based training provided a way of meeting their particular needs.

In October 1977 Taylor introduced a draft prospectus for the APT course to the governors. The main base for training would no longer be the college but a church, where the student would be placed as minister. The placement would be carefully monitored by the college, each student living near their church and spending the equivalent of three days a week working as a minister. Consideration would be given to the students' previous experience of ministry before accepting them for APT. One and a half days a week would be spent at college, with additional evening and weekend classes being undertaken, and also study weeks during the vacations. College work would be closely related to the actual experience of ministry, its content varying according to the needs of the students. The academic side of training would be covered through the university's Certificate of Religious Studies, a qualification designed for non-degree students. It would be a three-year course

The governors gave their approval, and the Baptist Union accepted it as adequate for the purposes of denominational accreditation. By the Spring of 1978 the first applications had been received, and five students were accepted to start their APT course in October[42]. The *Baptist Times* described it as "just what the doctor ordered" for two of them. Both had experience of ministry already, Gillian Boorne having previously served with the Baptist Missionary Society in Angola and Kenneth Harris for several years as a lay pastor[43].

The Brighton Grove community in the 1970s, with M.H. Taylor near the centre.

The initial response to APT was encouraging. The college invited John Nicholson, a Baptist minister on the governing body and then working with the British Council of Churches, to become a part-time tutor with responsibility for administering the scheme, especially by supervising the placement of students in churches. Initially this was for just one day a week, but a year later, when Nicholson was appointed association minister by the Lancashire and Cheshire Association, his time at the college was doubled.

There were, then, from 1978, four tutors at the college, all of them, apart from Taylor, employed in a part-time capacity. Student numbers were higher in 1978 than for several years. The annual report that year listed no fewer than ten new ministerial students, plus two new "open option" students, more than the total in the entire college during the previous session[44]. The introduction of APT was responsible, at least in part, for this turn-around.

While APT was being introduced, an additional boost to the college was the reception of a report on its work by a team of inspectors in February 1978. Periodic inspections were a requirement of Methodist colleges, and, when the time came for Hartley Victoria College to submit to this examination in November 1977, Northern decided to join them, in the true spirit of ecumenism. Three inspectors were appointed, Anthony Dyson from the university, John Turner from the Methodist Church and Douglas Sparkes from the Baptist Union.

In their report, much of which covered both colleges, the inspectors commented favourably on the way the relationship between the Baptists and the Methodists had developed. They advised that a joint board of studies be set up to formalise arrangements for joint courses. They commended the ecumenical worship and the way the building was used by both lay and ministerial students. They drew attention to the pressure tutors were under, and the danger of an "uncontrolled proliferation of responsibilities not subject to the control of corporate planning". They also highlighted several weaknesses in the training provision and warned about the risks involved in moving away from a full-time residential course[45]. Its general conclusion, however, was that the two colleges constituted a centre of excellence. Their continuing presence was needed as the only colleges in the north of England for both denominations, and deserved support from both Baptist and Methodist authorities nationally[46].

The report specifically recommended that the Baptists provide fuller instruction in denominational history and doctrine, and that a member of staff be appointed for the forthcoming APT course, a recommendation that was immediately implemented with the appointment of Nicholson. In an appendix directed specifically at the Baptist college, the inspectors referred to its reputation as having "a theological emphasis left of centre", adding that in their opinion this was unjustified. They pointed out that a significantly lower proportion of Baptist ministerial students was being trained at Northern than a decade earlier, and that the current number was "only just adequate". It was, they said, the responsibility of the governors to communicate more effectively the theological diversity in the college. They identified a tendency for the governors to agree a policy, but then give insufficient practical support and backing for its implementation, leaving Taylor in "an isolated position". This was partly, they acknowledged, the result of Taylor's personal ability, in particular "the cogency and power with which he can order the arguments he uses to support his case"[47]. It seems they felt that the governors were not bearing their share of responsibility for the college. One of the consequences was the decision to create a publicity committee, under the chairmanship of R.G.S. Harvey, to promote the interests of the college and to recruit candidates for the various courses on offer[48].

The inspectors' report and the governors' response to it came at a crucial time in the college's history. The effect was undoubtedly positive. The strengthening of the team of tutors with the arrival of Nicholson in 1978 was important in enabling APT to expand. Another important decision was on the horizon. Moore was due to retire in 1981, and a successor would have to be appointed. The inspectors encouraged the governors to take responsibility for this[49].

One of Taylor's duties was that of being the secretary of a body known as the Baptist Colleges Joint Consultative Committee. This consisted of representatives of the English, Scottish and Welsh Baptist Unions, the Baptist Missionary Society and the seven recognised denominational colleges. It was created in 1976 as a forum for discussing matters of mutual concern related to ministerial, missionary and lay training. The selection of ministerial students, the content of courses, settlement in churches at the end of training, financial support for students and in-service training for newly qualified ministers were all debated. Important though these topics were, the committee seemed to have little influence on decisions at the college.

Most of the college's annual reports in the mid- and late-1970s included an informal photograph of a large number of students, staff and family members taken in the college quadrangle *(one example of these is given on page 242)*. No attempt was made to distinguish ministerial from lay students, Baptist students from others, or students from staff. The informality was in marked contrast to the formal photographs of Baptist students and tutors taken in earlier years. Suits and ties had been replaced by open-necked, casual shirts and jumpers, the sober expressions by broad grins.

The photographs reflected the rapid transition in college life that had taken place. The atmosphere was experimental, informal and non-denominational. Baptist ministerial students did little together as a separate group. Academic courses taken at the university were very varied, the fifteen students successfully completing courses between 1975 and 1977 working between them for three different degrees and two different certificates. College-based training and corporate worship was conducted ecumenically, some involving lay as well as ministerial students. Some students were part-time.

Many at the college were proud of its reputation for theological radicalism, even though this was often misunderstood, and sometimes heavily criticised, by others. There was no doubting the revolution that had taken place. The process of doing theology had been given a new context, both ecumenically and in terms of its relation with the world outside the church. Its advocates maintained that this was the only way theological reflection could seriously and relevantly be undertaken. Brighton Grove was certainly an exciting and intellectually challenging place to prepare for ministry. Guest preachers at the weekly Eucharist included professors of theology with international reputations, leading figures from all the major denominations, and prominent men and women representing every theological point of view. The worship was unpredictable and stimulating.

There were opportunities for discussion and friendship with students from a wide range of backgrounds, studying many different subjects.

Critics, on the other hand, felt that in this melting pot of experiences and activities not enough care was given to providing a proper foundation for theological reflection. They doubted whether it could be described as theology, in any Biblical sense, at all. Could a college committed to such a radical transformation of ministerial training provide ministers for churches that, for the most part, did not understand most of what was going on, and were uneasy about what they saw and heard? Also, it was far from clear where the experiments in ecumenical training would lead. Given denominational divisions over ministerial recognition and funding, could ministerial training really be done ecumenically? Even among Northern's supporters, it was not always easy to find definite answers to such questions.

Thanks largely to Local Education Authority grants, the finances of the college were in a reasonably good condition, but the future was by no means secure. A lot depended on the impact of APT. Nothing like it existed in any of the other colleges. Could it be organised effectively? Could churches be found willing to be partners in the provision of training? Would it be popular with men and women seeking training for ministry? What effect would it have on the general life of the college? In 1978 APT seemed to have got off to a good start, but its fortunes over the next few years would be critical for the long-term future of the college as a whole.

---

1   Mrs W.J. Graham replaced Miss Wass in 1965.
2   Rev.Dr D.S. Russell, "Two in One", *Northern Baptist College Magazine*, no.1 (1965), p.10.
3   Rev.K.C. Dykes, "Baptists and unity – Obstacles in the Path" (*Northern Baptist College Magazine*, no.1 (1965), pp.10-13.
4   Cynthia Allegro, "There's a place for us" (*Northern Baptist College Magazine*, no.1 (1965) pp.15-17.
5   Rt Rev. Ambrose Reeves, "The Need for Action" (*Northern Baptist College Magazine*, no.1 (1965) pp.36-38.
6   Russell, "Two into One" p.10.
7   The Baptist Missionary Society also appointed one governor.

8   Governors Meeting, 16 October 1968. Dykes' illness prevented him being at this meeting.
9   Governors Meeting, 29 January 1969.
10 *Baptist Times*, 6 February 1969.
11 After his ministry in North Shields, Taylor was originally planning to take up a BMS appointment at Serampore College in India. The move to Birmingham occurred when this fell through.
12 Governors Meeting, 27 June 1969.
13 Beasley-Murray expressed his feelings in a letter to Dykes, dated 11 November 1967, following an address by Neville Clark, one of the authors of *Ministry Tomorrow* at a conference of principals and tutors. The letter is with the minutes of the conference at Northern Baptist College.
14 *Baptist Times,* 23 January 1969.
15 Author's conversation with Taylor in April 2000.
16 Michael Taylor, "The Church in Training: theological training and the Northern Baptist College: a basis for discussion" (unpublished, 1969).
17 *Ibid.*, pp.28-32.
18 *Ibid.*, p.64.
19 Education Committee, 15 April 1970.
20 Governors Meeting, 6 May 1970.
21 Education Committee, 21 April 1971. The proposed scheme for Anglican-Methodist unity was very much in the air at this time. Neither the joint training college nor the Theological Education Council materialised.
22 The text of Taylor's address was published, among others, by the Baptist Revival Fellowship.
23 Henton Davies expressed disagreement with Taylor's views immediately after the address, but this was not enough, in the minds of many, to eradicate his share of responsibility for it.
24 *Baptist Times* 1 July 1971.
25 The title of Pawson's address, which was later published, was dismissed by Henton Davies as "a polytheistic howler" (*Baptist Times,* 28 October 1971).
26 *Journal of the Baptist Revival Fellowship* no.110 (January/March 1972)
27 W.M.S. West, *To be a Pilgrim: a memoir of Ernest A. Payne* (Lutterworth Press: Guildford, 1983), p.171.
28 Governors' Meeting, 6 October 1971.
29 *Baptist Times*, 5 August 1971.
30 Governors Meeting, 25 October 1972 and 9 May 1973. In the event, the Methodists did stay.
31 Moore also had a part-time teaching appointment in a school.
32 By then the United Reformed Church had come into existence. The Congregational College, generally known as Northern College, was responsible for training ministers for both the URC and the Congregational Federation.
33 Governors Meeting, 9 May 1973.

34 His immediate predecessors, Dykes and Russell, accepted the practice of open communion, although Dykes was from a strict Baptist background.
35 *The Report of An Advisory Group and Other Related Documents made available by the Baptist Theological Colleges in England and Wales* (unpublished: 1974).
36 Governors Meeting, 17 October 1973.
37 Governors Meeting, 23 October 1974.
38 Education Committee, 26 March 1975.
39 Personal conversation between Goodbourn and the author, 15 October 2001.
40 *Baptist Times*, 16 March 1978.
41 Governors Meeting, 19 May 1976.
42 Strictly speaking, candidates did not apply for the APT course but were designated as APT students by the college after application for ministerial training. Of the five who started APT in 1978, two failed to complete the year and only two went on to complete their training successfully.
43 *Baptist Times*, 18 May 1978. The denominational newspaper provided positive coverage of Northern's initiatives during 1978, with prominent articles on the institute and the 1978 inspectors' report, as well as APT. This was no doubt helped by the fact that the editor, Geoff Locks, had taught Goodbourn, whose responsibility it was to get pieces to the newspaper, in Sunday School!
44 Open option students undertook the same training as ministerial students, but were unsure of their vocation to the ministry and had not been officially accepted as ministerial candidates.
45 A.O. Dyson, D.C. Sparkes and J.D. Turner, *Inspection of Northern Baptist College, Manchester and Hartley Victoria Methodist College, Manchester. February 1978* (unpublished), pp.6-7, 10 and 16.
46 *Ibid*, p.17. It should, perhaps, be noted that not long before this, Hartley Victoria's future was under serious threat of closure. Numbers at Northern were also causing serious concern about its future.
47 Dyson *et al*, *Inspection*, pp.20-24.
48 Governors Meeting, 17 May 1978. Harvey was trained at Manchester Baptist College in the 1950s. In 1982 he became General Secretary of the Baptist Missionary Society.
49 Dyson *et al*, *Inspection*, p.23.

Chapter Twelve
The Northern Federation for Training in Ministry: 1979-1999

Developing the new patterns of training

In the event, APT proved to be an astonishing success, and had a profound effect, not only on Northern Baptist College, but also on patterns of ministerial training in other places. The total number of ministerial students rose every year from a low of nine in 1978 to forty-one in 1985[1]. Full-time, college-based students remained at about the same level as before, never rising above twelve. APT students increased rapidly in the early years, levelling out at about fifteen from 1981. From 1983, the number of part-time students also increased quickly, so that by 1985 ministerial students were divided into three roughly equal sections: college-based, church-based and part-time.

The placement and supervision of fifteen or more APT students in churches over a wide geographical area, covering much of Lancashire, West Yorkshire and beyond, was a key element in the success of the course[2]. These tasks were undertaken by Nicholson. Earlier work had brought him extensive knowledge of local churches, both through the pastorate and as secretary of the Manchester and District Council of Churches. Responsibility for APT students and being Association Minister were complementary. Organisational skills and pastoral sensitivity were required for both, and the work of both the college and the association benefited.

APT was popular with both students and churches. It made training possible for those who felt called to ministry in Baptist churches, but for whom the traditional residential pattern was difficult or impossible. Smaller churches were able to enjoy regular ministry, often by mature students with significant pastoral experience, and to share with the college the important task of training. The college also benefited by being brought into a closer relationship with local churches, contributing directly to their ministry and mission.

There were from the start, however, doubts about whether such a course could provide an adequate preparation for ministry. Questions were asked about the adequacy of the University's Certificate in Religious Studies as a suitable academic qualification. The limitation of the student's experience to a single church, usually a small one, was felt by some to be too narrow. When the college reviewed the course after its first three years of operation, it was recognised that APT students sometimes found themselves "under very considerable pressure" because of the combined demands of college and church[3]. Probably the fiercest criticism came from other Baptist colleges, in particular Spurgeon's, with its conservative Biblical tradition. The annual meetings of principals and staff were often the scene of vigorous arguments about the value of the course. Ever since Taylor's 1971 address at the Assembly, many at Spurgeon's had regarded Northern with suspicion, if not hostility. The introduction of APT was taken as a sign that it had rejected serious theological scholarship as a basis for ministry. Taylor countered this objection by pointing out that APT students actually spent more time attending classes in theology and Biblical studies than Spurgeon's college-based students did, although this did little to alleviate the criticism[4]. From its inauguration, the Baptist Union expressed itself willing to accept APT as a recognised training programme for Baptist ministers. It went further, in allowing Home Mission grants to be given to support the student ministers.

The intention was to integrate church placements and training, and to divide the students' time equally between church work and college work, allowing time also for family and relaxation. At college, discussion groups and lectures were related to pastoral experience. Each church was encouraged to participate actively in the training process, mainly through the formation of church groups, which met regularly with students and tutors to review the students' progress.

The formation of a significant group of students undergoing a distinct programme of training had inevitable consequences on college life. APT students were in college for just two days a week, and to a large extent followed a separate course of study. On average, the APT students were older than their college-based counterparts, and were theologically more conservative, and more sympathetic to the charismatic movement. They were attracted more by the structure of the course than the college's reputation for radical ideas, and were not always at ease with the innovative style of ecumenical worship at the weekly Eucharist. Taylor felt that one of the weaknesses of the course was that it meant students could escape the intellectual challenge and threat of communal life in college more easily[5]. APT also represented a move away from the ecumenical approach to training. Although a small number of postgraduate Methodist students used the APT programme, neither the Methodists nor the Congregationalists embraced it for the purposes of ministerial training, with the result that it had a distinctively Baptist character.

The benefits of the new course contributed to the development of the pattern of training for residential students with the introduction of fourth-year internships for college-based students in 1981. These were run on similar lines to APT, and were organised jointly by the college and the URC/Congregationalists. In 1984 a new variant of APT known as community-based training was introduced. Students could be based in churches in deprived inner-city areas and, in addition to ministry within the church and college study, gained experience and training in community work under the auspices of the Salford Urban Mission. Between 1984 and 1987 three ministerial students were trained according to this pattern.

Alongside the establishment of APT, another important development that occurred during the early 1980s was the creation of a new programme of part-time training called the Christian Leadership Course (CLC). Although this was sponsored by the Manchester Christian Institute, most Baptists on the course were officially students of the college, having been accepted either as full ministerial students or as open option students seriously considering the ministry. At its inception, Goodbourn and Nicholson were appointed chairman and secretary of the committee responsible for CLC, Nicholson's hours being increased to allow for the extra work involved. It was run in conjunction with Northern (URC) College and included students being trained for ministry within the Congregational Federation, the United Reformed Church and the Moravian Church.

CLC was inaugurated in 1981. It offered a four-year part-time course for candidates intending to pursue ministry on a non-stipendiary and supplementary basis. It was designed for students who wished to continue their existing employment while being trained, and after ordination to exercise a part-time or spare-time ministry. Tutorial support and teaching was provided during weekends in Manchester and in regional tutorial groups. Students also attended the residential theology weeks run for the APT students. There had been a demand for training of this kind for some years, partially met through the 1970s by the North Western Ordination Course (by 1980 the Northern Ordination Course), in which a few Baptists had participated. Dissatisfaction with this, particularly because of its predominantly Anglican ethos, was partially responsible for the creation of CLC as an "ecumenical Free Church course"[6]. As with APT, the numbers of students grew rapidly and within a few years it became a major part of the college's work in providing ministerial training. In 1983 a similar, though shorter and less demanding, course for lay leaders was started by the institute, known as Church Leadership Training.

Another significant initiative taken by the Institute was the provision of training for the leaders of the predominantly black churches in Manchester. Inspired by the Centre for Black and White Christian Partnership in Birmingham, and supported by Manchester University, an evening course was developed by Goodbourn at Brighton Grove. In 1983 the first certificates in Religious Studies were awarded to its participants. It was part of a number of projects organised by the Institute to support leaders and members of black churches. It also arranged joint meetings of people from white majority and black majority churches in the city.

In 1981 Ernest Moore retired as tutor. Having been appointed a tutor at Rawdon twenty-five years earlier, he had been through the move to Manchester in 1964, and the revolution in theological training that had occurred since then. Always rather peripheral to the changes that had taken place, he had at one stage been encouraged by the education committee "to seek another sphere of service"[7]. He was replaced as tutor by Brian Haymes, who joined Taylor, Goodbourn and Nicholson on a full-time basis. Haymes had been trained for the ministry at Bristol Baptist College and received a PhD from Exeter University for his thesis *The Concept of the Knowledge of God*. He had sixteen years of pastoral experience in Bristol, Exeter and Nottingham, and had a special interest in the relations between Christianity and other faiths. The college's 1981 annual report described his main areas of responsibility as biblical studies and inter-faith dialogue. In practice, the college work of the tutors was not divided along subject divisions, although any university teaching they undertook naturally matched their fields of academic expertise. Taylor told the education committee that Haymes would be especially responsible for the college-based students, while Goodbourn concentrated on non-ministerial students and Nicholson the APT students[8].

Forming a training federation

The co-operation between the theological colleges in Manchester was formalised with the creation of the Northern Federation for Training in Ministry in October 1984. The idea of a more structured unity was raised during a review undertaken by Northern (URC) College of its work and future plans in 1980. It came to the conclusion that the best way forward involved the provision of training by the main Nonconformist denominations on one site. The parties that might be involved met to discuss how this could be achieved, and in 1981 both the URC and the small Unitarian college expressed their willingness to sell their premises. The governors of the Baptist college were not prepared to go this far, but in February 1982 agreed that their buildings could be leased to a new federation "for the purpose of continuing and developing ecumenical training for ministry in Manchester"[9]. The Methodists and the Northern Ordination Course were also involved, both already being based at Brighton Grove. The Moravians also came on board. Although it was decided that the Unitarians could not be members of any federation for doctrinal reasons, it was understood that they could have "associate standing".

For two years detailed negotiations took place over the legal and practical implications of forming a federation. Alongside Taylor, Jack

McKelvey, the Principal of the URC college, Graham Slater, since 1982 Principal of Hartley Victoria, and Ray Selby of the Northern Ordination Course were involved in these. The governors decided that the formation of a federation called for a change in the name of the college buildings. In view of their increasingly ecumenical use, "Northern Baptist College" was no longer appropriate. After a close contest between "Carey House" and "Luther King House", the latter was chosen. Both had strong Baptist associations, of course, but Luther King's contemporary significance, and his links with social justice, won the day over Carey's ecumenical and missionary credentials.

The federation was officially inaugurated at a service in the university chaplaincy in October 1984. The participants (including the Unitarians) committed themselves "to consult with one another over all that they do, to co-operate wherever possible and to share their resources"[10]. The college's 1985 Open Day provided an opportunity to celebrate the start of the federation and to officially rename the buildings. In view of the significance of Martin Luther King, Taylor was keen to have a speaker who would "be able to communicate effectively to a mainly white audience something of the black Christian experience" in Britain[11]. Paul Boateng, Chair of the Greater London Council's Police Committee and a Methodist local preacher, accepted his invitation to address the meeting.

The creation of the federation was an important symbolic step, and a statement of intent, but initially it made little practical difference to life in Luther King House. It was not until the URC and Unitarian college buildings had been sold, and their staff, students, books and furniture arrived in the summer and autumn of 1985, that its significance was really felt. Many courses were already run jointly, but being all together on one site created new opportunities for united worship and the development of deeper relationships among students and staff.

Brian Haymes: consolidation

A new name for the premises and the arrival of fresh faces from other colleges were not the only changes for Northern Baptist College in 1985. A succession of staff resignations made it one of the most significant periods in the college's history. Goodbourn had given notice the previous October of his new appointment as research officer with the Church of Scotland, and he left Manchester at Easter. He was replaced in June by Heather Walton. Unlike Goodbourn, whose appointment was shared with the URC and Congregationalists, Walton was appointed to a full-time post at the college. She came from the Methodist Division of Social Responsibility, where she had helped produce a report on black people and the Methodist Church. Her arrival was unprecedented in two respects. She was the first female tutor in the history of the college or its predecessors and the first non-Baptist.

Taylor handed a letter of resignation to the governors at their meeting on the college Open Day a few days after Walton's arrival. He had been appointed Director of Christian Aid and was to take up the appointment in October 1985. After fifteen years of remarkable leadership, the news caused understandable consternation. The sub-committee that had arranged Walton's appointment was hastily reconvened to start the search for his successor. A month later Haymes was interviewed and asked to take over as principal. His appointment was "ratified unanimously and joyfully" by the governors at their meeting in October. When the question of a service of recognition was raised, Haymes declined the suggestion, stating that "he was grateful to have

Brian Haymes

been recognized"[12]. Interestingly, Haymes was the first man trained at another college to be appointed principal at either Manchester or Northern.

In terms of its student numbers and finances, Taylor left the college in a healthy condition. Over forty ministerial students were due to start or continue their training that year, and there had been a surplus of over £11,000 in the college's general fund in the previous year. APT and CLC, which he, Goodbourn and Nicholson had created and established, had provided the college with two successful patterns of training, both of which by 1985 were being copied elsewhere. Church-based training, for example, was adopted by Spurgeon's College, and soon became an integral part of its training programme. Taylor had expanded Northern's work into the field of lay training. He had also been largely responsible for bringing the two other major Free Church colleges in Manchester together onto the Brighton Grove site and introducing a strong ecumenical spirit to the task of ministerial training. The federation and the Manchester Institute were significant institutional expressions of this. Taylor's personal qualities of intellectual and moral integrity, his leadership gifts and passion for social justice had been recognised not only by colleagues at the college, but also more widely as a magistrate and with the World Council of Churches. His membership of the WCC's Programme for Theological Education Commission had provided wide opportunities for debate and enriched his contribution to the college's own training programmes. Barrie White, principal of Regent's Park College, said of him that "he has never feared to press home the questions which he has believed need to be asked ... nor has he failed in finding creative answers to them"[13].

Circumstances had looked very different eight years earlier, when student numbers were at an all-time low and the college seemed in danger of losing its position as a place where Baptist ministers were trained. Taylor's commitment to ecumenism and radical change, especially when coupled with a reputation for liberal theology, had distanced him and the college from many of the churches they were supposed to be serving. The tide had been turned by the implementation of APT, and of CLC a little later. The inspectors' 1978 report, which recognised the value of what was happening, but also highlighted some shortcomings and provoked the governors to play a more active role in overseeing and publicising the college, also made a crucial contribution to the revival of the college's fortunes.

Perhaps the most significant factor in all that had been achieved since 1978 was the mutual friendship and respect among the tutors. Taylor, Nicholson and Goodbourn were together at the college from then until 1985, joined in 1981 by Haymes. Not only there, but also in the multiracial Moss Side Baptist Church and in innumerable other joint activities, their ability to complement each other and enjoy working together was vitally important. In bringing significant and varied experience of pastoral leadership in local churches, Nicholson and Haymes were well able to relate the many exciting new ideas and projects emerging from the college to the realities of church life.

The photograph of the tutorial staff in the college's annual report for 1985 pictured Haymes, Nicholson and Walton. Shortly afterwards, Nicholson was appointed Area Superintendent for the North East of England, leaving Haymes as the sole survivor of the four who had been in post at the beginning of the year. The staffing committee's work continued through the autumn to find at least two new tutors as soon as possible. Before the end of the year two Baptist ministers had been appointed. Ernest Whalley arrived from Bradford as a full-time tutor, and Keith Hobbs moved from Grimsby to take up Nicholson's position as joint tutor and minister for the Lancashire and Cheshire Association.

Apart from staff changes, 1985 also saw the erection of a block of ten married students' flats at Brighton Grove, supplied by the Baptist Housing Association. Planned for several years, these increased accommodation for married students on the site to twelve units. The year was also notable because it marked the death of Kenneth Dykes, whose name had appeared on the list of staff as principal emeritus since 1969. In one of his last duties as principal, Taylor gave a warm tribute to his predecessor at the funeral service on 15 July, an event that, given the circumstances of Dykes' enforced retirement, was not without a trace of irony.

At their first regular meeting in 1986, the governors were asked to ratify not only the appointments of Whalley and Hobbs, but also that of Richard Kidd. Kidd, a graduate of Cambridge University in mathematics who had undertaken theological study and training at Spurgeon's and Regent's Park Colleges and received a DPhil for a thesis in systematic theology, had been minister at Theydon Bois in Essex. The staffing committee felt that an increase in the number of tutors to five was justified by the growth of student numbers. Like Hobbs, the appointment was half-time, the college sharing Kidd with the Greenfield Baptist/Congregational Church at Urmston. Kidd and Haymes had worked together for several years as part of a group of Baptist ministers reflecting and writing on theological themes of relevance to the denomination[14]. In this unprecedented spate of new appointments, Walton (June 1985), Whalley (February 1986), Hobbs (April 1986) and Kidd (September 1986) all joined the team of tutors within little more than a year, during the course of which Haymes had also became Principal (October 1985).

Haymes and his colleagues faced a series of considerable challenges. The first was to familiarise themselves with their new situation, divide up their various responsibilities and establish good working relationships. They were thrown together in such rapid succession that there had been no time to plan how their individual abilities and personalities could best be used within the existing work of the college, or contribute to its future development. A second major challenge lay in taking over the direction of the various college courses. The situation was complicated, involving three distinct methods of ministerial training (APT, college-based and part-time). Each one was demanding in terms of administration, and there was a real risk of fragmentation, leading to the duplication of effort and a loss of unity in the college's work. Over and above ministerial training, and at times overlapping with it, was the provision of lay training. A third challenge was coping with new institutional relationships created by the formation of the federation, the arrival of the URC college at Luther King House, and changes at the university. When Haymes was appointed, the principal's duties included being warden of Luther King House as a university hall of residence. There were many practical issues to be resolved over finance and accommodation. More fundamentally, the significance of the federation and its relationships with the individual colleges, the institute, the university and, indeed, the wider Church were far from clear.

Haymes began by tackling the training courses for which the college was responsible. Their basic shape was maintained, but modifications were soon introduced. He believed that a greater degree of integration in training was required, and introduced a "New Integrated Programme" of ministerial formation, within which more than one "path" could be followed. The reforms were based on the principle that the process of ministerial formation entailed a balance of academic study, the development of practical skills and growth in personal spirituality. It took place in the context of the college, ministry in local churches and the community. Full-time students could still be based either at the college or in a church, but they would be regarded as following two variations of one course, rather than two separate courses. The church-based course was extended to four years, bringing it in line with the college-based course, and short community placements were introduced for both sets of students. The same university certificates, diplomas and degrees were made available to all, and training was undertaken together when the church-based students were in college. The university's introduction of a four-year part-time BA degree course was important in making this possible. For a while, the old-style APT course ran alongside the new integrated course. A new element for college-based students was the so-called "Monday programme". Led by Walton from her Moss Side home, it enabled students to experience first-hand the problems of poverty and unemployment in an inner-city area, and afterwards to share their reactions and thoughts in an informal group setting.

Dissatisfaction with elements of CLC also led to changes. A lack of clarity about the division of responsibility between the institute and the college became a problem once the strong link provided by Goodbourn and Nicholson had disappeared. Difficulties also arose over the maintenance of effective local tutorial groups, and with the level of staff-student contact[15]. It was decided to extend the course for Baptist ministerial students to five years from 1987, the fifth year designed specifically "as a preparation for Baptist ministry"[16]. It continued to be popular with students from a range of church backgrounds.

The relationship between the federation and the college was a constant topic of debate. It had been decided to lease the premises to the federation for a nominal sum. This probably helped persuade the other colleges to join, but it also led to serious financial deficits for the college and large surpluses for the federation until the imbalance was put right in 1989[17]. The other members of the federation made steadily increasing demands for accommodation at Luther King House, resulting in a decline in the number of rooms available for lay students from the university. In 1987 there were only five. This was not a financial problem, as the college made very little profit, if any, from this arrangement. It did raise a question of principle about the value of maintaining a mixed student community, however. The federation generally did not support the college's policy, that had developed over the years, of positively encouraging the presence of lay students as a contribution to ministerial training. Their role was regarded as simply to take up surplus space[18]. It was probably inevitable that this should be the view that prevailed, given the new and expanding ways in which Luther King House was being used.

The relationship between the institute and the federation sometimes also needed clarifying. Largely the brainchild of Taylor as a means of co-operation between the colleges, the institute's role had been inevitably affected by the formation of the federation; the institute's work as an ecumenical agency for lay and part-time training had developed considerably. This was reflected in the appointment of its own director, John Ponter, in 1985. Financial support for Ponter became the responsibility of the federation.

In 1987 the college was visited for the second time by a team of inspectors, this time as part of an inspection of the federation and its constituent colleges as a whole. Their report highlighted the need to resolve some of the uncertainties that existed in the relations between the various bodies using Luther King House, especially over finance, decision-making and future planning. It also urged the need to improve the federation's library and to appoint a librarian[19].

Several staff changes took place in 1989 and 1990. The most significant was the departure of Hobbs for the post of Baptist Area Superintendent for the North West. This brought to an end the joint appointment by the Lancashire and Cheshire Association and the college that had existed since Nicholson's appointment in 1978. Kidd was appointed to a full-time post, the sharing agreement with the Urmston church continuing with the appointment of a new part-time tutor, Martin Scott of Jarrow. At the same time, Whalley became part-time, dividing his duties at the college with those of ministry in the South West Manchester Group of URC and Baptist churches. From 1990, then, two of the five tutors were "tutor-ministers". In enabling the cost of an appointment to be shared, this brought financial advantages for church and college. More importantly, it enabled staff, like many of the students, to bring current experience of ministry to the training process. One of the initiatives spearheaded by Scott was the production of a college journal called *Theology Themes*, containing articles based on the lectures given at termly study weeks[20].

During the late 1980s and early 1990s, leaving students faced increasing difficulty in finding churches in which to commence their ministry. During this period about ten students finished their training each year, and each year one or more were designated in the autumn annual report as "still to settle". In 1993 as many as half had been unable to find a church. This was a national problem of the supply and demand for paid ministers and affected all the colleges. It was discussed at the joint colleges' consultative committee several times from 1987 onwards. One of the Northern representatives asked whether some kind of central selection system for ministerial students could be operated[21]. This did not prove generally acceptable, but in 1992 the college announced that it was voluntarily accepting a limit of forty on the total number of ministerial students in training at any one time[22].

The consultative committee also discussed a number of other matters of vital interest to Northern at around this time. One was the question of financial support for students. Changes in the funding of higher education nationally meant that grants from Local Education Authorities were no longer as readily available for theological students. This was posing serious problems for all the colleges. Support for training had been one of the objects of the Baptist Union's 1964 Ter-Jubilee Fund, from which the college had benefited. Twenty-five years later, the need for such help was considerable. The sale of Baptist Church House in London in 1990 meant that it became a realistic possibility. The Union agreed to designate the income earned by some of the capital realised by the sale for student support.

Another matter debated by the consultative committee was the question of women in ministry. Although settlement of women ministers in churches continued to be difficult, the number of women ministerial students had been steadily increasing. The college was particularly keen to eliminate any distinction between male and female candidates, and to encourage the acceptance of women ministers. In 1990, by which time more than one in four students were female, Northern joined with the other Baptist colleges in affirming the ministry of women and recognising the need to do more to support it[23]

Issues such as the supply of ministers, student funding and women in ministry involved all the colleges and, indeed, the denomination as a whole. They drew the colleges closer together and made the consultative committee and staff conferences important occasions for colleges and Union alike, enabling a greater sense of partnership and friendship to develop. This was a welcome contrast to the somewhat tense relationships of a decade before. Northern's ecumenical setting and its part-time training programme became increasingly seen as important contributions to the national provision of Baptist ministerial preparation, rather than marginal and radical[24].

In 1992 Haymes was elected vice-president of the Baptist Union, the first principal from the north to be given this honour since Henry Townsend in 1935. A few months later the governors were told that two legacies, amounting in total to about £3 million, had been left to the college. They came from the estate of two sisters, Ellen Bennett and Maud Reddihough, whose support for the college's work dated from links with Rawdon College before the amalgamation of 1964. It soon became apparent that interest on the capital would increase the college's annual receipts by £150,000 - £200,000, doubling its existing income. This was obviously going to make a big difference.

In order to decide how best to use the money, the college engaged in a wide-ranging consultation exercise with its supporters. Resulting from this, it was resolved to use the money, as far as possible, to fund new initiatives rather than merely to supplement the existing work of the college. These initiatives should be for the benefit not just of the college's work in Manchester but its extended work of training and education throughout the north and the midlands. Three specific ideas were put forward: the creation of a fund to support ministerial students and their families at the college, the establishment of partnerships with colleges elsewhere in the world, and the creation of a "learning community" in those parts of the country served by the college. It was envisaged that this third project would take the bulk of the money.

New partnerships and a new ecumenical degree

While the governors were drawing up more detailed proposals, and making decisions about the use of interest already received, Haymes announced his resignation as principal, having been appointed president of his old college in Bristol. Kidd, who had been acting as principal during Haymes' presidency of the Baptist Union, was appointed in his place. He took up his new post in 1994. By then there were some new faces on the staff team at the college. Susan Durber, a URC minister, had been appointed as a third part-time tutor in 1992, and the Mennonites Alan and Eleanor Kreider had been welcomed as "scholars in residence". Alec Balfe-Mitchell's contribution to the training programme of the college as minister of the United People's Church in Moss Side was recognised by his appointment as "minister tutor". Since 1994, other college appointments were made, including the arrival of Brian Howden from Lymm (1994) as tutor with special responsibility for church-based students, and more recently Rachel Jenkins (1996), Anne Dunkley (1999), who had already served the college part-time as a regional key-worker, and Sean Winter (2000)[25].

Richard Kidd

It fell to Kidd to oversee the implementation of the plans for the Bennett-Reddihough money. Links with churches overseas, particularly in developing countries, had existed for many years by means of regular visitors from abroad, visits overseas by students and staff, and the presence of foreign students at the college. Since 1985 students from Kenya and India had studied at Northern. Although few missionaries were now being trained at the college, a partnership with the Church in El Salvador resulted from the work of a past student in that country. David Quinney Mee, a missionary with the Baptist Missionary Society, had left the college in 1980 and gone to El Salvador in 1988. The extra financial resources now available enabled a number of exchange visits by students and staff to take place, and gifts to be made to help establish a new seminary. In 1993, Haymes and Kidd both went to South Africa to attend a conference of theological teachers. During his visit, Kidd made contact with the college of the Baptist Convention in Soweto, Johannesburg. Formal agreements between the college and the two colleges in El Salvador and South Africa were later signed, with regular exchanges and consultation taking place.

The creation of a learning community for the north and midlands was, as had been envisaged, a more substantial development. In May 1994 it was decided to allocate an annual sum of £50,000 for the project, mainly to fund the appointment of a full-time facilitator and two half-time development workers. The college had some experience to build on as it had recently established a course on church planting and evangelism as a joint venture with the Church Army, the Oasis Trust and Spurgeon's College; this was based in Sheffield for the north of England. It had also, with the federation, already been considering the possibility of establishing regional centres. The Community Learning Network was officially inaugurated in 1995. Jayne Scott was appointed the first full-time tutor to oversee its work. Married to fellow tutor Martin Scott, she came from an appointment as a training officer with the URC. The network was designed to respond to requests from churches and others for help with training and theological reflection, and to facilitate the setting up and leading of local groups. At the end of 1996 the governors heard that eight or nine initiatives were underway, covering such topics as attitudes to black Christians in Baptist churches and ministering to women in situations of a crisis pregnancy[26].

Predictably, regular income from the churches dropped substantially once news of the huge increase in the college's financial assets became public knowledge. Large deficits over several years had to be met by transfers to the general fund from the Bennett-Reddihough Trust Fund.

Discussions between the members of the federation concentrated on the search for closer integration and more effective management. By 1993 the need for change became more pressing because of developments at the university. The Faculty of Theology was being dismantled and the degrees offered by the Department of Theology and Religions did not meet the needs of ministerial students. The combination of academic study and practical experience of ministry that had been pioneered by the college, and was increasingly being adopted by the other partners in the federation, was no longer possible under the auspices of the department. The University's Extra-Mural Department, which had offered certificates and diplomas to external students, such as those studying through the institute, was also closing down.

A new opportunity presented itself, however, when it became possible for the federation to offer its own diplomas and degrees, validated by the university. The federation's board of studies recommended to its constituent colleges that it become "an affiliated college" of the university in order to take advantage of this[27]. The Baptists, as well as the Methodists, under their new Principal John Harrod, the URC and the institute were all persuaded of the merits of this course of action, and the work of designing the new qualifications was rapidly put in hand. The "Faith in Living: Ecumenical Christian Discipleship and Ordination Course" was approved by the university and became the basis of training in the federation from 1994 onwards. It was a modular course, integrating academic study and experience, leading to a certificate, diploma or BA degree in contextual theology. It was available for lay and ministerial students, on a full or part-time basis, and incorporated "creative methods of assessment". While the course was being designed and put in place, the federation itself was restructured by the creation of a Council, a business committee and the appointment of a Dean[28]. Soon post-graduate degrees were also being offered.

The restructuring of the federation and the development of its relations with the college took a further step with a proposal to transfer the ownership of Luther King House from Northern Baptist College to an ecumenical Trust. The process of achieving this was a complex one, but with the support of the governors it began in the summer of 1998[29].

The thirty-five years following the creation of Northern Baptist College were a time of considerable complexity and constant change. New ideas about theological education and ministry and changing patterns of church life resulted in the creation of new types of courses, the introduction of new kinds of staff appointments and the formation of new partnerships with other church bodies. At times it looked as though the college's constant process of innovation would lead to chaos. The pressure on staff to manage the various demands placed on them was enormous, and was commented on as a matter of concern in both the inspection reports that were made. The college under Taylor was a dynamic, creative place in which old boundary lines and presuppositions disappeared. Those who worked and studied with him acknowledged it to be an exhilarating place to work. In the long run, however, constant innovation was unsustainable. The integration that took place under Haymes, and the eventual consolidation of training within the federation, was a necessary response to what could have become a threatening lack of coherence.

In the 1970s, neither the Baptists nor the other Free Church denominations were ready to embrace the kind of changes that were being proposed at the college. The ideas put forward were unfamiliar and strange. Many of these had their roots in new ways of thinking derived from America or Asia, often brought to the college through Taylor's contacts with the World Council of Churches. Gradually, however, through the 1980s and 1990s, and not without great effort and many hours of discussion, these radical ideas took on a less threatening appearance. It became natural to think of ministerial training as something that could and should be done ecumenically. New ways of reflection integrated theology and practice and became known as practical or contextual theology; these became the norm. Church-based training, far from being a risky experiment, became mainstream. Part-time training was accepted as a valid route into ministry. Colleges were increasingly regarded as resource centres for the theological education and training of the whole church, rather than merely as places for training people for ordination. Initially regarded with suspicion, the college came to take its place, with others, at the heart of denominational and ecumenical thinking on ministerial training.

The college's circumstances provided it with the opportunity to embrace these new ideas earlier than most. The presence of several Nonconformist theological colleges in Manchester, all linked closely to the university, provided the stimulus and opportunity for increasing levels of co-operation. This was encouraged by the national drive for church unity in the early 1970s. Added to this was the fact that all three main Nonconformist colleges faced financial pressures, mainly because of their small size. In the case of the Methodists and the URC this problem was compounded by their uneconomic premises. Baptist premises were both modern and too big for their own purposes, so when Hartley Victoria was threatened with closure the advantages of consolidating the work on one site were obvious. Several years later similar reasoning led the URC college to the same conclusion. Russell's earlier insistence that the new college should have new premises proved, then, to be highly significant. The consolidation of the federation as the primary provider of training through its own Faith in Living Course was the consequence of changes at the university as much as the desire of the colleges to work more closely together.

However, while circumstances may have presented the college with the opportunity for moving forward, that opportunity still had to be grasped. There was nothing inevitable about the changes that occurred. Often they only happened because the college was prepared to make sacrifices to see them realised. In the case of two of the most important developments, the creation of part-time and church-based ministerial training, the initiative lay firmly with the college. Throughout these years, the Baptist college was the chief pioneer, bringing forward new ideas and urging others to help them become reality.

A thorough evaluation of the college's contribution to ministerial training in the second half of the twentieth century lies beyond the scope of this historical account. The story has its negative as well as its positive side. Fundamentally, the college existed to serve the Kingdom of God, but in practice this meant serving the needs of Baptist churches in a large part of England. Its reputation for radical ideas and innovation, sometimes proudly promoted by its supporters, undoubtedly helped establish close ties of co-operation and affection among some, but also alienated the college from many of these churches. Lack of resources, especially of staff time, also meant that the courses offered could not always be managed well. Supervision of those on part-time training and the integration of church-based students into college life were not always all that they should have been. In spite of this, however, the value of what was achieved and the interest in ministerial formation that was generated were highly significant. The college played a pioneering role in enabling ministers to be trained in ways that met the needs of a changing Church and society, both within the Baptist denomination and beyond.

---

1   The figure of 43 that is sometimes given includes two "open option" students.
2   It was sometimes made more difficult because the churches where students were placed called them to full-time ministry at the end of their training. Although this may have been a sign of success, it also reduced the number of churches available to the college for student placements.
3   Governors Meeting, 21 October 1981.
4   In 1986, Spurgeon's introduced church-based training of its own. By then Regent's Park College was also offering a similar course.
5   In personal conversation with the author, 15 April 2000.
6   Governors Meeting, 21 October 1981.
7   Education Committee, 10 January and 12 April 1972. A recommendation to this effect was not approved by the governors. Moore was at that time sharing his time equally between the college and teaching in a school.
8   Education Committee, 1 April 1981.
9   Governors Meeting, 15 February 1982.
10 Statement made at the inauguration of the federation and signed by representatives of the Hartley Victoria, Northern Baptist, Northern (URC) and the Unitarian colleges and the Northern Ordination Course. David Charley, chairman of the college governors, signed on behalf of the Baptists.
11 Correspondence in Northern Baptist College's Record Room.
12 Governors' Meeting, 28 October 1985.
13 *Baptist Times,* 13 June 1985.

14 The group, which also included Keith Clements, Paul Fiddes and Roger Hayden, produced two volumes of essays. One in 1981 entitled *A Call to Mind: Baptist Essays Towards a Theology of Commitment*, which was a response to the Baptist Union's *Call to Commitment* issued at the 1980 annual Assembly, and another in 1985 entitled *Bound to Love: The Covenant Basis of Baptist Life and Mission*. The group was inspired to work together in this way by Leonard Champion's 1979 plea for "a clearer, more coherent and more widely accepted theology" among Baptists (Keith W. Clements *et al*, *A Call to Mind* (Baptist Union: London, 1981), p.3).
15 Governors Meetings, 19 May and 27 October 1986.
16 Governors Meeting, 18 May 1987.
17 Financial Report, 1989.
18 Governors Meeting, 16 May 1988.
19 Governors Meeting, 30 October 1987. A summary of the inspectors' report was also given in the 1987 annual report.
20 *Theology Themes* began life in 1992 and continued until 1997, by which time the approach to study weeks had altered and production of the journal was no longer realistic.
21 Joint Baptist Colleges Consultative Committee, 10 September 1987.
22 1992 Annual Report. Nationally, the Baptist colleges accepted the need to keep the number of ministerial students being trained to a maximum of 63 a year (see the Baptist Union's 1998 report, *Partners Together: The Colleges and the rest of the Baptist Union of Great Britain*, p.13). At Northern, ministerial student numbers began to drop well below 40 from about this time onwards, leading to expressions of concern in the mid-1990s.
23 1990 Annual Report.
24 A document prepared by the principals of the colleges in January 1997 entitled *The Complementarity of the Baptist Colleges in Membership with the Baptist Union of Great Britain* describes this growing sense of partnership.
25 See the afterword for more details on the most recent developments.
26 Governors Meeting, 25 November 1996. The Network has since 1995 expanded and developed. In 2002 there were five field-workers, one for each of the five associations in the North and Midlands, working in conjunction with a full-time tutor based at the college.
27 Governors Meeting, 25 October 1993.
28 Governors Meetings, 23 May 1994 and 24 October 1994. John Sutcliffe, Ponter's successor as director of the institute, played a leading role in the creation of the new Faith in Living courses.
29 The process was completed in 2002 when the premises were conveyed to the Luther King House Educational Trust. It is not possible to describe the details of the negotiations and the hurdles that had to be overcome to achieve this, but tribute can, perhaps, be paid here to the college officers, particularly Michael Bradley and Graham Sutherland, who, under Kidd's leadership, enabled the college to take this further significant ecumenical step forward.

Conclusion

There are different aspects to the task of preparing people for Christian ministry. For the most part, the colleges have seen their responsibility as primarily for the ordained ministry. For Baptists, this is not an easy distinction to make, as lay and ordained ministries have never been clearly differentiated. In practice, however, it has almost always been recognised that God calls certain people to special tasks within the church, and that this requires special training.

These tasks have often centred on preaching. Preaching has meant more than simply a method of delivering a message. It represents the personal communication of Christian truth to the world and the church in ways that are relevant and effective. Traditionally, Baptists have seen Biblical preaching as lying at the heart of other aspects of ministry like evangelism, teaching, social action and pastoral care. College principals frequently emphasised preaching as the central task of ministry. New methods of communication, especially during the second half of the twentieth century, have sometimes threatened to make the whole concept of preaching irrelevant, but an awareness that the message of Jesus needs to be effectively delivered and understood has not disappeared.

It is not surprising, then, that the colleges have consistently seen a major part of their work as enabling their students to develop an understanding of the Bible. The standard of the teaching given has naturally varied. For all their personal qualities, it is impossible to imagine some of the early principals being able to cover the vast curricula they sought to teach, as well as all the other things they did, in anything other than a superficial manner. A serious consideration of what it meant to provide a theological education was not given significant attention until about forty years ago. Before that, theological tutors often seemed more concerned with getting the job done than thinking about what it was they were really trying to do. James Acworth, for example, was more of a practical man of action than a thinker and teacher, and while the construction of Rawdon College was a magnificent achievement, there is little evidence that it was the result of any clearly worked out strategy about the principles and direction needed for ministerial training.

The spirit of open enquiry and honest exploration, the basis of any genuine learning, has not always been present. Men like Henry Dowson and Edward Parker seem to have had little patience with anything other than what they were convinced their students needed to learn. Another danger has been the tendency for some principals and tutors, in the cause of intellectual discipline, to allow academic scholarship to dominate all else. Several of them, such as A.C. Underwood and J.T. Marshall, were primarily academics with little, if any, pastoral experience. Even W.E. Blomfield, with his long experience of ministry in Coventry, seemed to delight in imposing on his students strenuous demands that seemed to have little relevance to what they might be required to do once they left college.

Each tutor brought a particular set of abilities and experience to the job, and it would, of course, be unreasonable to expect each of them to be good at everything. It has been one of the major disadvantages of the small size of the institutions that there has been little chance of weaknesses and strengths being balanced out among a team of tutors. In view of the handicaps under which they worked, the achievements of many of them were remarkable. Strong personalities sometimes enabled things to get done that would otherwise have been impossible, but they could also become unhelpfully dominant, or lead to an unhealthy dependence on one person. Principals and tutors featured most prominently in college life, but they were not responsible alone for the training. Sacrificial service by many others, including in particular honorary college officers and principals' wives, frequently made an equally important contribution.

Learning to communicate Christian truth effectively can never be just a question of studying the Bible. The personal dimension of ministerial formation and the practical application of training are also vitally important. This was, perhaps, the particular strength of the early academies, as the colleges were usually called. The effectiveness of Steadman and Dan Taylor probably lay not so much in the content of their lectures as in their personalities, and in their willingness to involve their students in the practical business of ministry. The training provided by the Baptist Evangelical Society, when a student was attached to an experienced minister, was an attempt to keep a personal dimension in the process of ministerial formation. Its shortcoming was that it was dependent on the personality and gifts of the tutor. The development of small group-work and the "contextualisation" of theological education at Northern Baptist College has been a move in a similar direction. A thorough preparation for ministry is bound to be more personally involving than can be provided by a detached, academic education, and this demands much of both tutor and student.

The significance of the colleges can only be understood in the context of the life and work of the whole Church. They existed first to serve the churches of their own denomination, and in turn relied upon them for support. Success depended largely on a sense of common purpose and fellowship with the churches. All the colleges had to work hard to maintain meaningful relationships, and they frequently felt that the churches did not take their responsibilities for supporting their work seriously enough.

The provision of financial support was vitally important, but was only one element of this relationship. Links were expressed in a variety of other ways, including the identification by the churches of suitable candidates for training, the provision of volunteers to serve on college committees, the giving of invitations to tutors and students to exercise and develop their gifts in the churches, the readiness on the part of tutors to share their expertise beyond the confines of college life, and the willingness of churches to call students to be ministers when their training had finished. A close relationship between church and college also enabled the latter to hear the opinion of church members, respond to church needs and make a meaningful contribution to their life. Much depended on the loyalty of the alumni and the effectiveness of the colleges in nurturing relationships through personal contact and publications.

These links naturally fluctuated over time and from college to college. The early success of Horton depended a great deal on Steadman's work within the wider church community and his desire to see the college play an active role, not only in preparing men for future ministry but also in encouraging their participation in current opportunities for ministry. Later, Rawdon sought to maintain close relationships with its constituency through such means as the Friends of Rawdon scheme. Harold Rowse's involvement with the ministers of the north through their annual conference between the wars was also beneficial.

One of Manchester's assets in retaining the loyalty of the churches was its distinctive doctrinal stance. In general, however, its links with the wider church community do not seem to have been as close as was the case at Rawdon. Its connection with the university was financially helpful and gave the college a greater degree of independence. It was Midland College, however, that struggled most to receive the support it needed. Even before the denominational amalgamation of 1891, General Baptist churches sometimes preferred to support one of the Particular Baptist colleges, and afterwards it was not able to extend its constituency much beyond the east midlands.

Northern benefited from being the only college in the north, and from its official links with the Baptist Union. After the public relations disaster of 1971, Taylor and his colleagues worked hard at building and maintaining contact with the churches, relationships that bore fruit with the ready response to the launch of the Alternative Pattern of Training. Its introduction in 1978 created a new sense of partnership with local churches, and the formation of the Community Learning Network in 1995 helped make the notion of the college as a regional resource centre a realistic possibility.

It is difficult to evaluate reliably the effectiveness of a college's work. Once students have left, a fair assessment of their ministry and the ongoing significance of the college's part in preparing them for it would be a formidable exercise. One of the best indicators, however, is the trust and support a college receives from the churches it seeks to serve. In the long run, the churches' perception of the quality of ministers supplied by a college is the measure by which it will be judged. Any college needs the active partnership of the churches if it is to succeed. This responsibility is shared by both college and churches. With mutual respect, and a united commitment to nurture this partnership, William Steadman's ambition of cultivating pious and useful ministers of the Gospel can continue to be achieved.

Afterword

Richard L. Kidd

Reading this story as principal of the college in the run up to its bicentenary celebrations has been both challenging and inspiring. Prospectively it inspires, encouraging a lively spirit of hope for the future. Retrospectively it challenges at many points: it is, for example, very striking that, when the story is told, it is still overwhelmingly peopled with 'men', the majority of them, like myself, occupying the role of 'principal'. This is no criticism of Peter Shepherd's research which has been at every point both extensive and meticulous; it simply reflects the archival sources which are available for telling the story so far. It would be good to think that when this task is revisited, another century on perhaps, the sources available for constructing its later chapters will reflect an altogether more deeply collaborative venture: a story of women and men long-established in patterns of working as equally memorable members of a creative and valued staff community.

It would be good to feel that such a spirit of collaboration is already in the making and, believing this to be the case, this Afterword attempts a brief description of the College as some who are deeply involved with it day to day see it in the year 2004 - something we could not reasonably expect a historian to undertake within the main body of the text. In particular it will name three significant landmarks on a journey towards increased collaboration: in the wider ecumenical community of Luther King House, in partnership with five of the recently formed regional Baptist Associations, and in collaboration with local Baptist congregations, set to take an increasingly significant formal role in shaping its future life.

Tutors, 2004

Rachel Jenkins, tutor

Sean Winter, tutor

Anne Dunkley, tutor

David Buckingham, regional tutor

Afterword

David Lennox,
regional tutor

Gaynor Hammond,
regional tutor

Jo Williams,
regional tutor

Stephen Keyworth,
regional tutor

Concerning the ecumenical journey, it was a very significant landmark indeed when, in 2002, the main buildings on the Brighton Grove site were finally transferred into genuinely shared ownership with Methodist and United Reformed partners. From that point on the story of the college's fabric became the story of the Luther King Educational Trust, Northern Baptist College taking its seats alongside others on a newly formed Board of Directors.

By 2004, the House itself had long ceased to be a university Hall of Residence, and today it functions more on the model of 'conference centre', enjoying greatly enhanced facilities for the use and enjoyment of visitors as well as of the Baptists' own distinctive learning community. Every one of its Baptist ministerial students is at this time deeply rooted in a local congregation for the duration of his or her training, and their stays in the House take the form of weekly or weekend visits on a variety of patterns through the year.

As an Affiliated College of the University of Manchester, the ecumenical community of Luther King House now offers everything from a Certificate to a PhD under the guidance of Manchester University, each with a distinctive stress on contextualisation. This development has been accompanied by a notable increase in the number and diversity of Baptist users of the learning resources. Whilst today there are less than twenty ministerial students on track for accreditation as Baptist ministers, there are at least fifty Baptists studying as lay people, student ministers or ministers engaged with in-service training through one of the many programmes on offer. This shift of emphasis was given new status when, in the autumn of 2001, the Governing Body attempted a re-statement of the overall aims of the college in the light of clear trends in its developing commitments. The text reads:

1. To create a sustainable resource for the enabling and delivery of adult theological education amongst Baptists in the Midlands and the North of England.

2. To provide a centre in Manchester capable of responding to the Baptist Union of Great Britain's need for specific programmes leading to the accreditation of a variety of recognised ministries.

Afterword

3. To undertake both of the above consistent with the distinctive ethos which has taken shape over recent years: ecumenical, collaborative, contextual and critically responsive to prophetic challenges from the world church.

This was an uncompromising vote for the priorities of 'lifelong learning' and 'education for the whole people of God', both of which are now firmly established as hallmarks of our time.

2004 also marks the end of the first five years in a new collaborative experiment in staffing, building stronger partnerships with the five regional Baptist Associations of the Midlands and the North. Today we have just four full-time staff (including the principal) in Manchester and five (two-fifths time) Regional Tutors scattered across the constituency: Jo Williams in the North Western, David Lennox in the Northern, Gaynor Hammond in the Yorkshire, Stephen Keyworth in the East Midland, and David Buckingham in the Heart of England Baptist Associations. As part of a national Baptist Training Partnership these tutors facilitate the delivery of a wide range of modular courses, meeting the needs of local Baptist church members as well as the needs of those who are seeking formal accreditation as Lay Pastors and Lay Preachers.

The appointment of regional tutors has also made it easier to respond to individual requests for learning initiatives in local church communities throughout the area. Together this has enormously increased the learning influence of the college, and done more than any other initiative in recent years to raise the college's profile at church level widely across its traditional constituency. Two hundred years on, although in very different guise, this regional strategy is taking the college back into many of the places where, at earlier times, local churches featured so strongly in the story of its making. An increased profile is also re-awakening local churches and Baptist members to increased monetary giving, offering measured confidence that there can be a period of relative financial stability for some years ahead.

Finally, and in time for the bicentenary, the college is reconstituting its structures of governance in keeping with the reality of the present moment. This includes slimming the size of its governing body, emphasising regional representation, and involving local churches as members within a newly formed legal identity.

All of which encourages the belief that, in 2004, the college stands at a very hopeful moment in its story. We trust that the publication of this documentary account of its making will add fresh clarity to a wider understanding of the college's distinctive ethos and identity. We are impressed with and immensely grateful to Peter Shepherd for this careful and thorough work of scholarship on the college's behalf. Entering a third century cannot be allowed to pass unnoticed: our hope is that a programme of events designed to mark the occasion will add its own momentum to the continuing journey, working together in mission and ministry for the glory of God and the future of the college.

Appendix
The College Principals

1. New Connexion/Midland:
    Dan Taylor (London): 1798-1813
    Joseph Jarrom (Wisbech): 1813-1837
    Thomas Stephenson (Loughborough): 1825-1841[1]
    John Stephenson (London): 1842-1843
    Joseph Wallis (Leicester): 1843-1857
    William Underwood (Nottingham and Chilwell): 1857-1873
    Thomas Goadby (Chilwell and Nottingham): 1873-1889
    Thomas Witton Davies (Nottingham): 1892-1898
    Sidney William Bowser (Nottingham): 1910-1912[2]

2. Horton/Rawdon:
    William Steadman (Horton): 1805-1835
    James Acworth (Horton and Rawdon): 1835-1862
    Samuel Gosnell Green (Rawdon): 1863-1876
    Thomas George Rooke (Rawdon): 1877-1890
    Thomas Vincent Tymms (Rawdon): 1891-1904
    William Ernest Blomfield (Rawdon): 1904-1926
    Alfred Clair Underwood (Rawdon): 1926-1948
    Laurance Henry Marshall (Rawdon): 1948-1953
    David Syme Russell (Rawdon): 1953-1964

3. Accrington:
    David Griffiths: 1841-1849

4. Bury/Manchester:
    Henry Dowson (Bury and Manchester): 1866-1877
    Edward Parker (Manchester): 1877-1898
    John Turner Marshall (Manchester): 1898-1919
    Henry Townsend (Manchester): 1920-1949
    Kenneth Charles Dykes (Manchester): 1949-1964

5. Northern:
    Kenneth Charles Dykes: 1964-1969
    David Syme Russell: 1964-1967[3]
    Michael Hugh Taylor: 1969-1985
    Brian Haymes: 1985-1994

Richard Lawrence Kidd: 1994-

Notes
1   Between 1825 and 1837 there were two New Connexion colleges.
2   Between 1898 and 1910 there was no principal at the Midland College, although Bowser was often referred to as such.
3   Between 1964 and 1967 Dykes and Russell were joint principals.

Abbreviations

APT	Alternative Pattern of Training
BQ	*Baptist Quarterly*
BMS	Baptist Missionary Society
CLC	Christian Leadership Course
GBES	General Baptist Education Society
NBES	Northern Baptist Education Society
NES	Northern Education Society
URC	United Reformed Church
YMCA	Young Men's Christian Association

Bibliography

1. Manuscript and archival sources
Acworth, James, *Letters to Edward Steane 1836-1841* (Angus library).
Baptist Colleges Joint Consultative Committee Minute Book, 1976-2001.
Baptist Evangelical Society Minute Book 1861-1866 (NBC Record Room).
Baptist Revival Fellowship papers, 1971-2.
Barrett, J.O., *Letters to E.A. Payne, 1950-1961* (Angus Library).
General Baptist Association Minute Books, 1802-1891(East Midland Baptist Association Archive).
General Baptist Education Society Minute Book, 1825-1861 (Angus Library).
Godwin, Benjamin, *Letters to his son John* (1855: Angus Library).
Hopley, Thomas, *First Sermon Class Notebook 1818-1821* (Angus Library).
Inter-Collegiate Board Minute Book 1912-16 (Angus Library).
Lancashire and Cheshire Baptist Association Minute Book, 1837-1876.
London Baptist Education Society Minute Book (Angus Library).
Manchester Baptist College Minute Books, 1874-1965 (NBC Record Room).
Manchester Baptist College, proceedings in connection with the opening of the College, 1874 (Rylands library).
Northern (Baptist) Education Society Minute Books (NBC Record Room).
Northern Baptist College Inspectors Report, 1978 (NBC Record Room).
Northern Baptist College Minute Books (NBC Record Room).
Nottingham Baptist College Minute Books (Angus Library).
Principals' Conference Minute Book, 1959-1968 (NBC Record Room).
Rawdon College Brotherhood Minute Book (NBC Record Room).
Rawdon College Minute Books (NBC Record Room).
Steadman, William, *Letters to John Saffery of Salisbury, 1804-1824* (Angus Library).
Steadman, William, *Pastoral Charge addressed to George Sample on his ordination, 1818* (Rylands Library).
Taylor, Michael H., *The Church in Training: theological education and the Northern Baptist College: a basis for discussion, 1969* (the author).

2. Newspapers and periodicals
Baptist Magazine
Baptist Times
Baptist

Bradford Observer
Bradford Review
British Monthly
The Church
Collegian
East Midlands Baptist Magazine
Freeman
General Baptist Magazine
General Baptist Repository and Missionary Observer
Manchester Guardian
Midland College Students' Magazine
Northern Baptist College Magazine
Primitive Church Magazine
Rawdon College Magazine
Rawdonian

3. Books, pamphlets, articles, reports and unpublished theses
(place of publication is London unless otherwise indicated)

Anon.: "The General Baptist Academy of the Old Connexion", *BQ* vol. 3 no. 7 (July 1927) pp. 331-332

Avery, W.J., "The Late Midland College", *BQ* vol. 1 (1922-3) pp. 218-22, 263-9, 327-36.

Baptist Handbooks.

Baptist Theological Colleges in England and Wales, *Report of an Advisory Group and other Related Documents* (1974).

Baptist Union, *Forms of Ministry among Baptists: Towards an Understanding of Spiritual Leadership* (Didcot: 1994).

- *Ministry Tomorrow* (1969).
- *Partners Together: The Colleges and the rest of the Baptist Union of Great Britain* (Didcot: 1998).
- *The Doctrine of the Ministry* (1961).

Barrett, John O., *Rawdon College (Northern Baptist Education Society) 1804-1954: A Short History* (Carey Kingsgate Press: 1954).

Binfield, Clyde, *Pastors and People: The Biography of a Baptist Church. Queen's Road, Coventry* (Queen's Road Baptist Church, Coventry: 1984).

Bonner, Carey, *Floreat Rawdona* (score and lyrics: 1930).

Breed, Geoffrey R., *The Baptist Evangelical Society – an early Victorian Episode* (Fauconberg Press, Dunstable: 1988).

Briggs, J.H.Y., (ed) *Bible, Church and World* (BHS: 1989).

- *The English Baptists of the Nineteenth Century* (BHS, Didcot: 1994).
Brown, Kenneth D., "College Principals – A Cause of Nonconformist Decay?", *Journal of Ecclesiastical History* vol. 38 (1987) pp. 236-53.
- "Patterns of Baptist Ministry in the Twentieth Century", *BQ* vol. 33 no. 2 (April 1989) pp. 81-93.
- *A Social History of the Nonconformist Ministry in England and Wales 1800-1930* (Clarendon Press, Oxford: 1988).
Brown, Raymond, *The English Baptists of the Eighteenth Century* (BHS: 1986).

Carter, A.C., *A Popular Sketch Historical and Biographical of the Midland Baptist College* (Kingsgate Press: 1925).
Champion, L.G., "Reflections upon the present Curriculum of Theological Colleges", *BQ* vol. 19 no. 6 (April 1962) pp. 270-6.
Clements, Keith W. et al, *A Call to Mind: Baptist Essays Towards a Theology of Commitment* (Baptist Union: 1981).
Cooper, R.E., *From Stepney to St. Giles': The Story of Regent's Park College 1810-1960* (Carey Kingsgate Press: 1960).
Cross, Anthony R., *Baptism and the Baptists: Theology and Practice in Twentieth Century Britain* (Paternoster Press, Car;lisle: 2000).

Dakin, Arthur, *The Baptist View of the Church and Ministry* (Baptist Union. 1944).
Deacon, Samuel, *Barton Memorials* (Eliot Stock: 1889).
Dix, Kenneth, *Strict and Particular: English Strict and Particular Baptists in the Nineteenth Century* (BHS, Didcot: 2001).
Douglas, David, *History of the Baptist Churches in the North of England from 1648 to 1845* (Houlston & Stoneman: 1846).
Dowson, Henry, *The Centenary: A History of the first Baptist Church, Bradford* (Ward & Co.: ?1853).

Evans, P.W., "The Ideal Training for the Ministry", *BQ* vol. 3 no. 2 (April 1926) pp. 65-70.

Fancutt, Walter, "William Steadman's Hampshire Years", *BQ* vol. 16, (October 1956) pp. 365-9.
Fawcett, John, *An account of the life, ministry and writings of the late John Fawcett DD* (Baldwin, Cradock & Joy: 1818).
Fiddes, Edward, *Chapters in the History of Owens College of Manchester 1851-1914* (Manchester University Press: 1937).

Fiddes, Paul et al, *Bound to Love: The Covenant Basis of Baptist Life and Mission* (Baptist Union: 1985).
- *A Leading Question: The Structure and Authority of Leadership in the Local Church* (London: n.d.).
Ford, R.C., *Twenty-Five Years of Baptist Life in Yorkshire 1912-1937* (Yorkshire Baptist Association, Leeds: 1937).
Foreman, H., "Baptist provision for Ministerial Education in the 18th Century", *BQ* vol. 27 no. 8 (October 1978) pp. 358-69.

Gadsby, John, *A Memoir of the late Mr. William Gadsby* (Manchester: 1844. Second edition 1847).
General Baptist Association Year Books, 1882-1891.
Glass, David, "Baptist Beginnings in the West Riding", *BQ* vol. 3 no. 4 (October 1926) pp. 178-83.
- "Character Sketch of W.E. Blomfield" (*Baptist Magazine*, February 1924).
Goadby, Bertha and Lilian, *Not saints but men, or the story of the Goadby ministers* (Kingsgate Press: ?1908).
Goadby, J. Jackson, *Bye-paths in Baptist History* (Elliot Stock: 1871).
Gould, George P., *The Baptist College at Regent's Park: A Centenary Record* (Kingsgate Press: 1910).
Green, Bernard, *Tomorrow's Man: A Biography of James Henry Rushbrooke* (BHS, Didcot: 1997).

Haden, W.H., "A Doctrine of the Baptist Ministry", *BQ* vol. 6 (April 1932) pp. 49-56.
Hall, Robert, *On Terms of Communion (fourth edition)* (Leicester: 1820).
Harrison, Fred M.W., *It all Began here: The Story of the East Midland Baptist Association* (East Midland Baptist Association: 1986).
Hayden, Roger (ed.), *Baptist Union Documents 1948-1977* (BHS, 1980).
Haykin, Michael A.G., *One Heart and One Soul: John Sutcliff of Olney, his friends and his times* (Evangelical Press, Darlington: 1994).
Haymes, Brian, *A Question of Identity: Reflections on Baptist Principles and Practice* (Yorkshire Baptist Association, Leeds: 1986).
Hebden Bridge Baptist Church, *A brief history of the Baptist Church, Hebden Bridge, Yorkshire* (Yates & Alexander: 1878).
Horton College Annual Reports.
Horton College, *Jubilee Memorial* (Heaton & Son, Leeds: 1854).

Ivimey, Joseph, *A History of the English Baptists* (Isaac Taylor Hinton: 1830).

James, Sharon, "Revival and Renewal in Baptist Life: the contribution of William Steadman (1764-1837)", *BQ* vol. 37 no. 6 (April 1998) pp. 263-82.

Jennings, Bernard (ed), *Pennine Valley: A History of Upper Calderdale* (Smith Settle Ltd., Otley: 1992).

Johnson, Dale A., *The Changing Shape of English Nonconformity, 1825-1925* (Oxford University Press: 1999).

Kaye, Elaine, *For the work of Ministry: A history of Northern College and its Predecessors* (T & T Clark, Edinburgh: 1999).

Langley, Arthur S., "Some Notable Names in Midland Baptist History", *BQ* vol. 3 no. 6 (April 1927) pp. 280-6.

Lauer, L.E., "Women in British Nonconformity circa 1880-1920, with special reference to the Society of Friends, Baptist Union and Salvation Army" (*DPhil* thesis, Oxford University, 1997).

Lea, John, "Baptists in Lancashire 1837-1887: A Study of Mid-Victorian Dissent" (*PhD* thesis, University of Liverpool, 1970).

Lord, F. Townley, "The Office and Function of the Baptist Ministry", *BQ* vol. 3 no. 3 (July 1926) pp. 99-107.

Manchester Baptist College Annual Reports.

Marshall, L.H., *Rivals of the Christian Faith* (Carey Kingsgate Press: 1954).

Medley, William, *Centenary Memorial of Rawdon Baptist College* (Kingsgate Press: 1904).

Miall, James G., *Congregationalism in Yorkshire: A chapter of Modern Church History* (John Snow & Co.: 1868).

Middlebrook, J.B., "Rawdon: 1914-1921 – Years of Transition", *Rawdonian* no. 6 (January 1963) pp. 2-6.

Midland College Reports.

Moon, Norman, S., *Education for Ministry: Bristol Baptist College 1679-1979* (Bristol Baptist College, Bristol: 1979).

Munson, J.E.B., "The Education of Baptist Ministers, 1870-1900", *BQ* vol. 26 (July 1976) pp. 320-7.

Northern Baptist College Annual Reports

Parker, Irene, *Dissenting Academies in England: Their Rise and Progress and their place among the Educational Systems of the country* (Cambridge University Press: 1914).

Payne, Ernest A. (ed.), *Studies in History and Religion* (Lutterworth Press: 1942).

- *A Twentieth-century Minister: John Oliver Barrett 1901-78* (privately published: ?1978).
- *Henry Wheeler Robinson: Scholar, Teacher, Principal. A Memoir* (Nisbet & Co.: 1946).
- *The Baptist Union: A Short History* (Carey Kingsgate Press: 1959).

Poe, William Allen, "The Reverend Edward Parker", *BQ* vol. 32 no. 4 (October 1987) pp. 154-72.

Preston, Ronald, *The Faculty of Theology in the University of Manchester: the first seventy-five years* (Manchester University: 1979).

Price, Seymour J., "Dissenting Academies 1662-1820", *BQ* vol. 6 (July 1932) pp. 125-38.

Rawdon College Annual Reports.

Rawdon College brochures (1904, 1910).

Rignal, Charles, *Manchester Baptist College 1866-1916* (William Byles & Sons, Bradford: 1916).

Rinaldi, Frank, "The Tribe of Dan: The New Connexion of General Baptists 1770-1891. A study in the transition from revival movement to established denomination" (*PhD* thesis, University of Glasgow: 1996).

Robinson, H. Wheeler, *The Life and Faith of the Baptists* (Methuen & Co.: 1927).

Sellers, Ian (ed.), *Our Heritage: The Baptists of Yorkshire, Lancashire and Cheshire 1647-1987* (Yorkshire Baptist Association and Lancashire and Chshire Baptist Association, Leeds: 1987).
- "Other times, other ministries: John Fawcett and Alexader McLaren", *BQ* vol. 32 no. 4 (October 1987) pp. 181-99.
- "Thomas Dawson of Liverpool", *BQ* vol. 19 no. 8 (October 1962) pp. 359-65.
- "W.T. Whitley", *BQ* vol. 37 no. 4 (October 1997) pp. 159-73.

Shepherd, Peter, *The Making of a Modern Denomination: John Howard Shakespeare and the English Baptists 1898-1924* (Paternoster Press, Carlisle: 2001).

Shipley, C.E. (ed.), *Baptists in Yorkshire, Lancashire, Cheshire and Cumberland (augmented edition)* (BHS: 1913).

Steadman, Thomas, *Memoir of the Rev. William Steadman DD* (Thomas Ward & Co.: 1838).

Taylor, Adam, *History of the English General Baptists part II: The New Connexion of General Baptists* (1818).
- *Memoirs of Rev Dan Taylor* (1820).

Taylor, Thomas, *A Memoir of Mr. Joseph Harbottle* (Elliot Stock: 1866).
Town, W. N., "W.E. Blomfield", *BQ* vol. 7 (October 1934) pp. 162-6.
Townsend, Henry, *The Claims of the Free Churches* (Hodder & Stoughton: 1949).

Underwood, A.C., "The Early Relations of Horton Academy and Rawdon College ith Lancashire", *BQ* vol. 5 (July 1930) pp. 130-6.
- *A History of the English Baptists* (Carey Kingsgate Press: 1947).
Underwood, W., *Life of Dan Taylor* (Simpkin, Marshall & Co.: 1870).

Valentine, Theo V., *Concern for the Ministry: The Story of the Particular Baptist Fund 1717-1967* (Particular Baptist Fund, Teddington: 1967).

Watson, James Edward, "The Educational Activities of Baptists in England during the 18th and 19th Centuries with Particular Reference to the North West" (MA thesis, University of Liverpool: 1947).
Watson, Lily, *The Vicar of Langthwaite (new edition)* (James Clarke & Co.: 1897).
West, W.M.S., *Baptists Together* (BHS, Didcot: 2000).
- *To Be A Pilgrim: a memoir of Ernest A. Payne* (Lutterworth Press, Guildford: 1983).
Whitley, W.T. (ed.), *General Baptist Assembly Minutes 1731-1811* (Kingsgate Press: 1910).
- "A Treasurer and his College", *BQ* vol. 5 (April 1931) pp. 274-80.
- "Our Theological Colleges", *BQ* vol. 1 (1922) pp. 16-27.
- "The Influence of Whitefield on Baptists", *BQ* vol. 5 (January 1930) pp. 30-6.
- *A History of British Baptists (2nd (revised) edition)* (Kingsgate Press: 1932).
Wood, J.H., *A condensed history of the General Baptists of the New Connexion* (Simpkin, Marshall & Co.: 1847).
Wright, D.G., and Jowitt, J.A., *Victorian Bradford: Essays in Honour of Jack Reynolds* (City of Bradford Metropolitan Council: 1982).
Wylie, Robert J.V. (compiler), *The Baptist Churches of Accrington and District* (W. Shuttleworth, Accrington: 1923).

Yorkshire Baptist Association Year Books.

Index

Aberdeen University, 15
Accrington, 4, 66f, 81, 96n
Acworth, James, 49, 58n, 63-6, 70f, 74ff, 77n, 81f, 86, 95, 102ff, 108, 271
Ahern, V J, 236
Airedale College, 69ff, 73f, 110, 126n, 127n, 136, 200, 205
Aked, Thomas, 71
Aked, Charles, 166
Allan, J B, 185
Allegro, Cynthia, 199, 206, 218n, 224
Alternative Pattern of Training, 239f, 243-6, 247n, 249-52, 256, 258f, 274
America, 191f, 266
- War of Independence, 22
Angus, G H C, 204, 210, 213
Angus, Joseph, 63
Arkwright, Richard, 6
Arnold, Matthew, 102
Ashby de la Zouch, 24, 113
Asia, 266
Aubrey, Melbourn Evans, 177, 179
Avery, W J, 168

Bacup, 66
Balfe-Mitchell, Alec, 263
Bangor Baptist College, 138
Baptist, 100
Baptist Colleges Joint Consultative Committee, 243, 262
Baptist Convention of South Africa, 264
Baptist Evangelical Society, 81, 84f, 87, 89ff, 95, 120f, 273
Baptist Housing Association, 257
Baptist Magazine, 50, 143
Baptist Missionary Society, 17, 21, 27f, 33n, 38, 49f, 61, 96, 109, 112, 123, 158, 241, 243, 247n, 264
Baptist Register, 38

Baptist Repository, 62
Baptist Revival Fellowship, 233, 246n
Baptist Students Fraternal Union, 135
Baptist Theological Education Society, 82
Baptist Times, 138, 143f, 147, 155, 232, 247n
Baptist Training Partnership, 279
Baptist Union, 3, 11, 16n, 50, 61, 64, 74, 81, 96, 99, 106, 112, 116f, 126n, 129, 131ff, 144, 147f, 152-7, 164, 173n, 177-81, 183, 193, 199, 208, 212, 216, 217n, 219n, 223, 226, 231ff, 236, 240, 250, 261ff, 274, 278
- *Baptists and Unity* report, 228
- Commission on the Ministry, 227
- Corporation, 129, 211, 226
- *Doctrine of the Ministry* report, 227
- *Ministry Tomorrow* report, 227f, 236
- Scholarships, 163, 187
- Ter-Jubilee Fund, 208, 210f, 216, 226, 261
Baptist World Alliance, 152, 177, 186
Barrett, John, 203f, 218n
Barritt, Mrs, 206
Barton-in-the-Beans, 19, 24
Beasley-Murray, George, 228, 232
Bedfordshire Union of Christians, 22
Belgium, 83
Bennett, Ellen, 262
Bennett-Reddihough legacies/Trust Fund, 264f
Beveridge Report (1942), 191
Bidston, G, 198, 200
Bilbrough family, 163
Bingley, 26
Birchcliffe, 7, 10, 13, 19ff
Birrell, Charles M, 66, 70, 77n
Bissill, J, 52
Black, Cyril, 233

Index

Blomfield, Ellen, 145, 162, 183, 200
Blomfield, William Ernest, 145, 161-5, 172n, 173n, 181-5, 188f, 272
Board Schools, 101
Board of Studies (Manchester College), 153, 160, 197f
- (Rawdon College), 165
Boateng, Paul, 254
Bonner, Carey, 186, 190n
Boorne, Gillian, 240
Booth, Abraham, 28, 33n
Booth, Samuel Harris, 129, 132f, 147
Bootle, 198
Boston (Lincolnshire), 13, 23
Bowser, Sidney William, 139, 144ff, 165f, 168
Boxer Rising, 140
Bradford, 4f, 8, 11, 36, 41, 44f, 48, 64f, 69f, 72, 91, 120, 134, 177, 207, 217
- Mechanics Institute, 64
Bradley, Michael, 269n
Brearley Hall, 18f, 26f, 29, 32n
Bright, Joseph, 166
Bristol Baptist College, 26ff, 33n, 38f, 61, 64, 106, 131f, 200, 253, 263
Bristol Education Society, 17f
Bristol University, 132
British Council of Churches, 192, 217n, 223, 227
Brittain, John, 21
Broadley, Samuel, 48
Broadmead Baptist Church, Bristol, 15, 17
Broughton, 38
Brown, Robert, 143
Brown, Kenneth, 178
Brown University (America), 56n
Brunner, Emil, 196
Buckingham, David, 276, 279
Bull, Samuel, 153
Burdett, H W, 134, 140
Bury, 4, 79
Bury, James, 28

Calabar College (Jamaica), 198
Calvinism, 80, 92
Camberwell, 60
Cambridge University, 57n, 100, 109f, 114, 126n, 166
Canada, 123
Carey, William, 26, 254
Carlyle, Thomas, 102
Centre for Black and White Christian Partnership, 252
Chamber Hall, 79, 86-9, 91f, 106
Champion, Leonard, 200, 214, 269n
Charismatic movement, 223
Charley, David, 268n
Chartists, 46, 83
Chatham, 64
Chilwell, 4, 75f, 106
Chown, J P, 75
Christian Aid, 255
Christian Leadership Course, 251f, 256, 259
Christian Unions (university), 184
Church Army, 264
Church Leadership Training, 252
Church of England, 22, 68, 79, 84, 100, 106, 150n, 151f, 158, 170, 176, 179, 190, 223, 231, 235f, 238, 246n
Church unity, 176, 223
Clark, Neville, 246n
Clarke, Charles, 114f
Clement, A S, 198
Clements, Keith, 269n
Clifford, John, 61, 116f, 119, 125, 132, 135, 151f, 166, 168f, 177, 181f
Cloughfold, 66f
Clowes, Francis, 64, 70
Collegian, 135
Community Learning Network, 263f, 269n, 274
Congregational Federation, 246, 252
Congregational Institute (Nottingham), 69, 114f, 134, 146, 166
Congregationalists, 64, 67, 73, 81, 95,

152, 188, 235, 238, 251 (see also Airedale and Northern Colleges)
Conventicle and Five Mile Acts, 50
Cornwall, 38
Cooper, William Mansfield, 215
Coventry, 113, 145, 162, 173n, 206
Crabtree, William, 8-12, 36
Crosley, David, 16n
Crozier Seminary, 203
Culross, James, 131

Dakin, Arthur, 163
Dale, R W, 69
Daniell, C, 71, 74
Davies, Henton, 231, 246
Davies, Thomas Witton, 116-9, 130, 134, 136ff, 146, 168, 170
Davies, William Solva, 179, 193
Dawson, Thomas, 82f, 85, 119f
Dearden, A E, 140
Derby, 26, 113, 177
Didsbury Wesleyan College, 136
Disestablishment, 152
Dissenting Academies, 14
Doddridge, Philip, 14
Douglas, John, 166
Downgrade Controversy, 122, 125n, 129
Dowson, Henry, 63, 74f, 78n, 82f, 85ff, 89-92, 94f, 120f, 272
Dunkley, Anne, 263, 276
Durber, Susan, 263
Durham University, 125n
Dykes, Beryl, 196, 212
Dykes, Kenneth Charles, 193, 195-8, 205, 209-12, 215f, 219n, 224, 226ff, 234, 246n, 247n, 257
Dyson, Anthony, 241

East Midlands Baptist Association, 117, 166
Edinburgh University, 89, 162
Education Act (1870), 100
- (1902), 151f

Edwards, W, 172n
El Salvador, 264
Ellis, Herbert, 138, 153, 158, 160, 179
Estonia, 179, 186
Evangelical Alliance, 80
Evangelical Revival, 7, 11, 13, 17, 79
Evans, Benjamin, 28, 39, 41, 68f, 82f, 95
Evans, Caleb, 17, 27, 38
Evans, Dorothy, 197f
Evans, Hugh, 15, 17f, 38
Evans, John, 23
Ewood Hall, 26f

Fairbairn, Andrew, 110, 126n
Faith in Living courses, 265, 267, 269n
Farr, George, 194, 196, 210, 212, 219n, 226, 235
Farsley (Leeds), 120, 138
Farthing, George B, 140
Fawcett, John, 4, 7-11, 13ff, 17-20, 25-31, 33n, 39, 56n, 82, 95, 105, 169
Fawcett, Susannah, 7f, 14, 18
Federal Council of the Evangelical Free Churches, 152, 176, 189n
Fellowship of Independent Evangelical Churches, 184
Fiddes, Paul, 269n
Fisher, Geoffrey, 193
Forster, Marjorie, 206, 218n
Foskett, Bernard, 17
Foster, Henry, 7, 14, 16n
Foster, John, 26
Free Churches/Free Church Federal Council, 151, 176, 178, 189n, 192, 194, 217n (see also Federal Council and National Council)
Freeman, 73
Freeman, Stephen, 23
French Revolution, 22, 83
Friends of Rawdon, 205, 274
Fuller, Andrew, 21, 96n

Gadsby, William, 36, 80f, 96n, 217

Index

Gamston, Nottinghamshire, 13
Gates, Edith, 177
Geissler, Moritz, 88
General Baptist Education Society, 23, 53
General Baptist Home Missionary Society, 53
General Baptist Magazine, 25, 33n, 125
General Baptist Missionary Society, 52, 113, 117, 169
General Baptist Repository, 33n
Germany, 69, 88, 102, 113, 206
Gill, John, 32n
Girton College, 101, 125n
Glasgow University, 49, 53, 64, 113, 204
Glass, David, 133, 145, 181, 186f, 200, 218n
Glover, Richard, 129, 146
Glover, T R, 176
Goadby, Frederick, 76n
Goadby, Joseph, 24, 62, 76n, 113
Goadby, Thomas, 112-6, 118, 120
Godwin, Benjamin, 39, 41, 44, 46-9, 57, 68f, 89
Goodbourn, David, 235, 237, 238f, 247n, 251ff, 255ff, 259
Gospel Standard, 80
Gould, G P, 85, 165, 172n
Graham, Billy, 192
Graham, Mrs W J, 245n
Great War, 152, 158
Green, Samuel Goswell, 70, 74, 84, 88ff, 102, 105ff, 112f, 120, 129
Greenfield Baptist/Congregational Church (Urmston), 258, 260
Griffin, James, 131
Griffiths, David, 66f, 77n, 81, 84, 96n
Grimshaw, William, 7f, 11

Halifax, 5f, 21, 27, 32n, 33n, 177
Hall, Robert, 22, 29, 80
Halle Orchestra, 154
Hammond, Gaynor, 277, 279
Hamsterley, 89

Harbottle, Joseph, 66f, 81, 83ff, 96n
Hardy, Margaret, 177
Harris, Kenneth, 240
Harrod, John, 265
Hartley, James, 10
Hartley Victoria College, 235f, 241, 247n, 267
Harvey, Joseph, 83, 85
Harvey, R G S, 243, 247n
Havelock Hall, 168, 173n
Haverfordwest Baptist College, 117
Haworth, 7, 10
Hayden, Roger, 269
Haymes, Brian, 252, 255-9, 262ff, 266
Headingley College, 185, 200, 202, 204f
Hebden Bridge, 5f, 10, 25ff, 29
Heckmondwike, 15, 28
Hedger, Violet, 177
Heidelberg University, 163
Hemel Hempstead, 53
Henderson, W, 172n
Heptonstall, 5ff
 Book Society, 14
Hill, George (Rawdon), 111
Hill, George (Midland), 139, 141, 144
Hinton, James, 35, 56n
Hminga, Lal C, 199
Hobbs, J G, 204, 210, 213
Hobbs, Keith, 257f, 260
Holland, 186
Hollinwood Mission, 123
Honest To God, 233
Hopley, Thomas, 52
Horsfall, John/Cedric, 163f
Hough, William, 203f, 210
Howden, Brian, 263
Howe, John, 86, 94, 120
Howells, George, 185
Huddersfield, 7, 160, 178
Hughes, Hugh Price, 151
Huntingdon, Countess of, 15, 20
Huxley, T H, 102

Idle, 28
Independents, 8, 12, 15, 21, 27, 33n, 46, 50, 57n, 79
India, 192, 199, 239, 264
Industrial Revolution, 5f, 22, 44
Inter-collegiate Board, 156, 164 (see also United Collegiate Board)
Inter-Varsity Fellowship, 198
Italy, 206

Jamaica, 192, 199
- Baptist Union of, 199, 206
Jarrom, Joseph, 51ff, 55,
Jelleyman, David, 198
Jenkins, Rachel, 263, 276
Jones, Norman B, 227f
Jones, Richard, 235
Joseph Davis Charity, 181

Kenya, 264
Kershaw, John, 80
Key, Thomas, 46
Keyworth, Stephen, 277, 279
Kidd, Richard Lawrence, 257f, 260, 263f
King, Martin Luther, 254
Kinghorn, Joseph, 35, 80
Kreider, Alan and Eleanor, 263

Labour Party, 171, 175, 191, 222
Lady Margaret Hall, 101
Lancashire and Cheshire Baptist Association, 66, 84, 96, 97n, 120, 157, 241, 249, 257, 260
Lancashire and Yorkshire Baptist Association, 25, 27, 33n, 35, 43f, 54, 66, 80f
Lancashire and Yorkshire Baptist Itinerant Society, 43
Langdon, Thomas, 28, 64
Latvia, 186
Lay training, 256, 258
Leeds, 28, 36, 42, 44, 70, 72ff, 115f, 134, 160, 178, 202

- College of Science, 126n
- School of Medicine, 109, 126n
- University, 162ff, 165, 170, 185, 188, 200ff, 205, 208, 214
Leeds and Bradford Theological Circle, 185
Leicester, 4, 60, 64, 113, 187
Lennox, David, 277, 279
Leominster, 36f
Liberal Party/Liberalism, 151, 163, 175f
Lincolnshire Baptist Association, 13, 19
Littlewood, Thomas, 27f, 33n, 35f, 80
Liverpool, 26, 43f, 66, 101, 195
Living-Taylor, Maria, 177
Lloyd George, David, 152, 175
Local Education Authority grants, 196, 245, 261
Locks, Geoff, 247n
Lockwood, 26
Logan, James Moffatt, 106
London Baptist Education Society, 18, 28, 32n, 33n
London Baptist Society for Assisting Young Men, 15
London Missionary Society, 22
London University, 57n, 61, 65, 68, 74, 76n, 78n, 89, 96, 100, 102, 106, 110, 121, 136, 145, 153, 160, 163, 165, 178, 183, 205, 208
Longsight Mission/Students Settlement, 123, 140, 161
Loughborough, 4, 53ff, 59, 63, 113
Lowry, A S, 173n
Luther King House, 254, 266
Luther King House Educational Trust, 269n, 278
Luton Industrial Mission, 207

Macalpine, George/Macalpine family, 143, 163
McBain, Douglas, 232
McCorkendale, Miss, 136
McCurrach, W A, 140

Index 295

Mackay, John, 71
McKelvey, Jack, 253
Mackenzie, Azariah, 206
Maclaren, Alexander, 143, 154
McMaster University (Canada), 187
Magaramombe, G C, 206
Manchester, 4, 36, 43f, 66f, 69f, 72, 74, 80f, 92f, 101, 123, 154, 180, 208
- Christian Institute, 237f, 251f, 256, 258ff, 265
- College (Congregational), 73
- *Guardian*, 154
- Ship Canal, 128n, 154
- South West Group of URC and Baptist churches, 261
- Theological Education Council, 231
- University, 146, 154, 170, 212ff, 216, 244, 250, 252, 258f, 265, 267, 278
    - University Faculty of Theology/Department of Theology and Religions, 146, 153f, 157, 178, 197, 208, 265
Manchester and District Council of Churches, 249
Mann, Isaac, 40, 47
Mansfield College (Oxford), 126n
Manson, T W, 196
Marshall, John Turner, 111, 121ff, 126n, 130, 138, 140, 143f, 146, 153f, 155,157-61, 170, 172n, 178f, 272
- Marshall, Miss, 161
- Marshall, Mrs., 161
Marshall, Laurance, Henry, 163, 187, 200-4, 218n
Marshall, Newton Herbert, 135, 139, 144
Marshall, Ruth, 202
Marshall, Thomas, 116
Massachusetts, 113
Medical Missionary Scholarships, 182, 197
Medley, Samuel, 26f, 105
Medley, William, 70, 105, 107, 109, 111, 133, 140, 145, 162, 170
Mee, David Quinney, 264

Melbourne (Australia), 111
Methodists/Wesleyans, 6ff, 11f, 14, 19, 21f, 33n, 45, 50, 54, 67, 73, 81, 94, 152, 223, 231, 234f, 237f, 243, 246n, 251, 253, 255, 265 (see also Hartley Victoria and Headingley Colleges)
Middlebrook, John, 164f, 210, 212
Midlands Baptist Association, 127n
Mile End, 24
Mill, John Stuart, 102
Milligan, Robert, 70f, 76n
Mirfield College, 200
Mitchell, William, 16n
Monday Programme, 259
Moore, Ernest, 205, 210, 212, 235, 243, 246n, 252, 268n
Moravians, 252f
Moss Side Baptist Church, 257
Mursell, James, 200, 203, 209
Myrie, H S, 198ff, 218n

National Council of the Evangelical Free Churches, 189n
New Integrated programme, 259
Newnham College, 101
Newton, E M, 224
Nicholson, John, 241, 243, 249, 251ff, 256f, 259f
Noel, Baptist, 71
North Shields, 229
North Western Baptist Association, 84, 88, 97n, 120
North Western/Northern Ordination Course, 235f, 238, 240, 252f
Northamptonshire Baptist Association, 21, 33n
Northern Baptist Convention, 123
Northern College (Congregational/URC), 235f, 238, 246n, 251, 253, 258, 267
Northern College Magazine, 224
Northern Education Society/Northern Baptist Education Society, 4, 9, 15, 27ff, 33n, 35, 43, 46, 63, 68, 81, 145

Northern Federation for Training in Ministry, 253, 256, 258ff, 265ff
Northowram, 11
Nottingham, 4, 63, 75, 114ff, 166, 198
- University, 132
- University College, 114f, 118, 134, 146, 166

Oasis Trust, 264
Oncken, Johann Gerhard, 83, 88
Orissa (India), 52, 113
Owens College, 67ff, 74, 81, 92ff, 100, 122
Owens, John, 68, 93
Oxford University, 57n, 100, 109f, 162, 165

Pankhurst, Emmeline, Christabel and Sylvia, 154
Parker, Edward, 86, 88, 119-23, 131, 133, 137f, 272
Parker, Joseph, 151
Parker, Michael, 32n
Part-time training, 231
Particular Baptist Fund, 15
Pawson, David, 232, 246
Payne, Ernest, 193, 203f, 209f, 215f, 218n, 219n, 224, 226, 233
Pearce, Samuel, 38
Peel, Robert, 86
Pegg, Robert/Pegg Trust Fund, 114, 140
Peggs, James, 52
Peto, Morton, 71
Pike, J G, 52, 61, 76n
Pilling, Edmund, 189n, 204
Pitt, William (the Younger), 24
Poland, 186
Ponter, John, 260
Pratt, David, 8
Preston, 26f
Priestley, Joseph, 14
Primitive Church Magazine, 82, 86, 120
Primitive Communionist, 82

Queen's College (London), 125n

Rawdon, 4, 36, 70, 207ff
Rawdon Brotherhood, 209
Rawdon College Magazine, 203, 211, 213
Rawdonian, 134, 186
Rawtonstall, 179
Red Cross, 158f
Reddihough, John, 160
Reddihough, Maud, 262
Reform Act (1832), 50
Reform Act (1867), 101
Regents Park College, 76n, 106f, 112, 117, 132, 136, 139, 145, 162, 165, 177, 181, 185, 204, 228, 231, 258, 268n
Religious Tract Society, 107
Representation of the People Act (1918), 171
Rhode Island Baptist College, 15
Rignal, Charles, 158
Rippon, John, 24, 38
Roberts, E J, 166
Robinson, Henry Wheeler, 162-5, 170, 176, 181, 185
Robinson, John, 233
Robinson, Robert, 22
Robson, Harry, 164
Rochdale, 4, 6, 26f, 29, 33n, 35, 44, 80
Rodhill End, 16n, 31
Roman Catholic Church, 124, 179, 181, 238
Rooke, Thomas George, 107-11
Rotherham, 28, 127n
Rowley, H H, 196
Rowse, Harold Charles, 163, 181, 200, 274
Rushbrooke, James Henry, 135, 139, 166, 169, 177, 179, 186
Russell, David Syme, 204ff, 208-13, 215f, 219n, 224ff, 234, 247n, 267
Russell, Marion, 205, 212
Russia, 191
Rust, Eric, 201, 203f

Index 297

Ryland, John, 38
Ryland, Jonathan, 47

Saffery, John, 38, 42ff
St Andrew's University, 112, 183
St Mary's Baptist Church, Norwich, 85
Salford Urban Mission, 251
Salisbury, 38
Salt, Titus, 71, 76n
Sample, George, 43
Sandys, John, 18
Saxony Mission, 83, 88
Schofield, John Noel, 185
Scott, Alexander John, 68
Scott, C P, 154
Scott, Jayne, 264
Scott, Martin, 261, 264
Scottish Baptist College, 204
Scottish Universities, 57n, 65, 110 (see also individual universities)
Second World War, 191
Selby, Ray, 254
Senaticus Academicus, 109f, 116, 118, 122, 136, 153
Serampore College, 26, 165, 181, 202, 204, 246n
Shakespeare, J H, 132, 144, 147, 152f, 155f, 163, 166, 177, 184
Sharpe, Heckford, 224
Shaw, W Dale, 137, 143, 157, 172n, 179
Shaw, William, 83, 93f, 120
Sheffield, 264
Shred, John, 123
Sidmouth, Lord, 50
Skae, William, 105, 126n
Slater, Graham, 254
Smith, Rhoda, 236
Smith, Richard, 9-12, 25
Snaith, Norman, 202
South Africa, 264
South Parade Baptist Church, Leeds, 49, 64, 164
Southern Baptist Convention (America), 83, 123
Soviet Union, 191
Spain, 206
Sparkes, Douglas, 241
Spurgeon, Charles Haddon, 69, 80, 93, 107, 122, 125n, 126n, 129, 184
Spurgeons/Pastors College, 69, 127n, 132, 135f, 148n, 156f, 172n, 250, 256, 258, 264, 268n
Steadman, Sarah, 38, 40
Steadman, William, 4, 35-49, 51, 54f, 56n, 57n, 64ff, 68, 74, 82, 86, 89, 95, 203, 217, 272ff
Steane, Edward, 64
Stepney Academy, 33n, 50, 60f, 63, 65, 76, 82, 89, 102
Stevenson, John, 53, 59f
Stevenson, Thomas, 53, 59, 63
Stevenson, William, 63, 75, 112, 114, 116
Stocksbridge, 38
Stone Slack, 16n
Strict Baptists, 80, 83
Strict Baptist Convention/Strict Baptist Society, 83
Student Christian Movement, 184, 224, 228
Superintendents, 193, 197, 199, 226
Sutcliff, John, 7, 14, 17f, 21, 27, 31, 35, 46
Sutcliffe, John, 269
Sutherland, Graham, 269

Taylor, Adam, 20, 33n
Taylor, Dan, 4, 7, 10-13, 15, 17, 19ff, 23ff, 27, 29ff, 33n, 51, 54f, 60, 76, 113, 169, 272
Taylor, James, 23
Taylor, Michael Hugh, 195, 228-44, 250-7, 260, 266
Temple, William, 193
Test and Corporation Acts, 50
Thatcher, Margaret, 222
Thomas, Joshua, 37

Thomas, John, 153
Tissington, M H, 198ff
Townsend, Henry, 159ff, 178-81, 185, 189, 193-6, 218n, 262
- Townsend, Mrs., 161
Trevecca College, 15, 37
Trinity and All Saints College (Leeds), 213
Turner, John, 241
Tymms, Thomas Vincent, 111f, 130-3, 136f, 139-43, 145, 147f, 149n, 150n, 161, 172n

Underwood, Alfred Clair, 165, 168f, 176, 181-5, 188f, 200ff, 218n, 272
- Underwood, Mrs, 201
Underwood, Donald, 202
Underwood, William, 63, 75, 112f
Union Theological Seminary, 228
Unitarians, 14, 106, 238, 253ff
United Collegiate Board, 180, 184, 193
United Reformed Church, 223, 238, 246, 251-5 (see also Congregationalists and Northern College)

Venn, Henry, 7
Vicar of Langthwaite, 103
Victoria (Federal) University, 101, 110f, 125n, 132, 140
Viney, James, 40

Wainsgate, 5f, 7, 9ff, 17ff, 25f, 31
Wallis, Joseph, 60-3
- Wallis, Mrs., 62
Walton, Heather, 255, 257ff
Ward, John, 15
Ward, William, 26

Wass, M, 224, 245n
Watson, H L, 212
Watson, Lily, 103f
Watt, James, 6
Webb, James, 92, 94, 121
Wedgwood, Josiah, 6
Welsh Students, 48
Wesley, John, 6, 8, 11
West Midlands Baptist Association, 127n, 134, 167
West, Morris, 228
Western Baptist Association, 17, 33n
Westgate Baptist Church, Bradford, 8, 36, 42, 74, 89f
Westhill Training College, 186, 219
Whalley, Ernest, 257f, 261
White, Barrie, 256
Whitechapel, 21
Whitefield, George, 6ff, 10f, 20
Whitley, W T, 111, 157
William Temple College/Foundation, 207, 238
Williams, Charles, 84, 96n
Williams, Howard, 204
Williams, Jo, 277, 279
Winter, Sean, 263, 276
Wisbech, 4, 51ff, 55
Women, 124, 172n, 177, 199, 201, 262
Women's Social and Political Union, 154
World Council of Churches, 217n, 223, 227, 256, 266

Yeadon, Mrs, 108
Yorkshire Baptist Association, 77n
Yorkshire United College, 127n, 185
YMCA, 167